ADAMS
Streetwise®

COMPLETE
BUSINESS PLAN

ADAMS

Streetwise®

COMPLETE

BUSINESS PLAN

Writing a business plan has never been easier!

Bob Adams

Adams Media Corporation
Holbrook, Massachusetts

Published by Adams Media Corporation
260 Center Street, Holbrook, MA 02343

ISBN: 1-55850-845-7

Printed in the United States of America.

J   I   H   G   F   E   D   C   B   A

Library of Congress Cataloging-in-Publication Data
Adams, Bob
Adams Streetwise complete business plan : writing a business plan has never been easier! / Bob Adams
p.   cm.
Includes index.
ISBN 1–58062–845–7
1. Business planning. I. Title. II. Title: Streetwise complete business plan. III. Title: Complete business plan.
HD30.28.A3   1998
658.4'012—dc21   98–43071
CIP

Cover Photo: ©SPG International Corporation.
Cover background photo: ©SuperStock Incorporated.

This publication is designed to provide accurate and authoritative information with regard to the subject matter covered. It is sold with the understanding that the publisher is not engaged in rendering legal, accounting, or other professional advice. If legal advice or other expert assistance is required, the services of a competent professional person should be sought.
— From a *Declaration of Principles* jointly adopted by a Committee of the American Bar Association and a Committee of Publishers and Associations

This book is available at quantity discounts for bulk purchases.
For information, call 1-800-872-5627 (in Massachusetts, 781-767-8100).

This book is available in a full interactive software version for $99.95.
For information, call 1-800-872-5627 (in Massachusetts, 781-767-8100).

Visit our exciting small business Web site: www.businesstown.com

CONTENTS

CONTENTSCONTENTSCONTENTSCONTENTS

Part I
The Basics of Business Planning

CONTENTS

CONTENTSCONTENTSCONTENTSCONTENTS

Part II
Writing the Business Plan

CONTENTS

CONTENTSCONTENTSCONTENTSCONTENTS

Part III
Creating the Financials

CONTENTS

CONTENTSCONTENTSCONTENTSCONTENTS

Part IV
Sample Plans

INTRODUCTIONINTRODUCTIONINTRODUCTION

Introduction

Whatever business you are in, you are going to be a lot more successful if you have a solid business plan, and if you really follow it in running your business.

Business plans can't be just sugar-coated documents, with pie-in-the sky profit and growth projections, that you write only to raise money. Bankers and investors know that every business faces tough competition and a host of problems and hurdles—and they want to see how you are going to address each of these issues.

Even if you don't need financing, and even if your business is as small as a lemonade stand, you need a business plan to run your business at its full potential.

A good business plan allows you to look at all of the big issues facing your business in a balanced analytical way. A good business plan helps you take full advantage of your strengths and helps you to discover your competitor's weaknesses. A good business plan directs all of your business activities in a solid cohesive direction.

If you don't have a business plan—or if you don't really follow a business plan—you are leaving your success to chance.

It's a tough, competitive world out there! Don't leave your success to chance! Create a solid business plan—and follow it to success!

— *Bob Adams*

> Even a lemonade stand needs a business plan to maximize its potential.

CHAPTER 1

Creating Your Business Plan

CREATING YOUR BUSINESS PLAN

Getting Started

The hardest part of creating a business plan is getting the energy together to get started. At first it seems like a daunting task. But once you get going, you'll find that writing the plan is not as tough as it seems. Start with some of the easy steps first. Describe your business and your product or services. Talk about the market you are targeting. And explain what stage of development your company is in. If you get hung up on a particular part of the plan—skip it for now—and come back and fill it in later. Don't worry about making a perfect first draft—just get some thoughts down to get the process going and you can always come back and polish it up later.

Creating a business plan may be easier than you think.

Keep in Mind Your Audience

Throughout the writing of your business plan you want to keep in mind your intended audience and why you are writing the plan. For example if you are trying to attract equity investors, you will want to emphasize the big upside profit potential. At the same time you need to be especially careful to adequately disclose the risks and uncertainties in your business, because investors often look for someone to blame (read "s-u-e") if their investment disappears. If you are trying to get debt financing, you want to emphasize not the huge upside profit potential—but the certainty that the debt can be repaid. In fact talk of big profits may scare away debt financiers because high profit potential usually means high risks. If you are writing a plan to help you run the business better, you may skip or write very simple sections with general background information on the company and the industry, and instead focus in more depth on the areas of your plan that are currently most important to you.

Strategy Is the Core of Your Business Plan

Basically the first half of the business plan is geared toward helping develop and support a solid business strategy. You look at the market, the industry, customers, and competitors. You look at customer needs and the benefits of current products and services. You evaluate the strengths and weaknesses of each competing firm and look for opportunities in the marketplace. All of these steps are largely aimed at helping you create a strategy for your business. The second half of the business plan is largely to execute your selected business strategy. Your products and services, your marketing and your operations should all closely tie in with your strategy. So while it may be easy to select a smart-sounding strategy for your plan, I recommend you give a lot of thought to the strategy that will set the course for your business.

> A good business plan leads you to a strong strategy— then helps you execute it.

Think Competitively Throughout Your Plan

In today's crowded marketplace, you're probably going to have serious competition no matter how creative your business concept is. That is why you need to think competitively throughout your business plan. You need to realistically identify where you will do things in similar manner as your competitors, where you will do things differently, where you have real strengths, and where you have real weaknesses. To try to run a major aspect of your business significantly better than your competitors may be a very difficult challenge. Hence, you are often better to focus in planning on being different than your competition and competing with them less directly. Can you find a particular market niche to focus on? Can you find a unique strategy? Can you position your products differently? Can you use different sales or marketing vehicles?

Don't Overreach with Your Business Plan

A lot of business plans sound good on paper, but don't work in the real world marketplace. It's difficult to attract people to a new product or service. Just because it's better doesn't mean people are going to switch to it! People or companies have established buying patterns and are currently doing business with someone else. To get them to do business with you, you need to do more than to attract them to your business. You've got to steal them away from someone else's business. It's also quite possible that when you enter the marketplace your competitors may react with their own new products or services or by cutting their prices. And while it's easy to overestimate sales projections, it's just as easy to underestimate costs—especially for a start-up. There are always going to be a hefty amount of cost overruns, expensive problems, and items that you simply overlooked. So forecast conservatively and try to have an extra cushion of cash tucked in reserve.

> You've got to steal customers away from someone else's business.

CHAPTER 2

Getting a Bank Loan

What Are the Three "C's"?

Traditionally bankers look at what are called the three "c's"—character, credit, and collateral. Character means more than not having a criminal record. It means that the banker feels confident that you are not going to suddenly disappear for parts unknown if the business runs into trouble. Specifically bankers like to see ties to the community such as long residence, family ties, and home ownership. A clean credit history is important. A couple of late credit card payments shouldn't be a factor, but missing mortgage payments for three months in a row will require a good explanation. Bankers like good character and good credit, but they live for solid collateral. Equipment, buildings, and trucks—that's the kind of stuff that bankers really like for collateral—solid value and likely to be worth a lot even if the business goes bust. Inventory, raw material, and goods are second choices for collateral—they will lose their value more quickly than fixed assets but still be worth something.

> Bankers like good character and good credit, but they live for solid collateral!

Can You Get a Business Loan?

The criteria for business loans varies much more widely than for consumer loans and often varies quite a bit from one banker to the next at even the same bank! However, here are some rules of thumb to give you an idea of your chances of getting a loan.

- Getting a loan for a new business is tough.
- Fixed assets such as machinery or buildings can almost always be financed.

- Current assets such as inventory or goods in process increase your loan chances.
- 2+ years of profitable operation greatly increases your loan chances.
- The larger the owner's investment in the business the better your chances of getting a loan.
- Loans to small corporations will often have to be personally guaranteed by a shareholder.
- It is difficult to get loans to offset operating losses.
- It is usually possible to get a loan to modestly expand a profitable business.

How to Get the Bank's Money, Even When the Bank Says "No!"

Banks have much more lenient standards for lending to consumers than to businesses. So what you can do is borrow the money from the bank as a consumer and then turn around and personally invest the funds in your business. Just make sure that you never lie about how you are going to use the proceeds on a loan application. For example, you could apply for a home equity loan to tap any available equity in your house. Then take the funds and invest them in your business. The bank feels safer because their statistics show that home equity loans are much more likely to be repaid than loans for brand new businesses. No equity in your home? Maybe you can get a car loan.

A lot of businesses are financed with consumer loans.

Getting an Appointment with a Bank

Don't just show up in person—first make an appointment by phone. Ask the receptionist in the bank or the loan department for the name of the appropriate person who would handle your loan request. Of course it would be better, but not necessary, to get a referral from a friend or advisor such as your lawyer or accountant. When you get the name of the appropriate loan officer simply ask for an appointment. Don't offer any more details over the phone, unless the loan officer requests them. The more details you offer over the phone, the greater the chances you won't get the appointment at all. Sound confident. Sound matter of fact. Sound like you don't even need the money—that's the kind of person that loan officers like to lend to.

Sound like you don't even need the money.

CHAPTER 3

Attracting Equity Investors

ATTRACTING EQUITY INVESTORS

Talk with Your Lawyer First

People don't invest in small companies to lend a helping hand. They invest to make money. And they expect to make a lot of money. If they expected to make just a 10 percent or even 15 percent return on their investment they would invest in largely less risky major public companies. Instead they invest in small companies because they expect to get huge returns on their investments. Often these returns do not materialize. Even if the company is successful in the eyes of the founders, it may not meet the expectations of outside investors. And disappointed outside investors will often look for someone (read the company founders) to sue. This is just one reason you need to consult with a highly experienced business lawyer (not your family lawyer) before you to try to seek equity capital. There are also a lot of laws restricting how equity money can be raised from the public. And you need to be careful to structure any equity deal in your best interest—including all of the fine print.

Venture capitalists actually finance a very small percentage of new businesses.

Venture Capitalists

Venture capitalist firms get a lot of attention in the financial press and they look at a lot of deals. But chances are that you are not going to get a nickel from them. Venture capitalists finance a very small percentage of new businesses. And most firms have fairly specific criteria for the type of situation they are interested in. Venture capitalists are typically looking for a company that has a realistic possibility of becoming a very large business within 5–7 years, large enough for a major public offering, or for sale to a Fortune 500 company. This would allow them to cash out their

ATTRACTING EQUITY INVESTORS

investment, which they hope will have multiplied in value. Contrary to popular belief, many venture capital deals are not limited to high tech companies, and many are for second or third round financing. Because venture capitalists are approached with many potential deals everyday, you should try very hard to get a personal referral to get your plan carefully considered.

Relatives

I know that you hate to ask relatives for money—it feels like begging—but I've done it. And you can do it too. When you need money for a business, you just have to swallow your pride. Approach your relatives very much like you'd approach any other outside investor. Explain not how they can help you out—but how they can make money. Have a written agreement—and have your attorney read it. A written agreement with relatives will not only help avoid legal problems but will also help avoid potentially bitter family relations. Even with your parents, siblings, or spouse, keep your business relationship formal. When I borrowed money from my father he was tougher than the bank—demanding interest every 30 days. But by adhering to his strict terms, I was able to borrow money from him on more than one occasion.

Swallow your pride and ask for the money.

Employee Investors

One of the most common sources of equity money is potential employees, especially people you either worked with in the past or you have personally known in the same industry. By offering equity to potential employees, you not only get an equity investment but you also get (presumably) a talented and com-

ATTRACTING EQUITY INVESTORS

mitted employee. Usually employees who have invested in a company are willing to take a significantly below market salary—but they will expect that the principal founder does likewise. While raising equity from potential employees has obvious pluses, it also can raise a bunch of serious issues. What happens if the employee's work proves less than satisfactory? What happens if the employee decides to join or start a competing company? These are all issues that need to be addressed with a good business attorney before you even approach a potential employee-investor.

Public Offerings

In the United States, the securities laws have changed to make it easier and less expensive to do a small public offering. But despite the allure of going public, I would suggest that you think twice before pursuing this option, especially for a relatively new or small business. For one, I have seen business people underestimate what has proven to be an incredible stress of taking their company public. For another, there are a lot of hidden legal issues in running a public company. For example, if you take your company public, you will need to be very careful about any public statements you make (or neglect to make) about the company's expected future performance. Sadly enough, there are a bunch of attorneys that make a living suing small public companies on frivolous grounds when quarterly earnings fall short of expectations.

Going public is not a step you want to take lightly.

CHAPTER 4

Planning for Profits

PLANNING FOR PROFITS PLANNING FOR PROFITS

No matter how small or large your business, you've got to aggressively plan the work—and then work the plan!

How to Really Jump Ahead

On a discussion panel, I was recently asked: "Was there a particular turning point when your small business really jumped ahead?" Absolutely. I always made up plans and budgets, but it was about five years into my business before I really began to proactively use them. Before this point in time, my sales projections were miles off and more importantly—I was always thinking up excuses for making unplanned expenditures, often for advertising that seldom matched my expectations. I'd finish the year way over budget, with profit margins a fraction of what my plan called for. I learned that a lot of expenditures seem like a great decision if you look at them in isolation—but when you look at them in the context of the whole budget—they often look a lot less enticing.

> A lot of expenditures appear enticing when viewed in isolation.

Sharply Focus Your Plan

Too many people equate annual planning with budgeting. Worse, when they budget, they simply extrapolate last year's numbers into next year's plan, perhaps increasing by 5 percent here and 6 percent there.

Big mistake! The annual planning process is your best chance to really manage the business—and to get key people to "buy-in" to the total plan by actively participating.

Even if you're running a one-person business you want to get a few words into your annual plans, not just numbers. You don't need a full-fledged hundred page business plan—in fact, a big detailed plan takes focus away from what matters. What matters is the few big things that the business is going to strive to do better or different next year. The annual planning process should be focused around these few, important changes.

Don't Jump into Budget Numbers

Before you start doing any nitty-gritty budgeting for your annual plan, here are the crucial first steps:

1. Review the company's business strategy. Do changing market conditions or heightened competition mean that it's ready for an overhaul?
2. Establish just a few major goals for the next year. These are usually quantitative goals such as to increase sales by 18 percent or to increase profit margins by 15 percent—but they may be qualitative goals such as to improve the quality of a product or customer service. It is very important to have very few major goals—otherwise, with too many goals, the company will lose focus and be less likely to hit any of them.
3. If your company is big enough to have departments, have one or several specific goals for each department. To take this one step further, you may want to have specific goals for individual people within each department.

Even for annual planning, your business plan needs text—not just budget numbers.

Sales Projections Need Extra Attention

Once you've reviewed the company's strategy and set up company-wide, as well as department strategies for the next year, then it's time to start cranking out budget numbers.

I always begin with sales, because sales numbers will drive many of the other numbers. Unfortunately sales numbers, particularly of new products, are difficult to project. So I'll try to have at least three people, typically a project manager and the sales manager and myself, work up new product sales projections together. If you're really unsure of sales projections, consider multiple scenario's based on "weak," "likely," and "good" sales projections.

> Consider multiple scenarios for different sales projections.

After you've got the sales numbers, each department should work up their budget numbers. Once they're tentatively approved, the controller puts its all together into one big happy plan! But more often than not, I'm not completely satisfied with the overall profit margin, so I'll work with the different department heads to cut costs and drive it up.

Benchmark Your Costs

One of the best ways to establish cost goals for annual planning is to benchmark your costs with other firms in your industry. Don't get too wrapped up in the detail, focus on the total picture for major categories. For example, if your marketing costs are 23 percent of sales and the industry average is 16 percent, it's time for some cost-cutting. Benchmarking is a great way to get department managers to understand why they need to control costs.

Often industry associations provide standard industry costs, and occasionally they might be mentioned in articles in trade magazines.

You may want to consider hiring a consultant to put together a study of a half-dozen or more firms very similar to yours. Being a third party, the consultant will keep each firm's individual numbers confidential, by providing only average and median cost information to each company, as an incentive for participating. What's worked best for me is when another publisher foots the bill for the consultant, but shares the results with us in exchange for us agreeing to share our numbers.

Underpricing Kills Profits

Many small businesses have thinner profit margins than larger firms because they tend to underprice their products or services. So why not just raise prices? I know the feeling—you're scared that your competition might swoop in like a bird of prey and your customer base might shrivel overnight!

For years we credited much of the success of our best-selling resume book, *Resumes that Knock 'em Dead*, to it's relatively low, $7.95 price. But my sales manager insisted we could charge more, so when we brought out a new edition, I nervously increased the price by 25 percent to $9.95. What happened to sales? Unit sales surged over 20 percent. Total revenue soared 50 percent and profits skyrocketed!

Still unsure about raising prices? Remember, you can always cut them back. A Chinese restaurant I eat at has rolled the price of its lunch buffet back and forth like a ping pong ball, between $5.95 and $6.25, four times over the least two years.

> Try experimenting with higher prices.

Is the Marketing Working?

You've probably heard the familiar maxim: "20 percent of my advertising brings in 80 percent of my business, but I don't know which 20 percent!" Well, I bet that in your business there is at least one marketing expense that you have strong suspicion isn't carrying its weight—so cut it and see what happens!

One year I tried cutting three-quarters of the promotional budget for my leading book. What happened? The sales continued to creep upward and the profit margin of the entire company jumped markedly higher.

It's often by eliminating the marketing expenses previously considered most sacred that you gain the most. For example, in the book industry many of the leading publishers have recently stopped spending lots of money for big booths at the annual national trade show—it simply was costing them too much money for too little return.

> It's often by eliminating the most "sacred" marketing expense that you gain the most.

The Easiest Way to Profits

Let's say your overall profit margin is 5 percent—not an uncommon level for many smaller firms. But if you can cut your costs by just 5 percent, your profit will almost double. On the other hand, to get the same increase by boosting sales, you would have to increase sales by 100 percent.

Chances are cutting costs just a little bit would be a lot easier.

To attack your costs take a look at every single expense item starting with the biggest items! Get competitive bids for every product and every service that you buy! Remember, despite what they may teach you at business school, there is no such thing as fixed costs! Often lease rates, mortgage rates, and utility rates can be negotiated downward, especially if the market has shifted.

Review Your Product Mix

A seasoned banker once told me about a firm with several highly profitable divisions and one marginally profitable division. The company sold the marginally profitable division, and suddenly the performance of the remaining divisions dramatically improved!

I've tried this! It works! When the economy around Boston hit rock bottom in late 1980s I closed my job advertising newspaper—which was 50 percent of our revenue the previous year. By being able to put all of my energy into the other part of my business—book publishing—it took off, and revenue doubled, more than making up for the newspaper closing.

Even a marginal business or product line that isn't losing money is draining resources—time and focus. Close it and move on!

> Counting each paper clip may **double** your profits!

Outsource Judiciously

One of the battle cries in business today is to determine the one thing that your business does best, become even better at it, and outsource absolutely everything else. There is certainly a lot to be said for taking a careful look at every function in your business and asking yourself if you should outsource it. But take a hard look at the numbers before you decide to jump on the out-

> Save money when you can by doing it yourself.

source bandwagon! For example, we hoped that by outsourcing the warehousing of our books to our printer in the mid-west we could save lots of money in freight costs. But a careful analysis showed that we would save almost nothing in freight costs, and that outsourcing would have nearly doubled our warehouse and handling costs.

CHAPTER 5

Q & A

Q&AQ&AQ&AQ&AQ&AQ&AQ&AQ&AQ&AQ&AQ&A

Business Ideas

Q: I want to start a business, but what type?

A: Wait. Hold onto your job before you have firmly decided on a particular business and established a solid plan for starting your business. You will be investing a large amount of money, time, and energy in this business—so don't rush the process. Be sure that you are not going to say "I wish I had started a bowling alley instead," six weeks after you open a pizza parlor!

Q: What business offers good income, but few risks?

A: Consider a service business. Generally service businesses require less investment than other kinds of businesses. Retail, wholesale, and manufacturing businesses require large investments in some combination of inventory, raw materials, finished goods, receivables, equipment, space leases, and/or leasehold improvements.

Service businesses are also less likely to get clobbered by powerful national firms. And profit margins can be sky-high, even with a relatively small level of sales.

With a service business you are less likely to become a billionaire, but you are also less likely to end up flipping hamburgers for someone else after your business fails!

Q: Should I keep my business idea secret?

A: First, let me assure you that there are literally millions of ideas for new businesses floating around and you can't be paranoid about people stealing your particular idea. It is

> Service businesses are less likely to get clobbered by powerful national firms.

unlikely that any people hearing of your idea will become so excited about it that they will junk their current work pursuits to pursue it.

Also, you should be asking for feedback on your ideas, preferably from potential customers, before you invest your life savings in a new business. And, you will need to be able to tell investors, lenders, employers, and suppliers about your idea or they will not be able to provide support, services, and/or backing for your business.

While it is conceivable that your idea is so strong that you may create the next Microsoft or Wal-Mart, chances are overwhelming that a company based on your idea is going to be a lot riskier than a company based on an existing business that you are trying to execute with a new twist.

Q: What's the best way to learn about a business?

A: There is no substitute for working in the business. Even if you work for a very short period of time in an entry-level capacity you are going to get a much better grasp of how that business works than you would through research or reading.

For example, I decided to start a newspaper while I was in college. Instead of waiting several years to work my way through each position on a newspaper staff, I worked for five days as a proofreader. Proofreading a newspaper is not much different or more fun than proofing a term paper, but it placed me in the middle of a working newspaper office. It allowed me the time to observe the more interesting and important work that everyone else was doing. I was able to start up my newspaper with a working knowledge base, as

> There is no substitute for working in the business.

well as the help of some very motivated, but equally inexperienced friends.

An alternative approach, if you are buying a business, is to have the seller work with you for a short period of time to show you how things are run. Be sure to write any such understanding into the purchase and sales agreement, including holding back part of the payment until you have learned how to run the business.

You can also contact the trade association connected with your industry and see if it offers any seminars or has information packets about getting started in that particular business.

> There's a lot to be said for starting a business part-time.

Q: Should I keep my job when I start a business?

A: If you have a good job and are starting a relatively small and simple business, I would strongly suggest you keep your existing job while starting your business. In a fairly uncomplicated business, such as a lawn care service or local retail store, you can hire hourly workers to do the core work during business hours for less than you are earning in your full-time job. Then you can do the more critical work, such as quoting jobs or developing promotional schemes at night or on weekends. The cash flow of a new business invariably starts slowly and tends to be more erratic than most people anticipate. Holding onto a salaried job can really help you make it through the slow seasons typical of a new business.

My grandfather actually started his shoe factory, by no means a simple business, while retaining his full-time job as a sales manager for another shoe firm. He even got his boss to finance his new venture!

Preparing the Plan

Q: Should I hire an expert to prepare the financials?

A: It's better to prepare them yourself. A potential lender or equity investor wants to see not only that the numbers look good, but also that you understand them inside and out. If you can't answer highly detailed or thorny questions about how you arrived at your numbers, you aren't going to get your funding.

Q: How detailed should budgets be?

A: Budgets in business plans to raise money should have little detail beyond breaking expenses out by departments or functions. You should, however, have supporting details available on request.

Similarly, when creating annual plans, even for a very small, one-person business, I suggest that you have two levels of detail. One should be a budget summary that has just one entry for projected sales of each major product or service line, and just one entry for projected costs in each functional area such as marketing, cost of goods sold, etc. A budget summary is very important in helping you get a handle on the cost structure of your business and its major trends.

Then have a separate, more detailed budget for each functional area. But don't get buried in detail. I would suggest a maximum of ten to twenty entries for projected expense categories if your business is small.

> Have two levels of budget detail.

Q&AQ&AQ&AQ&AQ&AQ&AQ&AQ&AQ&AQ&AQ&A

Cash flow is it!

Q: How can I benchmark costs and profits?

A: You need to get data for firms in your industry, perhaps from an industry association. Sometimes trade magazines and newsletters publish statistics for their industries. Compare your numbers with firms of similar size in the same industry.

Q: Which pro forma is most important?

A: Cash flow! It's nice to project a profit, and knowing you have a solid balance sheet can make you feel good, but if you run out of cash, your business will be dead in the water!

Just about all small businesses will feel a cash crunch sooner or later, and for most businesses it will happen sooner, later, and fairly regularly. But if you keep your cash flow projection up to date, you can take steps to avoid cash shortages before the problem becomes acute. Otherwise, you will go merrily along your way until one day you may find you have no money in the bank, your bank credit is exhausted, your payroll is due, your key vendors are howling for payment, the IRS is calling, and customers are still paying their bills slowly. Remember, cash crunches happen all the time in successful, profitable, growing businesses too!

Q: What tone should I have in the plan?

A: Keep the tone of your business plan factual. Don't use hyperbole or generalizations to describe the potential of your business plan. Investors and lenders don't want to hear phrases like "this business has incredible potential." They want to use the more factual information you present to reach their own conclusions.

Q&AQ&AQ&AQ&AQ&AQ&AQ&AQ&AQ&AQ&AQ&AQ&A

Q: How much detail should I go into?

A: Keep your plan succinct. Whether creating a business plan to raise money or an annual plan to run your business, keep it succinct. People tend to use too much detail when creating plans. If a business plan is too long, it might be skimmed. If an annual plan is too long, focus on what is really important might be lost.

Getting Equity Money

Q: What's the most common reason venture capitalists pass on funding proposals?

A: They often aren't impressed by the management team. Ideally they want to see someone in the group who has already participated in a highly successful start-up. Lacking this, they want to see that people with solid and relevant experience are already committed for the key positions.

They are most likely to reject proposals that are still at the idea stage. The later the development stage the firm is in, the greater the chances for funding.

Venture capitalists aren't satisfied with a business that has only moderate profit potential. They are looking for companies that will not only be profitable but have the possibility of quickly developing into a huge business and returning to investors a large multiple on their initial investment.

If your business plan is not well thought out or well presented, venture capitalists aren't going to have confidence in your ability to run the business.

> Venture capitalists like to see highly experienced entrepreneurs, developed businesses, and sky-high growth potential.

Q&AQ&AQ&AQ&AQ&AQ&AQ&AQ&AQ&AQ&AQ&A

> The longer you can wait
> to share equity, the more
> you will get to keep.

Q: How much equity will I give up?

A: This primarily depends on what development stage your firm is at and how much money you are seeking relative to how much capital you have already raised. If your firm is up and running and showing profitable sales, and you are looking for additional capital to finance your expansion, you will probably need to give up only a small portion of equity. On the other hand, if your firm is only at the idea stage and the outside investors are going to contribute over 90 percent of the funding, then you will probably have to give up at least half, if not more, of the equity.

Q: What do investors focus on most?

A: People, people, people.

In seeking equity money from venture capitalists or other outside investors, you will increase your chances of success if you get someone committed to your management team who, if not known personally by a potential investor, at least will have a recognizable name. If you can't manage this, you should consider getting one or more people on your Board of Directors whom potential investors may be familiar with.

Alternately, you can include as exhibits to your plan any positive media clippings you can find, such as items from trade publications about members of your management team. If you don't have any clippings, try contacting relevant publications to get media coverage about your start-up business proposal.

Annual Planning

Q: How long should annual planning take?

A: As a rule of thumb, I would suggest that you begin the annual planning process four to six months before the beginning of the next calendar year.

Many large corporations begin planning several years in advance, and this is why larger firms have a well-deserved reputation for moving as slow as dinosaurs. For a smaller, growing firm, it is a waste of time to do any detailed planning more than a year in advance; the company, your markets, and your competitor's plans will have changed too much to make such long-term planning valuable. The closer you are to the upcoming year when you plan, the more relevant your plans will be.

On the other hand, though, if you wait until the last minute to start annual planning, then you will have to rush through the process to get it done. The emphasis then will be on getting the plan done, not making it as good as possible. You and everyone working on a plan need to have enough time not only to get the plan done, but to do it well. You should also have time to weigh major alternatives and reconsider how well each function contributes to the overall plan after you've completed it.

Q: Should all functions get equal attention?

A: No. If some parts of your business will change little during the next year, there is no reason to summarize these areas in great depth.

> Small companies shouldn't plan more than a year in advance in great detail.

Remember that the role of the owner or CEO is to be sure that the planning efforts focus primarily on the areas that will really matter to the success of your business. Often planning can become focused on rivalries between different functions or lost in debates about factors that are relatively insignificant or not within your control. The CEO needs to see that plenty of attention is given to larger issues, such as:

- How many new products should we launch next year?
- Why is our marketing budget so high as a percentage of sales?
- What are the risks of increasing prices on our core products or services?

Q: What should I watch out for?

A: Most of all, you want to keep the emphasis on considering major alternatives and new initiatives and re-examining the ways the firm is currently doing its business. You want to be sure you and the other managers (if there are any) don't spend all of your time just making sales and expense projections—that's just forecasting the future, not managing the business. For example, if you are currently shipping your product to local customers with your local delivery truck, you don't want to just project how much it will cost to run the truck next year. Instead you may want to consider selling the truck and contracting out the work to an outside delivery service.

> Doing a business plan provides a chance to "rethink" the business from the bottom up.

Q&AQ&AQ&AQ&AQ&AQ&AQ&AQ&AQ&AQ&AQ&A

Q: Are salespeople too optimistic in forecasting?

A: Yes. But there are some who try to be very conservative so they have less pressure during the year or so they can look better when they deliver sales that are way over budget. After you work with different people, you will find how people in every functional area tend to approach the budgeting process, and you can work with each one to be as realistic as possible. Also, I'm a big believer in frank and open discussions about budgets, and I think that people from other functional areas can often offer constructive suggestions and serve as a reality check for one another.

Q: How often should I create pro formas?

A: If your business is growing, start from scratch once each year. Additionally, the cash flow pro forma should be updated on a monthly basis. The cash flow is the most critical pro forma statement. If you run out of cash, you effectively are out of business!

If major changes are anticipated during the year, you may want to update your profit and loss pro formas at that time. Balance sheets really need to be updated only yearly if you are concerned about violating any bank loan agreements you have made that references your balance sheet.

> Cash flows should be updated monthly.

Using the Business Plan

Q: Who should help with planning?

A: Involve everyone.

Both for business and annual plans, you need to have key employees create their area budgets. Then work with them until you are satisfied. Have key people get together to get the plan in sync and to get any disagreements out in the open. The more input people have in creating the plan, the more responsibility they will feel toward it.

> Don't run your business just by the numbers.

Q: Isn't the budget what really matters?

A: No. Annual plans are not just budgets.

If an annual plan includes any financial projections, I find that almost everyone tends to focus on them almost exclusively, de-emphasizing the qualitative aspects of planning. While you do need to use numbers to run a business, numbers alone lead to a shallow plan. Companies run just by the numbers lose direction, drift from their strategy, and never realize their full potential. It is essential to the planning process to articulate clearly what the direction of the company will be for the coming year and what the role of each person will be in supporting the direction of the company overall.

Q: Exactly how do I use the annual plan during the year?

A: Use the annual plan to improve performance.

In the real world nothing ever goes exactly according to plan but your annual plan gives you a way of measuring your company's actual performance against projected performance. Meet with key people at least once a month to review how the company is performing relative to the plan. The emphasis should not be on browbeating those managers whose areas are underperforming, but on how performance can be improved in the future.

Q: How rigidly should I stay within budget?

A: You should be more concerned in seeing that each function stays within its entire budget. For example, if the marketing department spends much more than projected on publicity but makes up for it by spending that much less on advertising, that's fine.

Don't be terribly concerned about staying within budget if sales are above budget. But more than once I have let expenses soar above budget because sales were above budget. Then, later in the year, I discovered that expenses rose more quickly than sales. So if sales are increasing, make sure expenses increase only by a like percentage.

Q: Should the budget be redone in mid-year?

A: Generally, no. It just takes too long and too much effort to make it worthwhile.

If your sales are running way above budget, try to be sure that expenses are not rising disproportionately. Watch out particularly for new, discretionary expenses that were not on the budget—they can always be added to the budget for the following year.

If your sales are running a little below budget, try to cut expenses in a few limited areas.

However, if your sales are running way below budget, I strongly recommend reworking the entire plan and carefully re-examining each and every item of the budget.

> Keep your budget on course without being too rigid.

Q & A Q & A Q & A Q & A Q & A Q & A Q & A Q & A Q & A Q & A Q & A

Q: Do I need a budget if I'm frugal anyway?

A: Believe me—I've tried this approach, and it never worked. Running a business of any size is too complex to do by the seat of your pants. I've found that even if I try to be cheap as dirt on every expense, without a concrete plan, costs can still mushroom out of control and wipe out profitability.

Q: How can I quickly update cash flow?

A: Since any pro forma takes quite a while to carefully update, there may be times when you need a shortcut to get a ball-park estimate. I would first revise sales estimates and changes in collection cycle (the amount of time it takes you to get paid from customers who buy on credit) and any costs that directly change with sales, such as costs of goods sold in a product business, or the costs of labor and major supplies in a service business.

Strategy

Q: Shouldn't I just aim to be the best?

A: Aiming to be the best isn't a strategy. Everyone tries to be the best. Strategy is the means you choose to make your business the best option for existing and for potential customers. For example, offering a more personalized service than that offered by your competitors would be a strategy.

Also, attempting to be the best in every aspect of your business is tantamount to setting yourself up for failure. It is unrealistic to try to achieve and sustain superior performance throughout all areas of your business operation. A wiser goal

> A quick and dirty cash flow update is much better than none at all!!

is to try to be good in all areas but select only those one or two areas that are crucial to distinguishing your business from the competition in which to strive for perfection.

Q: Can you suggest a strategy for a car wash business?

A: You could use strategy to widen your gap of direct competition to boost your profit margins. For example, you could develop add-on premium services such as hand drying, high-luster waxing, detailing, or shampooing of car interiors. Not only should services like these offer higher dollar sales and higher profit margins, but they might also enable you to raise prices for your basic car wash service as well.

Q: How important is strategy?

A: On a scale of one to ten, it's a fifteen! If you don't have a strategy, it is quite possible that you could work eighty hours per week all year long and only break even or possibly even lose money. With a great strategy you might be able to work one day a week and make piles of money!

Football provides a good analogy. If a football team works very hard but initiates the wrong plays, it won't be going to the Super Bowl. If the team continually executes passing plays against rivals that are terrific at interceptions, it might as well have forfeited the game before it began!

Q: Do personal service firms need strategies?

A: Absolutely. A common, yet good strategy in competitive personal service businesses is to specialize. The more you can be recognized as a specialist, the less competition you will have

> Strategy is the heart of your business.

and the higher rates you can charge. Initially you may want to take any client that comes along. At the same time, however, you should start writing newspaper or trade magazine articles or giving seminars that focus on your particular area of expertise. As your ability to profit through higher-priced specialty work increases, you can proportionately, phase out your lower-priced less specialized work.

> Franchisers make money in several different ways.

Franchising

Q: How does a franchiser make money?

A: Usually a franchiser sells the right to a franchise for a hefty fee over the actual out-of-pocket costs of setting up the business. Then the franchiser receives ongoing payments—usually a percentage of the sales, not the profits. Most franchisers also sell supplies and services to franchises.

Q: How should I weigh initial versus ongoing fees?

A: If you are buying into a successful franchise, you should be more concerned about the ongoing charges. These costs are paid yearly. And, since these fees are typically extracted from sales, not profits, they can cut your profits to shreds. For example, if your pre-tax profit margin is 10 percent, but your franchise fee is 5 percent, your profit is halved! If you are buying a less established franchise, be leery of up-front costs. You could lose your investment altogether if the business fails.

In either case you should examine all costs and contracts, and talk to current franchise owners before signing.

Q: Is it worth it to pay a percentage of sales?

A: This is the $64 million dollar question you must ask yourself. Many people who buy franchises think it is a great deal when they are able to turn an early profit, but in later years, with experience under their belts, they come to view the franchise fees as onerous.

You need to evaluate what you are getting by buying into a franchise and how valuable what you are buying will be to you in several years. If you are just using the franchise as a means of learning industry skills, then you might be better off working for someone else for a period of time instead. If, on the other hand, you already have industry skills and business expertise and want to apply them through an established brand-name business in a competitive market, the franchise route may be right for you.

Q: Are there other costs to watch out for?

A: Often you will have to pay a percentage of local, regional, or national advertising costs as a separate fee over and above the franchise fees. You may also be required to purchase supplies and services directly from the franchiser.

How to weigh if a franchise is worth it.

Q: Any other issues I should consider?

A: If you are relatively inexperienced in running a business, buying a franchise may be a much better option for you than starting a business from scratch. But do be aware that even a franchise isn't a foolproof expressway to business success.

In addition to issues that may be peculiar to the particular industry you are buying into, there are general issues that should be considered. Can you sell the franchise easily, and how? Can the franchise fees be increased for any reason? Are new competitors affecting market share? What level of applicable industry or business skills did the typical franchise owner possess before he or she bought into the franchise?

Get out and talk to as many current franchise owners as you can before making any commitments. This just can't be overemphasized.

> Buying a business is often a good choice.

Buying a Business

Q: Am I safer with a start-up than buying a firm?

A: Probably not. An up-and-running business showing any profits means that you have established customers, marketing avenues, and sales momentum. If you put the energy and talent that it takes to start a new business into improving an existing business, you should be able to dramatically increase earnings and recoup your purchase price very quickly.

Q: Are businesses priced realistically?

A: Most people selling a business have a very inflated idea of what it is worth and this view is often reflected in the asking price. Few small businesses sell for anywhere near the asking price, and selling prices at half or even less are quite common. This is especially true when hard assets such as real estate are not a major factor. Remember, a business is a much less liquid asset than a house. In other words, relatively few people are interested in buying a particular type, size, and location of business.

Q: Should I buy a one year old firm?

A: Don't do it. Other than hard assets, when you purchase a business you are buying goodwill and forward momentum from an established pattern of doing business. Even if the business really is profitable, the owner couldn't have created much goodwill or developed an established market position in such a short period of time. Furthermore, I'd always worry about the real reason the business is being sold so quickly— if the new opportunity looks terrific to the seller, then his current business, obviously, looks less terrific. In addition, with a service business, you need to ascertain how much of the business' success has been due to the personal characteristics or contacts of the proprietor.

Q: Should the seller sign a non-compete?

A: Absolutely! An aggressive person can regain market position overnight in a new business through personal contacts, industry reputation, and market knowledge. You should at least have the seller agree to sign a non-compete clause. If you are really concerned, you should also consider paying for the business in partial payments over a period of time.

> Examine what you are reallying buying.

After I negotiated to purchase a magazine from the Harvard Business School, a former licensee announced that it was going to compete with me despite a non-compete agreement. I persuaded Harvard Business School to pay the related legal fees and retain title during my first year of operation to ensure the validity of the non-compete agreement.

CHAPTER 6

Front Matter

FRONT MATTER FRONT MATTER FRONT MATTER

Cover Letter

Try to talk with potential investors **before** sending them a copy of the business plan.

Name of Addressee
Title of Addressee
Company of Addressee
Address of Addressee
City/State/Zip of Addressee

Date . . .

Dear (Addressee):

To follow-up our phone conversation, I am forwarding you the requested copy of the business plan for (name of business).

(Name of business) is in the business of (type of business). We are well-positioned to succeed in this field because (success factors). Our current situation is (describe current situation).

We are currently seeking financing in the amount of $(amount). The funds will be used for (purpose of funding).

I will call you again in a few days, once you have had a change to review our plan. In the meantime do not hesitate to call me if you have any questions.

Sincerely,
(Name)
(Phone)
Enc.

FRONT MATTER FRONT MATTER FRONT MATTER

Cover Letter

As this cover letter indicates, I would try to first have phone contact with a potential investor or bank lender before sending them a business plan.

And ideally I would try to present the plan to them in person. This of course would save you the need to write the letter—but, more importantly, it will greatly increase your chances of getting financing.

If you do modify this letter or write your own—keep it short—one page at the most! The longer the letter the less chance any of it will be read.

In your letter be as factual as possible. First be sure to explain to the reader what business you are in. Then emphasize why your business will succeed, not how much it will succeed. Focus on what makes your business different from the competition.

Then state exactly how much money you want and what you will use it for. Don't be shy about asking for money. Bankers and investors are there to loan money. One of their very first questions is going to be "How much do you want?" Followed by "What are you going to use it for?" The sooner you answer these questions the more likely a potential financier will read your business plan.

Like your business plan, make sure your cover letter is carefully proofed and edited.

Remember that presentations to potential investors can raise security law (and related fraud law) concerns. If you are seeking to raise money first check with the appropriate regulatory agency. (In the US this would be the Securities and Exchange Commission and regulators in all states that you are seeking investors to insure either compliance with, or exemption from, appropriate regulations.

Non-Disclosure Statement

I would like to receive a copy of the Business Plan for (Name of Business) solely for the purpose of possibly investing in this business.

I acknowledge that the Business Plan contains confidential, proprietary information, release of which may cause substantial financial damage to the owners of the Business Plan.

In consideration for being given an opportunity to review the Business Plan, I agree not to make any copies of any portion of the Business Plan, not to disclose the Business Plan or any of its contents to any third party, and not to make any use of the Business Plan other than to consider possibly investing in (Name of Business.)

I agree to return the Business Plan and any accompanying documents to the owners of the Business Plan promptly, when I have completed my review of the plan, when I no longer have interest in considering the possibility of investing in the plan, or upon request of the owners of the plan—whichever comes first.

Signed: _____

Date: _____

Non-Disclosure Statement

To protect the confidentiality of your business plan get a signed non-disclosure statement *before* you release it.

Sending an unsolicited business plan with an accompanying "Non-disclosure Agreement" will not bind the recipient in any way. He/she can ignore the agreement and do whatever he wants with the plan. This is why you should ideally send out the non-disclosure agreement first and wait to send the business plan until you have received back a signed agreement.

Be sure to have your qualified business lawyer review the non-disclosure agreement to make sure that it is suitable for your purposes.

Unless their is something unusually secretive about your business I would not ask a commercial banker to sign a confidentiality agreement. Yes, there is a very, very slight chance that the banker might possibly not keep the information confidential, and an even smaller chance that by signing such an agreement he or she would be more likely to keep the plan confidential. But by asking the banker to sign a confidentiality agreement there is a very good chance that you will come across as either someone not comfortable in dealing with bankers, or as a very paranoid, non-trusting person.

On the other hand, I would consider it much more acceptable to ask potential equity investors to sign non-disclosure agreements. This is a much more commonly accepted practice.

> Generally, asking a banker to sign a confidentiality agreement is very awkward.

FRONT MATTER FRONT MATTER FRONT MATTER

Title Page

Keep the title page simple and clean.

NAME OF BUSINESS
_____

BUSINESS PLAN
_____

DATE
_____

CONTACT:
Name
Title
Address
Phone

This business plan is confidential.

FRONT MATTER FRONT MATTER FRONT MATTER

Title Page

Resist the temptation to make your title page too fancy. Many bankers and potential investors would consider a colorful or decorative title page to be inappropriate.

Also resist the temptation to fill your title page with lots of information. Especially resist the temptation to put any kind of "sell copy" on the title page—it will detract from the authoritative look you want your plan to have.

So keep it simple.

You may or may not want to include a note that the plan is confidential and should not be shared with third parties. You could also say merely "Confidential information." How confidential the information is kept will have a lot more to do with who you distribute the plan to, rather than what kind of confidentiality notice you attach to it.

Some people number each business plan they distribute to help keep track of them and to help keep the information confidential.

Some people put the number of years the business plan covers on the title page. I don't think this is necessary.

But I do think it is important to list the contact person and their phone number on the front of the plan.

> Just writing "confidential" on your business plan is **not** enough to protect you.

FRONT MATTER FRONT MATTER FRONT MATTER

Contents Page

A detailed, well-organized contents will entice people to more carefully review your plan.

Very few people will actually want to include all of the sections listed here in their plan.

SUMMARY
- Business Concept
- Current Situation
- Key Success Factors
- Financial Needs

~~VISION~~ GOALS
- FINANCIAL Vision Statement
- Milestones

MARKET ANALYSIS
- Overall Market
- Market Changes
- Market Segments
- Target Market AND CUSTOMERS
- Customer Characteristics
- Customer Needs
- Buying Decisions

COMPETITIVE ANALYSIS
- Industry Overview
- Nature of Competition
- ~~Industry Changes~~ IN THE INDUSTRY
- Primary Competitors
- Competitive Products
- Opportunities
- Threats AND RISKS

STRATEGY
- KEY Competitive Capabilities
- KEY Competitive Weaknesses
- Strategy
- Implementing Strategy

PRODUCTS/SERVICES
- Description
- Positioning
- Competitive Evaluation
- Future Products

SALES & MARKETING
- Marketing Strategy
- Sales Tactics
- Advertising
- Promotions
- Publicity
- Trade Shows

OPERATIONS
- Key Personnel
- Organizational Structure
- HR Plan
- Product/Service Delivery
- Customer Service
- Facilities

FINANCE
- Assumptions
- Starting Balance Sheet
- Profit & Loss
- Cash Flow
- Balance Sheet
- Ratios

EXHIBITS
- Resumes
- (TAX RETURNS '98 '97
- BROCHURES

FRONT MATTER FRONT MATTER FRONT MATTER

Contents

Just like the title page, the contents page should be simple and straightforward. If your plan is short, such as less than seven pages, you may want to skip the contents altogether.

A long contents will not impress investors. So don't feel that you have to use all of the sections of the plan. We anticipate that almost no one will want to use every single section of the plan.

If you want you could match page numbers to each part or section of the contents. After the body of your plan is finished, simply enter the page numbers opposite the matching wording in the contents. Most professionally-prepared plans I have seen however, do not include page numbers.

As another alternative you could simply number each major section of the business plan sequentially. As still another alternative you could have secondary numbering for each subsection of the plan (i.e. "1-1, 1-2, 1-3").

Remember, the contents, not the contents page is going to raise the money you need.

CHAPTER 7

Summary

SUMMARYSUMMARYSUMMARYSUMMARYSUMMARY

Business Concept

Identify the type of business or industry that you are in and your target market. Present the basic facts about the purpose of the business, describe its major characteristics, and note significant differences from competitors. Give a quick sketch of your future vision for the company. If you want to go into more detail, you may also add specific goals, a summary of your mission statement, or briefly summarize your business philosophy.

Select and edit the <u>one</u> statement that best applies. (For example, choose the "Basic Business Concept Statement" or the "Emphasis on Business Mission Statement" or another statement and edit this <u>one</u> statement to suit your needs. See the sample business plans in Chapters 16 and 17 for examples.)

☐ **Basic Business Concept Statement**

(This check-box headline on these statements is for reference only and should not appear in your finished plan)

We are part of the ^NATIONAL CONSTRUCTION .... industry.

Our target market is ... PRISONS, CONSTRUCTION OUR CUSTOMERS WILL BE CEILING CONTRACTORS, DETENTION EQUIPMENT CONTRACTORS, AND GENERAL CONTRACTORS.

Our primary (product or service or product line or service line) is HEAVY GAUGE SECURITY ACOUSTICAL CEILING SYSTEMS.

Important characteristics of this ..... PRODUCT .... are IT'S
(PRODUCT OR SERVICE)
DURABILITY TO STAND UP TO VANDELIZM AND ABILITY TO REDUCE NOISE.

Our ... CEILING SYSTEMS ..... differs from competitors in that BUT WE
(PRODUCT OR SERVICE) DON'T
DIFFER FROM MOST COMPETITORS BY OFFERING A HEAVY GAUGE LINE, A LIGHT GAUGE LINE AND THE INSTALLATION OF BOTH.

SUMMARYSUMMARYSUMMARYSUMMARYSUMMARY

Our intention is that the company will become _INVOLVED_
IN THE MANUFACTURING AND INSTALLATION
OF ENCLOSURES FOR BUILDING MECHANICALS AND
OF DETENTION FURNITURE.

☐ **Emphasis on Business Mission Statement**

We (produce or provide) . . . .
(DESCRIBE PRODUCT OR SERVICE)

. . . .

. . . .

The mission of our business is to . . . .
(PRODUCE PRODUCTS OR DELIVER
. . . . **that** (deliver superior value, offer outstanding
SERVICES)
quality, offer the best price, are the most technologically
advanced, provide highly personalized solutions, specifically
designed for the needs of., are individually tailored for the needs
of each customer, for a specific market niche . . . .

. . . .

will build a brand name franchise, will lead their markets, are
the most innovative in the industry, are professional in every
way, etc.). **We intend to fulfill this mission by giving extra effort
to** (customer service, sales, engineering, production, research,
customer's needs, changes in the market, superior workmanship, customer satisfaction, addressing customer needs, etc.).

EXPERT ADVICE

Business Concept

Keep the business concept short and succinct. You want the reader to quickly understand just the very basics of your business. The more detail you go into here, the more you risk confusing them. You will have plenty of opportunity to get into more detail throughout the entire business plan. Don't worry about getting into the subtle differences between your firm and your competitors. And don't start out tooting your horn too loud! Especially in this introductory part of the plan, keep your tone matter of fact, and you will be more likely to build credibility with potential financiers. If this is a plan for an already existing business, you may want to talk about what the concept was when the business first started and whether or not the original business concept still applies today.

SUMMARYSUMMARYSUMMARYSUMMARYSUMMARY

☐ **Responding to New Needs Statement**

In the . . . . industry today, there is a much greater awareness
(RELEVANT FIELD)
than ever before of the need for . . . . This has occurred
(NEW NEEDS IN THE RELEVANT FIELD)
as a result of . . . ., and creates tremendous opportunities for
(CHANGES IN THE FIELD)
businesses that specifically respond to this situation. We intend to distinguish ourselves from the competition by offering (high quality, superior, technically
advanced, state-of-the-art, highly personalized, highly customized, high performance, guaranteed, etc.) . . . . which address these
(PRODUCTS OR SERVICES)
new needs much more effectively than current companies in our market area.

☐ **Entering a Fast Growing Industry Statement**

The . . . . industry has expanded rapidly in the past several years
(INDUSTRY)
and growth is expected to continue at a strong pace for the foreseeable future. This
offers excellent opportunities for new companies to enter this market. We intend
to address the needs of customers in this market who seek . . . .

. . . .

We will address this need by providing . . . .

. . . .

Distinguishing characteristics of our (business or product(s) or service(s)) will be

. . . .

. . . .

SUMMARYSUMMARYSUMMARYSUMMARYSUMMARY

☐ **Expansion of Existing Service Business Statement**

We have been successful in providing .... services, with a
(TYPE OF)
special emphasis on .... We have an excellent
(AREA OF SPECIALIZATION)
reputation and are best known for our .... ,
(SPECIFIC SERVICE CHARACTERISTIC)
which differentiates us from our competitors. The company is profitable and has
great potential for growth and for becoming a market leader. To best take advantage of our growth opportunities, the company would like to ....
.... These expendi-
(NEW DEVELOPMENTS OR EXPENSES THAT FINANCING IS REQUIRED FOR)
tures will allow us to finance and support our planned growth, without sacrificing
the quality of service for which we are known.

☐ **Become a Market Leader Statement**

Our goal is to become one of the leading .... in the
(TYPE OF BUSINESS)
.... We intend to accomplish this goal by offering
(GEOGRAPHICAL AREA)
a set of .... that meet client needs better than any
(PRODUCTS/SERVICES)
competitor by (utilization of state of the art technology, building a superior workforce through careful hiring and continuous training and development, closely
meeting the needs of each customer, by differentiating our products by ....
....
by offering superior service). We will also create a high level of visibility and awareness for our .... by a consistent and carefully target-
(PRODUCTS/SERVICES)
ed marketing strategy.

SUMMARYSUMMARYSUMMARYSUMMARYSUMMARY

☐ **Change of Strategic Direction Statement**

The company was formed in . . . . to . . . .
           (YEAR)   (INITIAL PURPOSE)

Historically, the target market for our . . . . has
                           (PRODUCTS OR SERVICES)

been . . . . , which we have reached through a variety of
     (TARGET MARKET)

advertising and publicity channels. However, at this point in time, due to signifi-

cant changes in the field, including . . . . , a
                       (INDICATE CHANGES)

new strategic direction is warranted. We now plan to shift our focus to

. . . . We expect to maintain some of the current
     (NEW TARGET MARKET)

. . . . , but also to add new . . . .
  (PRODUCTS OR SERVICES)   (PRODUCTS OR SERVICES)

such as . . . .

. . . .

. . . .

. . . .

Current Situation

Present the facts—company name, owner's name, date of incorporation—and put it in the larger context of the industry as a whole. What stage is the company at now? If it's a new company, has it made any sales yet? Is all the staff hired? If it's an existing company, for how long has it been in business? Is the situation stable? Are sales and profits consistent? How does it compare to other firms in the industry? What are the major challenges or opportunities facing the firm? How are you going to respond to them?

Select and edit the <u>one</u> statement that best applies.

☐ **Basic Current Situation Statement**

The company was founded as a (sole proprietorship, partnership, corporation, S corporation, limited liability company) in ....WISCONSIN...... on (2/25/99). Currently the compa-

(LOCATION)   (DATE)
ny is (well established in its market, becoming established in its market, highly profitable, profitable, in a start-up mode, about to ship its first product, ready to begin operations, seeking money to begin operations, seeking seed money, etc.) The major challenge(s) the firm is facing at this point is (are) ..
.OBTAINING. LEADS. TO. SELL,.....................
....
It intends to respond to it (them) by .CONTRACTING....

EXPERT ADVICE

Current Situation

Think of your intended audience for this plan. If you are seeking money to finance a start-up, the potential investors reading the plan will want a fair amount of detail about how far developed your business is. If you are seeking financing for an existing business, you will want to mention instead the sales and profitability of the company and why financing is needed. If you are writing a plan to help you, the manager, correct a particular problem or improve a particular aspect of the company, you will find it useful to clearly identify in writing what the issue is, how it came about, and the end result that you hope to achieve.

SUMMARYSUMMARYSUMMARYSUMMARYSUMMARY

WITH A NATIONAL LEAD PROVIDER. THE SERVICE WILL SCREEN THE LEADS FOR OUR NEEDS AND FORWARD PLANS AND SPECIFICATIONS TO GENERATE ESTIMATES

The major opportunity(ies) available to the firm is (are) *REDUCING COSTS BY ELIMINATING MANUFACTURES REPRESENTATIVES. WITH THE LEAD SERVICE, REPS ARE OF LITTLE VALUE.*

The firm intends to take advantage of it (them) by ~~SELLING DIRECT~~ *USING HIGHLY COMPETITIVE PRICING AND SELLING DIRECT WITH OUR OWN SALES PEOPLE.*

☐ Start-up Company Statement

We are a start-up, incorporated in .... in the State of .... The principal
(YEAR)   (STATE)
owners are ...., whose title is .... ;
          (NAME)   (TITLE)
................., whose title is ...., and
(NAME)   (TITLE)
................., whose title is .... Other key person-
(NAME)   (TITLE)
nel include................., ..., and
           (NAME)   (NAME)
................., who bring special expertise in the areas
(NAME)
of ...., ..., and
   (AREA)   (AREA)
.... respectively. With this team of experienced and tal-
(AREA)
ented individuals, the company will be positioned to meet an emerging, under-
served need for .... We are currently (in the ini-
               (NEED TO FOCUS ON)
tial planning stage, in the research and development stage, about to finish plans
for our first product, finalizing plans for our operation, about to make firm com-

SUMMARYSUMMARYSUMMARYSUMMARYSUMMARY

mitments to begin operations, ready to begin production, seeking seed money, seeking additional capital) **to** . . . .

The major challenges we face before beginning operations are . . . .

. . . .

. . . .

We hope to begin business by . . . .

. . . .

. . . .

☐ **Existing Business Statement**

We have been in business for . . . .

. . . .

years with sales in our past fiscal year ending . . . . reaching . . . .
                                                (DATE)

. . . .

In recent years our sales have been (growing rapidly, growing moderately, growing slowly, growing steadily, growing, stable, flat, declining slightly, declining, erratic). **Recently we have been** (highly profitable, profitable, moderately profitable, marginally profitable, at break-even in terms of profits, nearing break-even, experiencing slight losses, experiencing losses, performing erratically in terms of profitability.) **Factors influencing our recent performance include** . . . .

. . . .

Upcoming challenges that we face include . . . .

SUMMARYSUMMARYSUMMARYSUMMARYSUMMARY

We intend to meet these challenges by . . . .

The largest opportunity(ies) that we face is (are) . . . .

We hope to take advantage of this opportunity by . . . .

☐ **Existing Business Facing Changing Market Statement**

Our company was formed in . . . . as a . . . . under
       (YEAR)   (FORM OF BUSINESS)
the laws of the State of . . . . We have seen massive changes in our
                   (STATE)
industry in recent years. New technologies, increased consumer awareness, and
global competitive pressures are largely responsible for these changes, and for
many companies providing . . . . in this marketplace,
                      (PRODUCTS/SERVICES)
it has been a challenging time. Competition has been fierce, product life cycles
have been shortening, market shares have been changing rapidly, profitability for
many firms have been erratic and some players have experienced severe financial
problems. We have survived in this difficult atmosphere, but challenges remain.
The most pressing challenge facing us is . . . .

We intend to face this by . . . .

SUMMARYSUMMARYSUMMARYSUMMARYSUMMARY

Other important issues we face are . . . .

. . . .

At the same time the market is very large and a successful player in this industry can potentially enjoy high profitability.

☐ **Innovative New Business Statement**

While the . . . . field is currently dominated by a few
(RELEVANT INDUSTRY)

large companies, our research shows that the situation is ripe for a new company

with a new approach. We believe we can successfully enter the market by offering

. . . . that . . . .
(PRODUCTS OR SERVICES) (DESCRIBE UNIQUE BENEFIT OF YOUR PRODUCT OR SERVICE)

. . . .

This differs from current . . . . in that . . . .
(PRODUCTS OR SERVICES)

. . . .

We believe that buyers will find the competitive benefit of our (products or services) compelling enough that we will be able to build sales quickly and establish a solid market position. We have (performed market surveys, spoken with prospective customers, studied historical market research, spoken with retailers, spoken with sales people, done focus groups, observed the success of a similar business approach in other markets) to confirm that customers are interested in our new approach.

A summary of our (interviews with prospective buyers, our market research, our telephone survey, discussions with retailers, findings from relevant industry studies) is included at the end of this business plan.

SUMMARYSUMMARYSUMMARYSUMMARYSUMMARY

☐ **Growing Business Statement**

. . . . is a . . . . . . -year old business, operating in the State
(COMPANY NAME)   (# OF)

of . . . . at . . . . There are   cur-
(STATE)   (BUSINESS LOCATION)   (# OF)

rent owners: . . . . owns . . . . . of the outstanding stock,
(NAME)   (%)

. . . . owns . . . . . . , and . . . . owns
(NAME)   (%)   (NAME)

. . . . In the last complete fiscal year, the Company had gross revenues of
(%)

. . . . and total operating expenses of . . . . , for a net profit of
(\$)   (\$)

. . . . Projections for the current fiscal year show a . . . . growth in net
(\$)   (%)

profits. In the next few years, it is estimated that our segment of the

. . . . industry will also grow by at least . . . .
(RELEVANT INDUSTRY)   (%)

This growth will be driven by . . . . ,
(GROWTH FACTOR)

. . . . , and
(GROWTH FACTOR)

. . . .
(GROWTH FACTOR)

We know that we are not the only company to see the business opportunities created by this expected growth, but we do feel that our . . . .
(TYPE OF)

. . . . is a unique response to the situation that
(PRODUCT/SERVICE)

will help us stand out in what will be a crowded marketplace.

☐ **Ready to Expand and Move Out of Home Office Statement**

The company was founded as a (sole proprietorship, partnership, corporation, limited

liability company) in . . . . The principle owner(s) is (are) . . . .
(DATE)

. . . .

SUMMARYSUMMARYSUMMARYSUMMARYSUMMARY

with ..... ownership. .... is also the founder and CEO.
（%）   (NAME)
To date the business has been operated from the founder's residence in

....
(LOCATION)

At this point the business is ready to step up it's level of business activity,
including moving to a commercial facility. The company plans to (buy, lease, sub-
lease, rent) approximately .... feet of (grade A office space, office space, industrial
(FEET)
space, warehouse space, retail space, space that is suitable) for ....

....

The company also plans to hire ....
additional people, primarily in .... positions. While
(FUNCTION)
sales last year were $........ , they have been gaining momentum, and sales this
($)
year are expected to reach $......... . The company expects to expand largely by
($)
(increasing its customer base, finding new customers, adding new products, adding new
services, increasing revenues with current customers, entering new markets, expanding our
target market) to ....

....

☐ **Seeking Initial Investors or Partners Statement**
At this point, we have refined our business concept and developed an extensive
plan for taking this concept to market. We are now seeking initial equity investors
or partners.

SUMMARYSUMMARYSUMMARYSUMMARYSUMMARY

☐ **Seed Money in Place Statement**

. . . . (COMPANY NAME) . . . . has raised . . . . (S) through the company founders and other private sources. The breakdown of initial investment by source is as follows . . . . (LIST INITIAL INVESTMENT SOURCES) . . . .

. . . .

These funds have been utilized to . . . . (USES OF SEED FUNDS) . . . . , which is proceeding successfully at this time. When the remaining capital requirements have been met, ... (OBJECT OF SEED FUNDS) . . . . will already be complete, and the Company will be able to focus on . . . . (NEXT OBJECTIVES) . . . .

☐ **Purpose of Creating this Plan Statement**

The purpose of writing this business plan is to (attract additional equity investment, obtain a bank loan, establish a line of credit, secure financing, re-evaluate our entire business, develop an overall business strategy, establish better control and direction of the business, correct the following problems . . . .

. . . ., address the following issues

. . . .). Specifically what we would like to accomplish is

. . . .

The current situation has come about because . . . .

. . . .

SUMMARYSUMMARYSUMMARYSUMMARYSUMMARY

Key Success Factors

Explain the factors that will help insure that your business will be successful. What has been responsible for your success to date if you are an established business. What is your real strength, your ace in the hole if you are a new business?

Select and edit the <u>one or two</u> statements that best apply.

EXPERT ADVICE

Key Success Factors

Every firm has plenty of success factors built into their business that can help them succeed. Here you want to zero in on just a few that can really make a difference. Especially for start-ups, you might want to focus on your key people

☐ **Key Success Factors Statement**

The success of our business (has been, is, will be) largely a result of

> COMPLIANCE WITH THE SPECIFICATION AT A LOW PRICES, REDUCED COSTS AND AGGRESSIVE SALES EFFORTS BY USING OUR OWN SALES FORCE AND a NATIONAL LEAD SERVICE INSTEAD OF INDEPENDENT REPS, OUR KNOWLEDGE OF THE BUSINESS AND OUR CONTACTS.

...t have a great new
...pt or positioning
...n't been tested in the
... the other hand, if
...erienced people, they
...ed. And they have
...gible to show for it—
... An established busi-
...arefully try to identify
...ss factors that have
...ucceed in the past.
...n your most suc-
...cts or services. Why
...ceeded? Are there
...ntributed to the suc-
cess of these items that could lead to the success of future ones?

). In particular what really sets us apart from the competition

is .OUR. SALES. APPROACH AND PRICE STRUCTURE.

(OVERALL SUCCESS FACTOR)

SUMMARYSUMMARYSUMMARYSUMMARYSUMMARY

This translates into a benefit for customers because *THEY OBTAIN THE REQUIRED MATERIALS AND SERVICE AT A COST SAVINGS.*

☐ Key Success Factors Listed in Order of Importance Statement

There are several key factors that can be identified as being particularly important in our firm's (ability to succeed, success to date). In order of relative importance these factors are:

1. *LOW COST BY SELLING W/O REPS*
   (SUCCESS FACTOR #1)
2. *LEAD SERVICE MAXIMIZES EFFORTS*
   (SUCCESS FACTOR #1)
3. *REPUTATION & CONTACTS*
   (SUCCESS FACTOR #1)
4. *FLEXIBILITY BY OUTSOURCING (TAP INTO VENDOR'S EXPERTICE)*
   (SUCCESS FACTOR #1)
   AND SUPERIOR SERVICE

☐ Management Team Statement

Our major asset is our highly talented and experienced management team. The (number of) individuals compliment each other well, combining backgrounds in a diverse group of important areas. . . . . brings
(KEY PERSON #1)
expertise in . . . .

. . . . brings expertise in . . . .
(KEY PERSON #2)

. . . . brings . . . .
(KEY PERSON #3)

. . . .

Together, these strengths cover many major operational aspects of the business with solid experience and a proven record of success. (Refer to the resumes at the end of the business plan for more information.)

☐ **Reputation and Contacts in the Industry Statement**

While our company has not yet registered any sales, we have a terrific reputation and a wealth of important contacts in the industry because of the key people already (on board, hired, involved in the business as an employee or investor). These individuals will help us to attract top employees for other positions that remain to be filled, will help us get in the door at major customers, will help us generate visibility in the media, and will generally lend a level of instant credibility to our entire business. Here is a summary list of key hire to date and a brief summary of their background (for more information see their resumes at the end of this business plan): . . . . (. . . . . years of experience
(KEY PERSON #1)   (#)
in . . . .
at . . . .)

. . . . (. . . . . years of experience in
(KEY PERSON #2)   (#)
. . . . at
. . . .)

. . . . (. . . . . years of experience in
(KEY PERSON #3)   (#)
. . . . at
. . . .)

.... (..... years of experience in
(KEY PERSON #4)   (#)

.... at

....)

☐ **Prototype of Proprietary Technology Statement**

In the initial development phase, we were able to create an operational prototype

of .... A (patent/copyright) has been applied for
(TYPE OF PROTOTYPE)

and is now pending. This new product offers an important advantage over exist-

ing alternatives because. . . . .

. . . .

☐ **Aggressive Sales Force Statement**

From the perspective of the customer there is relatively little difference from one

product or service to the next. Buyers do not tend to systematically weigh through

all the possible options when making a purchasing decision. The ability of the

salesperson to get access to the buyer and to persuade the buyer to buy from him

or her is a powerful competitive advantage. We (have, will have, are developing) an

aggressive sales force that will give us that competitive edge. Important elements

in this competitive edge include (our highly experienced sales manager, highly talented

salespeople, a careful recruiting plan for sales people, a careful selection process for sales-

people, a thorough training program for salespeople, a generous incentive-based compen-

sation structure, a strong sales support program, an ability to generate high quality leads

through our marketing efforts).

SUMMARYSUMMARYSUMMARYSUMMARYSUMMARY

☐ **Ability to Develop Products that Closely Match Customer's Needs Statement**

Important to our success (is, will be, has been) our ability to develop new products and services that closely match our customer's needs. By following a systematic process to create our . . . . we (assure, will
(PRODUCTS OR SERVICES)
assure) that we are meeting our customer's needs better than our competitors. To initiate ideas for new product ideas we first begin with (input from our current customers, input from buyers we know from our past experience, a detailed study of what products or services have been most successful, focus groups of customer's needs, conversations with potential buyers about what they like and dislike about current products or services). Then we develop a . . . . concept and discuss it
(PRODUCT OR SERVICE)
with (a focus group, key buyers, our larger customers, potential buyers). We then incorporate their feedback into our final design.

☐ **Ability to Deliver Highly Personalized Service Statement**

We are very customer-focused, committed to solving all of our related customer's needs and doing everything we possibly can to keep them satisfied. This approach (has, will, insures) that we retain a highly satisfied clientele, that we get a high rate of repeat business and that we get referrals. Also, especially once we have worked for a customer, we find that the customer is less likely to move to our competition on pricing considerations.

☐ **Low Cost Structure Statement**

We have an extremely low cost structure. And just as importantly we are determined to keep our costs low. This allows us to charge low prices, while maintaining our high quality, and still have a good profit margin.

☐ **State of the Art Technology Statement**

More so than most of our competitors we are current with the latest technology. We can deliver our customers cutting edge solutions. This gives us an opportunity to develop business with the larger, richer corporations who are willing to pay a substantial premium for the best solutions available today.

☐ **Reputation Statement**

Over the years we have developed a strong reputation throughout our . . . . This reputation is based upon . . . .
(MARKET AREA, INDUSTRY)

. . . .

Along with our reputation we have developed a sizable customer base, currently totaling over . . . .

. . . .

Our reputation has also proved important in our ability to attract new customers.

SUMMARYSUMMARYSUMMARYSUMMARYSUMMARY

Financial Situations/Needs

State specifically how much financing you will need, what type of financing, when you will need it, what the financing will be used for, and when you will be able to pay it back. For a start-up business, explain any sources of start-up capital you have already tapped and other sources you plan on using through at least the next year or until operations are underway. You can also here give the reader a quick financial snapshot of your company and refer them to the finance section or financial statements for further information.

Select and edit the <u>one</u> statement that best applies.

☐ **Basic Financial Needs Statement**

At this time we are seeking $ 20,000 (in equity investment, in a
_($)
credit line, ~~in an asset-backed loan~~, in lease financing, in a short term

Financial Situations/Needs

This is not the time to be shy. Start right out by stating how much money you need. And be sure to include plenty for a cushion in case you have underestimated expenses or overestimated sales. The costs of starting a business tend to run a lot higher than expected because it is impossible to foresee every cost that you will have to incur. (In addition to being specific about the amount of money you are seeking.) Also, be as specific as possible about any other details of the ... ou are seeking. If you ... bank financing, for ... ate whether you are ... ne of credit (for an on- ... cing need) or a term ... u will pay back at a ... nt in time. If you are ... estors for a new busi- ... ill want to emphasize ... y the founders have per- ... ested in the business.

IT WILL BE USED TO PAY FOR THE LEAD SERVICE, WORKING CAPITAL AND FOR A DOWN PAYMENT ON A BREAK PRESS DIE. FINANCING OF THE DIE AVAILABLE FROM SELLER. WE WILL BE ABLE TO PAY DOWN THE CREDIT LINE ON ~~THE~~ START TO JANUARY 2000.

SUMMARY*SUMMARYSUMMARYSUMMARYSUMMARY*

public within . . . . years allowing investors to cash out, sell to a larger corporation in
(YEARS)

about . . . . years allowing you to cash out your full equity investment).
(YEARS)

☐ Expansion of Existing Company Statement

The company has had sales of . . . . . , ... , and . . . . . over the past three years.
(\$)   (\$)   (\$)

We are currently seeking the infusion of . . . . . in new capital for expansion of the
(\$)

business, which we believe will allow us to grow to the sales of \$ . . . . . within
(\$)

. . . . years, and profits of \$ . . . . . .
(YEARS)   (\$)

☐ Growing Company Statement

The company's financial objectives are to reach . . . . . in sales by . . . . , with
(\$)   (YEAR)

a gross margin of . . . . . . A loan of . . . . . is needed to achieve this objective, in
(%)   (\$)

the form of a . . . . -year note to be paid back by . . . .
(#)   (MONTH, YEAR)

☐ Start-Up Financing Statement

In order to effectively launch the business, we project a total need for . . . . . in
(\$)

start-up financing. Principal uses of funds are . . . . ,
(APPLICATION OF FUNDS)

. . . . , and . . . . To
(APPLICATION OF FUNDS)   (APPLICATION OF FUNDS)

date we have raised \$ . . . . . from the three company founders and their relatives.
(\$)

The additional funds we need to raise is \$ . . . . . . We project that the company will
(\$)

be profitable by . . . . We project that within . . . . years of reaching break-
(YEAR)   (YEARS)

even that this new investment could be cashed out by either the founding partners
purchasing this investment stake or by replacing the investment stake with bank
financing.

SUMMARYSUMMARYSUMMARYSUMMARYSUMMARY

☐ **Start-Up Financing in Detail Statement**

We seek to raise a total of $ . . . . . in capital to get our business started and finance
(\$)
start-up negative cash flow that we anticipate will last the first . . . . . months of
(#)
operation. Here is the break-out of the financing we are seeking:

Company founder $ . . . . . Equity capital. 100% committed.
(\$)

Other key managers $ . . . . . Equity capital. 100% committed.
(\$)

Relatives of founder $ . . . . . Subordinated debt. 100% committed.
(\$)

Outside investors $ . . . . . Equity capital. 25% committed.
(\$)

Equipment financing $ . . . . . 3–10 year leases. 75% committed.
(\$)

Bank financing $ . . . . . Secured credit line tentative commitment letter.
(\$)

☐ **Bank Financing for Existing Business Statement**

This coming year, we project our financial need to peak at $ . . . . . in the likely sce-
(\$)
nario. This would be . . . . . % . . . . than our peak borrowing during
(%) (HIGHER, LOWER)
this year and . . . . . % . . . . than our peak borrowing during the
(%) (HIGHER, LOWER)
. . . . . previous years. Our worst case scenario shows our peak borrowing to be
(#)
$ . . . . As shown in the financial statements the company is currently in a solid
(\$)
financial position. Indicators of our financial strength are (our balance sheet, our
income statement, our debt to equity ratio of . . . ., our current ratio
of . . . ., etc.).

☐ **Financial Snapshot of Robust Business Statement**

With sales growth of an average of . . . . . % and net profit growth of an average of
(%)

SUMMARYSUMMARYSUMMARYSUMMARYSUMMARY

. . . . . % over the last . . . . . years, our business is on a roll. We are outpacing our
_(%)   _(#)
competitors and continuing to improve our market position. Our balance sheet
has been strengthening as we increase our retained earnings and decrease our
reliance on our credit line. Our current business can easily sustain the current
rate of growth without any new financing.

☐ **A Rapid Expansion Program Statement**

We intend to begin a rapid expansion as outlined in detail in this business plan. In
order to accomplish that goal, we will require additional capital. At this point we
are seeking $ . . . . . .As shown in our cash flow projections, we anticipate that this
_($)
will conservatively cover our cash needs for the next . . . . . years.
                  _(#)

CHAPTER 8

Vision

VISIONVISIONVISIONVISIONVISIONVISIONVISION

Vision Statement

Here is where you describe your vision of what you would like your company to become in the future, such as 5–10 years from now. Try to capture, in relatively few words, the essence of what you envision as the future, major distinctive characteristics of your company. You want to particularly emphasize how your company will be different from other companies in its industry, and how it will be different than the start-up or existing company that it is today.

Select and edit the <u>one or two</u> statements that best apply.

☐ **Basic Vision Statement**

Our vision of what our company will become in the future is . . . .

. . . .

Distinctive characteristics of the company will be . . . .

. . . .

The company will differ from it's competitors in that . . . .

. . . .

The company will have developed particularly strong capabilities in . . . .

. . . .

Our company will be recognized as . . . .

. . . .

VISIONVISIONVISIONVISIONVISIONVISIONVISION

☐ **Financial Vision Statement**

Our sales objective is to reach $ ..~5 MILLION~.. in sales by ..2005.. . We
(($)) (DATE)

plan to achieve a net profit margin of ..15.. % of sales. We
(%)

intend to reach these objectives largely by (developing new prod-

~EXPANDING OUR PRODUCT LINES AND SERVICES~
~TO THE PRISON MARKET.~

that will help set the standard in our market.

☐ **Personalized Service Statement**

We want to be thought of as the firm that offers highly personalized service. Our goal is not necessarily to be the largest firm
in our market—but instead the firm that really cares about the
unique, individual needs of each of its customers.

EXPERT ADVICE

...ion Statement

...part of the business plan
...s or breaks it. If you don't
...where you want your busi-
...to go—it's probably not going
...anywhere. Potential outside
...tors, lenders, key customers,
...employees all want to know
...your future vision is of your
...ness. But most of all you, the
..., need to have a clear vision of
...company's future. In your
...n statement, don't get carried
...y talking about how your firm is
...g to be so much better than
other firms. Instead focus on how
your firm is going to be different
than other firms. It's a lot easier to
succeed not by beating the competition, but by doing everything you
can to avoid competition. Don't get
into specifics here such as sales or
profit goals, instead give the broad
view of how you see your company
in the future.

VISIONVISIONVISIONVISIONVISIONVISIONVISION

☐ **Niche Market Leader Statement**

We intend to be a market leader in the . . . .
(DESCRIBE MARKET NICHE)
We want all prospective customers to know that we are the firm that focuses exclu-
sively on this . . . . and that we also serve it bet-
(MARKET NICHE)
ter than any other firm.

☐ **Value Leader Statement**

We intend to be the value leader in our field. We want to be known for very low
prices. But we also want to be known for dependable quality at a low price. In one
word, we want to be known for "value."

☐ **Industry Innovator Statement**

We want to be seen by our customers as the industry innovator. We particularly
want to be known as a company that is trying hard all the time to find new ways
of doing business that will benefit its customers.

☐ **Most Professional Statement**

We intend to be a stand-out in our market as the most professionally operated
firm. We will be sure that our target customers know that choosing us as a supplier is the safe choice for consistent, high-quality service.

VISIONVISIONVISIONVISIONVISIONVISIONVISION

☐ **Balance Between Stakeholders Statement**

Unlike the shareholder centered companies of old, our vision is to strike a balance between the different important stakeholders in our firm. We see the three pivotal stakeholders as 1) the customers; 2) the employees; 3) the owners. By striving to serve all three equally, we believe that we will also ultimately best serve the interests of each group individually.

☐ **Technological Leader Statement**

We will be seen as on the cutting edge of technology in our industry. When a company wants leading edge solutions—we intend to be the first name to come to mind.

☐ **Resolution of Current Problem/Issue Statement**

We expect by .... to have resolved the ....
(DATE)   (DESCRIBE MAJOR CURRENT PROBLEM OR ISSUE
.... We expect to have overcome this issue by ....
FACING COMPANY)   (SUMMARIZE HOW
.... We expect to have become a
YOU ENVISION OVERCOMING THE PROBLEM YOU ARE NOW FACING)
smoothly functioning organization, with high employee morale, high profitability, growing sales, and we expect to have achieved recognition as a leader in our market.

VISIONVISION**VISION**VISION**VISION**VISION**VISION

Milestones

This section is a nice feature, but is often not included in business plans and you should not feel compelled to include it either. List a few of the key events or points in time that will be important markers of progress toward the successful achievement of the goals of this business plan. Generally you will want to list between 5 and 10 milestones.

Select and edit the <u>one</u> statement that best applies.

☐ **Basic Milestone Statement**

Important milestones (for launching this business, for taking this business to the next level, for this year, for achieving our goals) are

1. SALES OF 1 MILLION DOLLARS FOR YEAR 2000
   (MILESTONE)   (TARGET DATE)
2. OFFER ENCLOSURE PRODUCT   1/2002
   (MILESTONE)   (TARGET DATE)
3. SALES OF 3 MILLION   FOR YEAR 2003
   (MILESTONE)   (TARGET DATE)
4. OFFER DETENTION FURNITURE   1/2004
   (MILESTONE)   (TARGET DATE)
5. SALES OF 5 MILLION   FOR YEAR 2005
   (MILESTONE)   (TARGET DATE)

☐ **Milestones for a Product Business Start-Up Statement**

1. Presentation to investors begins.

2. Financing completed.

3. Product prototype completed.

4. Package design finished.

5. Manufacturing/vendor selection finalized.

VISIONVISIONVISIONVISIONVISIONVISIONVISION

6. Sales force in place.

7. Distributors lined up.

8. First product ships.

☐ Milestones for a Service Business Start-Up Statement

1. Business plan completed.

2. Financing arranged.

3. Hiring for business opening completed.

4. Advertising/promotion begins.

5. Service begins.

☐ Milestones for an Existing Business for Next Year Statement

Important milestones for our business the upcoming year are:

. . . . (SELECT THE MOST IMPORTANT MILESTONES AND ADD TARGET DATES)

Filling the . . . . (NEW KEY POSITION)

Shipping the . . . . (NEW PRODUCT)

Launching an upgrade of . . . . (DESCRIBE PRODUCT OR SERVICE)

Launching a new advertising campaign.

Adding . . . . (DESCRIBE NEW SALES METHOD) . . . . to our sales effort.

EXPERT ADVICE

Milestones

You might be thinking: "Why have milestones? As a company we're going to do our best to succeed, and we'll simply tell outside investors and lenders this too!" But, milestones get people excited about reaching goals. It gives employees (including the CEO) something tangible to strive for. It motivates. And it challenges. It also prioritizes and helps lead the company to really push for the milestones that matter. (Of course it only prioritizes if you have just a very few milestones, not a long list of them). It also instantly gives both insiders and outsiders a very specific idea of what you aim to accomplish and—very importantly—when you hope to accomplish it by.

VISIONVISIONVISIONVISIONVISIONVISIONVISION

Beginning the . . . .
(NEW SERVICE)

Obtaining new financing . . . .
(DESCRIBE)

Changing vendors for . . . .
(DESCRIBE)

Reaching break-even sale volume of $ . . . . .
($)

Achieving sales of $ . . . . .
($)

Achieving profitability of . . . . .
($)

Entering the . . . .
(DESCRIBE)

Beginning a new research and development effort for . . . .
(DESCRIBE)

Moving to new facilities.

Adding an additional facility.

Enlarging current facilities.

Installing a new computer system.

New . . . . installed.
(DESCRIBE NEW EQUIPMENT)

Launching a Web site.

New catalog available.

Major convention / presentation.

Planning process complete.

CHAPTER 9

Market Analysis

The Overall Market

Define and describe the overall market that you are competing in. If possible, give the size of the market and cite the source of your information.

Select and edit the <u>one or two</u> statements that best apply.

☐ **Basic Market Overview Statement**

The overall market for ....SECURITY ACOUSTICAL COLLINGS.... in the (world, coun-
(PRODUCT OR SERVICE)

try, region or town) is approximately $ 10 MILLION , according to data from
(\$)

DSA, NATIONAL REP AGENCY ... . The market is growing by about ..2. % per
(SOURCE OF DATA)   (%)

year. Growth is expected to continue at this pace for the foreseeable future. Sales are

relatively steady and not subject to significant cyclical or seasonal variation.

☐ **Market Overview by Distinct Product Group Statement**

The overall size of the industry is currently $ ..... in the (world, country, region,
(\$)

town). Because the industry includes a very diverse group of product types with

significantly different characteristics, it is more meaningful to break out analysis

of the industry into roughly three .... groups.
(PRODUCT OR SERVICE)

The first group .... has sales of $ .... Currently
(SPECIFY GROUP)   (\$)

growing at about ..... % per year, this group is expected to reach a sales level of
(%)

$ ..... by the year .... The second group ....
(\$)   (YEAR)   (SPECIFY GROUP)

has sales of $ .... Currently growing at about ..... % per year, this group is
(\$)   (%)

expected to reach a sales level of $ ..... by the year .... The third group
(\$)   (YEAR)

MARKET ANALYSIS MARKET ANALYSIS

.... (SPECIFY GROUP) .... has sales of $ .... Currently
(\$)
growing at about ..... % per year, this group is expected to
(%)
reach a sales level of $ ..... by the year .... We intend to
(\$)   (YEAR)
compete in the ....
(SPECIFY GROUP)
group and this market analysis will be focused on this group.

☐ **Market Overview for Local Service Business Statement**

We estimate the total current market for .... at
(SERVICE)
about $ ..... in .... We have
(\$)   (TOWN OR CITY)
derived this number totaling the number of employees providing
service at the .... current service establishments, then
(NUMBER OF)
multiplying each employee by our estimate of their average
billings per year. The current market for this service appears to
be growing because .... of these firms just opened their
(NUMBER)
doors in the last two years and all of the firms appear to be prospering. Furthermore, as discussed in the customer needs section
of this plan, the overall market may be able to grow further if a
new business can offer new service dimensions that meet needs
not currently being served by existing competitors.

EXPERT ADVICE

The Overall Market

You may be thinking "Why should I have any discussion of the overall market since I'm only going to compete in one small niche or market segment?" An overall discussion of the market gives context to your plan and to your business. It also enables employees, investors, and customers to feel better about your company. "We're part of the multi-billion dollar residential landscaping industry," sounds a lot more motivating than "we mow a few lawns and remove weeds." An overall discussion of the market or industry may also help bring to mind business opportunities or market or product extensions. Unless you are raising a large amount of equity capital it is not essential to have multiple authoritative sources and absolutely precise market information. But you should identify your sources and clearly note where you have made estimates.

MARKET ANALYSIS MARKET ANALYSIS

☐ **Market Overview for Local Business on Per Capita Basis Statement**

The . . . . with . . . . population has
(PROPOSED MARKET AREA)   (ENTER AMOUNT)

. . . . of . . . . businesses. This works out to
(ENTER AMOUNT)   (TYPE OF BUSINESS)

. . . . per capita. On the other hand nearby markets with com-
(DIVIDE POPULATION BY BUSINESSES)

parable demographics have a much higher number of businesses of

this type per capita. Statistics for other markets include

. . . . : . . . . ;
(MARKET AREA 2)   (BUSINESSES OF THIS TYPE PER CAPITA)

. . . . : . . . . ;
(MARKET AREA 3)   (BUSINESSES OF THIS TYPE PER CAPITA)

. . . . : . . . .
(MARKET AREA 4)   (BUSINESSES OF THIS TYPE PER CAPITA)

These statistics indicate a relatively low level of competition in the proposed

market area.

☐ **Market Overview of Stable, Mature Market Statement**

Particularly because this . . . . has been readily
(PRODUCT OR SERVICE)

available for many years, the market growth in units has pretty much been in line

with the population growth. The market growth in dollar volume, however, has

been slightly higher because the typical unit sold is either a higher grade

. . . . or has more features. Similarly future
(PRODUCT OR SERVICE)

growth, beyond keeping pace with the general population growth, will need to

come from selling customers into more expensive products.

MARKET ANALYSIS MARKET ANALYSIS

☐ **Market Overview for Market about to Explode Statement**

Potential buyers for this .... number approxi-
                                          (PRODUCT OR SERVICE)
mately .... in the (world, country, region, city). Basically anyone who
             (ENTER NUMBER)
meets the following criteria can be considered a potential buyer ....

....

Because this product is in its relative infancy and is only being purchased by early
adopters, it is difficult to say what percentage of potential buyers will actually purchase the product in the next few years. Estimates of sales potential vary widely
from $ ..... to $ .... In any event, the market is clearly poised for dramatic
           ($)   ($)
growth. At this rate, dollar sales are growing at a rate of ..... % annually and unit
                                                                    (%)
sales are growing at a rate of .... annually. There is no slowdown in
                                    (ENTER UNITS)
sight for growth, and as more and larger competitors enter the marketplace, it is
possible that growth will even accelerate in the near future.

☐ **Market Overview for Product/Service for Corporate Market Statement**

Once considered a .... for only the largest cor-
                                (PRODUCT OR SERVICE)
porations, now many mid-sized and even smaller firms are buying this
.... as well. Because the market for this product
        (PRODUCT OR SERVICE)
is expanding, it is difficult to draw exact boundaries on the size of the potential
market, but generally any company over a size of .... is almost certainly
                                                          (ENTER SIZE)
using this .... and any company over a size of
                (PRODUCT OR SERVICE)
.... is likely to be at least seriously considering adopting it. We would
  (ENTER SIZE)
estimate   the   total   number   of   companies   currently   using   this

MARKET ANALYSIS MARKET ANALYSIS

. . . . at . . . . The market in dollar
(PRODUCT OR SERVICE)   (ENTER AMOUNT)

size has been estimated at $ . . . . . and is considered to be growing at the rate
($)

of . . . . . %.
(%)

☐ **Market Overview for Market on Verge of Decline Statement**

Once a growth area, the market for . . . . is now
(PRODUCT OR SERVICE)

flat and is likely to decline in future years as more and more users substitute

. . . . The market is expected to shift
(ALTERNATIVE PRODUCT OR SERVICE)

gradually, with industry observers projecting a decline of about . . . . . % over the
(%)

next . . . . years. Beyond this point in time, conversion rate to the
(YEARS)

. . . . is difficult to project with estimates
(SUBSTITUTE PRODUCT OR SERVICE)

varying more widely. In any case this market is not going to disappear

overnight and will be a major factor for some time to come. The current

sales   in   this   market   of $ . . . . . will   dwarf   those   of   the
($)

. . . . for some time to come.
(PRODUCT OR SERVICE SUBSTITUTE)

MARKET ANALYSIS MARKET ANALYSIS

Changes in the Market

Summarize important changes and trends in the overall market including any indication you have of what the future holds. Include implications of the changes.

Select and edit the <u>one or more</u> statements that best apply.

☐ **Basic Trends Overview Statement**

The most significant development in this marketplace recently has been . . . . Major implications of this trend include . . . . Other important trends include . . . . Implications of these trends are . . . .

☐ **Overview for a Fast Growing Local Service Market Statement**

The growth in demand for this service in the local market, as well as in most other markets, outstrips the population growth. Last year growth was estimated to be about . . . . . % nationwide _(%)

EXPERT ADVICE

Changes in the Market

You want to particularly focus on any major trends, or any minor trends that may possibly affect your business, however remotely. Give attention to emerging new markets, shifts in the nature of competition, consolidation of industry competitors or customers or suppliers, demographic shifts in markets, and the emergence of product substitutes. A careful analysis of changes in the market can potentially be very important for formulating other parts of your business plan such evaluating opportunities, examining possible risks, analyzing competitors, weighing your competitive strengths, determining strategy, positioning products or services, and even determining marketing plans.

MARKET ANALYSIS MARKET ANALYSIS

and we have every reason to believe that the local market grew at about the same rate. Beyond population growth, demand for this service is being fueled by the following factors (more people in the target age group, higher disposable incomes, more awareness of the general availability of the service, increased advertising and competition by service providers). Because of the continued presence of these factors, we expect growth in demand for this service to continue at approximately the current rate for the foreseeable future.

☐ **Overview for Service Being Provided to Corporations Statement**

The ongoing trend of corporations to downsize and outsource services such as
. . . . has led to very strong growth. Last year growth was
      (SPECIFY)
estimated at . . . . . % according to . . . . Because so much
    (%)   (SOURCE)
of the growth is coming from companies who have not previously outsourced this service, there is a tremendous potential for new players in this marketplace. New players have the potential to achieve significant sales volumes without having to take customers away from existing competitors. Growth is expected to continue unabated for some time to come.

☐ **Overview of Shift in Growth from Domestic to World Markets Statement**

While the growth in the domestic market for this . . . . has
                      (PRODUCT OR SERVICE)
been slowing in recent years, overseas markets are showing much more promise. The demographic information (such as rising income levels, higher education levels, and more familiarity with technology) are suggesting that the overseas markets are ripe for dramatically higher growth rates. Although the sales in overseas markets are cur-

MARKET ANALYSIS MARKET ANALYSIS

rently dwarfed by domestic sales, the firms selling overseas are experiencing very fast growth rates and there is every reason to believe that these fast growth rates will continue for years to come, and that eventually the overseas markets may even be larger than the domestic market.

☐ **Shift Toward More Emphasis on ~~Features/Benefits~~ Statement** _PRICE_

As the market for _SECURITY ACOUSTICAL CEILINGS_ continues to mature, buy-
(PRODUCT OR SERVICE)

ers have become _INTERESTED IN PRICE, AS A RESULT, ~~SALES BUYERS~~ CONTRACTORS_

in the key featur _ARE BUYING ON PRICE AS LONG AS THE PRODUCT_

MEETS THE SPECIFICATION. ~~AND THEIR~~

As a result many

tures and perform

to serve their nee

☐ **Shift Towards N**

The market is co

approximately

size of the mark

average price per

of the typical unit sold has been increasing. As a result, while the market continues to grow significantly in dollar sales, increasing approximately ..... % during
(%)
the last year, the dollar volume growth lags significantly behind the growth in unit sales. Also the growth in dollar volume fluctuates more rapidly and is highly sus-ceptible to when major players introduce or find widespread acceptance for the next upgrade of products commanding higher price points.

MARKET ANALYSIS MARKET ANALYSIS

☐ **Shift Toward More Female Buyers Statement**

Once overwhelmingly purchased by men, the buying decision for
.... is now increasingly being made by women.
(PRODUCT OR SERVICE)
This trend is being fueled by the changing role of women in society—including
higher income levels, higher levels of professional achievement, and higher education levels. The market for this .... continues
(PRODUCT OR SERVICE)
to grow among men and they still compose the larger market segment, ... %
(%)
for the last year for which numbers are available. But the market for women is
growing much more rapidly at ..... % as opposed to a growth rate of ..... % for
(%)   (%)
male buyers. As a result, some industry competitors are beginning to either shift
the nature of their marketing to be more inclusive of women or are embarking on
separate media campaigns specifically aimed at women.

☐ **Shift Toward Younger Buyers Statement**

Just several years ago the market for this .... was
(PRODUCT OR SERVICE)
predominantly people over the age of .... , with over ..... % of sales to
(AGE)   (%)
this age group in the year .... But in the last year, sales to the
(YEAR)
over .... had fallen to ..... %. The biggest growth is taking place in
(SPECIFY AGE)   (%)
the .... group which now comprises over ..... % of total market sales.
(SPECIFY AGE)   (%)
This shift is apparently being caused by higher disposable income and
more sophisticated tastes among younger people. As a result some industry
competitors are beginning to position some or all of their
.... toward the younger generation.
(PRODUCTS OR SERVICES)

MARKET ANALYSIS MARKET ANALYSIS

☐ Shift Toward Smaller Companies Statement

While once only larger and midsize companies were considered viable prospects for this . . . . (PRODUCT OR SERVICE), now smaller companies are increasingly purchasing it. Companies with sales of as little as $ . . . . . ($) or as few as . . . . (NUMBER) of employees are now expanding the use of this . . . . (PRODUCT OR SERVICE). Part of this trend is being fueled by lower costs and wider availability as well as an increased tendency to view the . . . . (PRODUCT OR SERVICE) as an integral part of any forward-looking company's business operation, not just a "nice to have" option.

☐ Shift to Home-Based Businesses Statement

Beyond the overall growth in the market of potential small business users, there is another very important trend shaping the market. This is the growth of home-based businesses. More and more people are running businesses out of their homes and many of the people running these businesses are sophisticated individuals who often previously worked at larger corporations. Running a home-based business has increasingly lost the negative stigma that once accompanied it, and especially with recent advances in technology, has become a very viable option for many people. Home-based businesses often have different needs from their office-based counterparts. They also frequently have a different attitude to business that has important implications for positioning, marketing strategy, and advertising.

MARKET ANALYSIS MARKET ANALYSIS

Market Segments

Carefully defining market segments is crucial for establishing or reviewing your business strategy, your product positioning, and your marketing strategy. Different markets tend to be segmented in different ways. Carefully consider the most meaningful way your market is segmented—especially considering the viewpoint of potential buyers. For example, is the market segmented by price point? By different product/service functions? By features? By target consumer groups? By geography? By specialty? By sales channel? By delivery method? Also bear in mind that many markets are segmented in more than one way.

Select and edit the <u>one or two</u> statements that best apply.

☐ **Basic Segmentation Statement**

The market is primarily segmented by (price point, product function, features, target consumer groups, geography, specialty, sales channel, delivery method, or . . . .

. . . .

). The number one segment in size is defined as . . . .

. . . .

It comprises approximately . . . . . % of the total market. And it is growing (faster, (%) slower or about the same) as the total market at the pace of about . . . . . % per year. (%) The number two segment in size is defined as . . . .

. . . .

It comprises approximately . . . . . % of the total market. And it is growing (faster, (%) slower or about the same) as the total market at the pace of about . . . . . % per (%)

year. The number three segment in size is defined as ....

It comprises approximately ..... % of the total market. And it is growing (faster,
(%)

slower or about the same) as the total market at the pace of about ..... % per year.
(%)

The number four segment in size is defined as ....

It comprises approximately ..... % of the total market. And it is growing (faster,
(%)

slower or about the same) as the total market at the pace of about ..... % per year.
(%)

☐ **Quick Approach to Segmentation Statement**

The basic market segments are:

1. .... % of total market.
   (DESCRIBE SEGMENT)   (%)

2. .... % of total market.
   (DESCRIBE SEGMENT)   (%)

3. .... % of total market.
   (DESCRIBE SEGMENT)   (%)

4. .... % of total market.
   (DESCRIBE SEGMENT)   (%)

☐ **No Segmentation Statement**

While there are obvious differences including features, pricing, and other attributes from one firm's .SECURITY. ACOUSTICAL. CEILING. to the next, the market
(PRODUCT OR SERVICE)

has not become segmented. Each competitor is more or less competing for the
same customer and each SECURITY ACOUSTICAL CEILING. is overwhelmingly
(PRODUCT OR SERVICE)

aimed at accomplishing the same function without significant competitive differ-
entiation. While firms go to great length to tout their competitive differences, they
still are basically competing within the same marketplace for the same customers.

MARKET ANALYSIS MARKET ANALYSIS

☐ **Increasing Segmentation Statement**

Until recently, buyers were thought to have relatively similar needs, and while there was some differences from one . . . . (PRODUCT OR SERVICE) . . . . to the next, there were not clearly defined segments and all industry participants more or less competed with one another head on. But recently this has begun to change with market segmentation emerging—although it is much more obvious in some potential markets than others. The most clearly segmented parts of the market are . . . .

. . . .

In these segments, buyers are responding well to . . . . . . (PRODUCT OR SERVICE) . . . . offerings aimed at specific needs. However, buyers are not responding as well to attempted segmentation in other parts of the market such as attempts to segment the market by . . . .

. . . .

☐ **Professional/Consumer/Institutional Segments Statement**

The market is divided by its three distinct user groups: professional—businesses buying the . . . . (PRODUCT OR SERVICE) . . . . for business use; consumer—individual consumers buying the . . . . (PRODUCT OR SERVICE) . . . . for personal use; and institutional—schools and government agencies buying the . . . . (PRODUCT OR SERVICE) . . . . for use at their facilities. The professional segment is estimated to be . . . . . % of the market; the consumer segment . . . . . %
(%)   (%)

of the market; and the institutional segment ..... % of the market. _(%) The basic products being sold into each market are quite similar or in many cases identical. However there are substantial differences in customer needs and concerns and the selling and marketing strategies used by competitors are quite a bit different from one market to the next.

☐ **Luxury/Standard/Economy Segments Statement**

The market can be broken into basically three segments: the (luxury or high performance) segment for consumers that are more interested in higher quality or the most features and are less concerned with price; (the standard or midrange) segment for consumers who want to strike a balance between quality, features and price; and the (economy or basic) segment for consumers who are most concerned with price. While some .... (PRODUCTS OR SERVICES) .... are on the borderline between these groupings, this segmentation applies to most offerings and most potential consumers are generally likely to only consider options within one segment at any one time.

EXPERT ADVICE

Market Segments

Market segmentation is usually not as straightforward as it first appears. Most markets are segmented in more than one way. If you overlook a particular type of market segmentation, you could miss a possible major advantage for your business—especially if you are trying to enter a new market. First look to buyers to understand market segmentation. What products or services do buyers tend to group together, and which do they tend to group separately? It is important to sort out which product and service differences are distinct enough to qualify as a unique market segment or niche. There is no easy hard and fast rule.

MARKET ANALYSIS MARKET ANALYSIS

☐ **Secondary Segmentations Statement**

In addition to the major segmentation of the market, (some, all, one) segment is also segmented by (price point, product function, features, target consumer groups, geography, specialty, sales channel, delivery method, or . . . .).

The size and growth of the sub segments that are most relevant for us are as follows. The . . . . is approximately $ . . . . . and growing
(SUB SEGMENT #1)   ($)

at approximately . . . . . % per year. The . . . . is
                    (%)   (SUB SEGMENT #2)

approximately $ . . . . . and growing at approximately . . . . . % per year.
                ($)   (%)

Target Market and Customers

Define and describe the target market segment or customers that you are primarily going to focus on in your business. Unless you have a clear idea of your target market, you may not want to complete this section until after you have completed the strategy section.

Select and edit the <u>one</u> statement that best applies.

☐ **Basic Consumer Target Market Statement**

Our target market is ..THE.. PRISON.. INDUSTRY,.....................

....

Our target market is ~~defined by consumers that~~ CONTRACTORS...............
(DESCRIBE TARGET CONSUMERS)
Common characteristics of CEILING.. MANUFACTURES.. serving this market
(PRODUCTS OR SERVICES)
are .THAT. THEIR.. CORE. BUSINESS.. IS.. SOMETHING. ELSE......

....

We are well-suited to serve this market because ..IT. WILL. BE. OUR.. MAIN.
FOCUS.. WE. HAVE.. CONTRACTS.. NATIONALLY. AND. HAVE..
KNOWLEDGE. OF THE.. INDUSTRY,

☐ **Basic Business Target Market Statement**

Our target market is ....

....

Our target market is defined by companies (with sales between $ ..... and $ .....)
(\$)   (\$)
in (industries) in the (city, metro area, region, nation). **Other common characteristics**

MARKET ANALYSIS MARKET ANALYSIS

that define our core market are . . . .

. . . .

We are well-suited to serve this market because . . . .

. . . .

☐ **Multiple Tiered Targets Statement**

Our primary target market segment will be . . . .

. . . .

We feel that this market will be easier to enter and also holds more long-term promise because of its high growth rate. We will also give secondary emphasis to the following markets . . . .

. . . .

Because the . . . . used by these different market
(PRODUCTS OR SERVICES)
segments are highly similar, we believe we can effectively cover all of these different segments without spreading our efforts too thin, however, we will give our
major marketing effort to our primary target market.

☐ **Multiple Markets, Equal Focus Statement**

We will focus on (two, three, four, etc.) target markets
. . . . Each of these mar-
(DESCRIBE EACH MARKET)
kets shows good promise and can be well served by the same business because of
their highly similar . . . . needs.
(PRODUCT OR SERVICE)

Niche Market Focus Statement

We intend to focus very narrowly on one particular market niche: . . . . (DESCRIBE NICHE). Buyers and potential buyers with these needs are not being specifically targeted or particularly well served by other companies. While this market niche is small enough not to attract a lot of attention from the national corporations, it is large enough for us to realize our growth expectations for the next 5–10 years. It is also a niche that we believe our company will be uniquely well-qualified to address because of . . . .

. . . .

Local Service Business Statement

We intend to direct all our efforts to within the town of . . . . (NAME TOWN). To reach our sales goals over the next five years we estimate that we will need to achieve about . . . . . . (%) percent market share—not enough to be likely to initiate an aggressive competitive response to our market entry. While we could easily travel to surrounding towns to provide service, we feel that from a marketing standpoint we are much better off focusing on one town. We can build sales momentum more easily by focusing on one town—for example we can buy larger ads

EXPERT ADVICE

Target Market and Customers

How you define your target market may have a major impact on the success of your business. Many small and new businesses would be better off if they specialized in a particular market or product niche. The more a business specializes, the less it will compete directly with other businesses. Also, the smaller a market niche a business chooses, the less chance that a much larger firm will compete with it at all. For some businesses your choice of target market may be the most important element of your strategy—especially if your choice of target truly sets you off from the competition. If choice of target market appears to be a crucial business decision, you may wish to complete this section later after you have completed the strategy section of your plan.

MARKET ANALYSIS MARKET ANALYSIS

in one local newspaper and we can more quickly build a word-of-mouth reputation. The demographics in this town, especially . . . .

. . . .

appear particularly good for our business.

☐ **Focus on Specific Companies Statement**

Our business will narrowly focus on just a handful of companies that our firm, or key employees at our firm, have had a prior relationship with. These companies are . . . .

. . . .

Our relationships and past experiences with these companies makes us uniquely well suited to serve their needs and gives us a strong competitive advantage. By limiting our focus to these very few firms, we can insure that we will remain extremely responsive to their needs and be able to offer unparalleled service.

Customer Characteristics

Analyzing customer characteristics helps you position and refine your products and services and develop your marketing strategy. Include characteristics that are more common among your target buyers than in the general population, but don't limit yourself to characteristics that are necessarily shared by all or even most buyers.

Select and edit the <u>one</u> statement that best applies.

☐ **Basic Target Consumer Characteristics Statement**

Our target consumers tend to be (male, female), aged .... , (ENTER RANGE)
(single, married, married with children, etc.), ... , with a (EDUCATION LEVEL)
household income of .... , (works full-time, part-time, is a (ENTER INCOME)
student, is a homemaker, is retired), typical occupations include
.... , they live in (cities, suburbs, towns, specific neigh- (ENTER OCCUPATIONS)
borhoods, etc.). They tend to read .... (LIST TYPES OF OR SPECIFIC MAGAZINES AND
.... , they tend to listen to .... , (NEWSPAPERS) (LIST TYPES OF OR SPECIFIC RADIO STATIONS)
they tend to watch .... , and they tend to (LIST TYPES OF OR SPECIFIC TV SHOWS)
access the Internet (often, occasionally, seldom). They often
belong to the following community organizations ....

....

EXPERT ADVICE

Customer Characteristics

At this point you want to group together all of the characteristics of your prospective customers, even if you aren't sure yet how any particular characteristic may help you make decisions on business strategy or tactics. You could simply list characteristics that are more common among your customers than the general population. You could create a composite "picture" of your typical buyer. Or you could tier your discussion to first discuss characteristics shared by all potential buyers; second discuss characteristics shared by most potential buyers; and third discuss characteristics present among just some buyers. If you have a clear target market segment or market niche or geographic market in mind, you will probably want to limit your discussion to characteristics of buyers within this part of the market.

MARKET ANALYSIS MARKET ANALYSIS

They often participate in the following non-business activities . . . .

. . . .

Other pertinent characteristics include . . . .

. . . .

☐ **Basic Target Company Characteristic Statement**

Our target companies tend to have sales between $ . . . . . and $ . . . . . , they tend to
have between . . . . . and . . . . employees, they tend to be in the following indus-
try(ies), ...

. . . . ,

and they tend to be located in . . . .

. . . .

These companies tend to be (start-ups, relatively new firms, established firms), (fast
growing, growing, stable, experiencing stiffening competition), and (privately-held or publicly held). Other pertinent characteristics include . . . .

. . . .

☐ **Basic Buyer at Target Company Characteristics Statement**

The key decision-maker at the companies we are targeting tend to hold the posi-
tion of . . . . and usually report to . . . .
(ENTER POSITION) (ENTER
SUPERVISOR) . . . . They tend to be (male, female), aged . . . . , (single, married,
(ENTER RANGE)
married with children, etc.), ... , with a household income of . . . . ,
(EDUCATION LEVEL) (ENTER INCOME)
they live in (cities, suburbs, towns, specific neighborhoods, etc.). They tend to read the

MARKET ANALYSIS MARKET ANALYSIS

following trade publications ....(ENTER SPECIFIC PUBLICATIONS), the following business publications ....(LIST TYPES OF OR SPECIFIC MAGAZINES AND NEWSPAPERS), and the following consumer publications ....(LIST TYPES OF OR SPECIFIC MAGAZINES AND NEWSPAPERS).They tend to listen to ....(LIST TYPES OF OR SPECIFIC RADIO STATIONS), they tend to watch ....(LIST TYPES OF OR SPECIFIC TV SHOWS OR ENTER LITTLE OR NO TV), and they tend to access the Internet (often, occasionally, seldom). They often belong to the following industry and business organizations . . . .

. . . .

They frequently attend the following trade shows, conferences, seminars, and charity events . . . .

. . . .

They tend to participate in the following activities outside of the workplace . . . . .

. . . .

☐ **Additional Company Business Buyer Characteristics Statement**

Our target buyers make approximately . . . . (ENTER AMOUNT) of purchasing decisions per month. They tend to meet with approximately . . . . (ENTER NUMBER) of salespeople per month. Common preferred methods of communication are (in-person visits, phone, e-mail, fax, or letters). They usually (answer or don't answer) their own phone. (Or their phone is usually answered by an assistant or is on voice mail.) They control or influence budgets in the range of . . . . (GIVE RANGE) Expenditures for . . . . (PRODUCTS OR SERVICES) like ours consume approximately . . . . . (%) % of their budget. Our . . . . (PRODUCT OR SERVICE) category is a (must-have purchase item, an important purchase item, a highly desirable purchase item, a clearly useful but not important purchase item, a marginal purchase item).

☐ **Tiered Evaluation of Customer Characteristics Statement**

All of our prospective customers share the need for . . . .

. . . .

Almost all of our customers have the following characteristics . . . .

. . . .

Many, but not all, of our customers have these characteristics as well . . . .

. . . .

In addition, some, but less than a majority of our customers have these characteristics . . . .

. . . .

☐ **Customer Characteristic Groups of Particular Interest Statement**

Of particular interest are the customers with . . . .

. . . .

characteristics because they compose a highly identifiable group with specific needs, yet they are not being well served by any current product or service offering.

MARKET ANALYSIS MARKET ANALYSIS

Customer Needs

Be highly specific about the benefits the purchaser derives from the product/service and the needs that it fulfills. Include direct and indirect, tangible and intangible benefits. For example, by buying a new sofa a buyer gets not only a place to sit, but also improves the decor of the house, impresses friends, and enjoys seeing it in the living room.

Select and edit the <u>one</u> statement that best applies.

☐ **Basic Customer Needs Statement**

The most obvious needs this *SECURITY ACOUSTICAL CEILING* addresses is the
(PRODUCT OR SERVICE)

following *CONCEALMENT AND PROTECTION OF THE BUILDINGS MECHANICALS (PLUMBING, ELECTRICAL, HVAC),*

Additional needs that it meets are *IS THAT IT REDUCES NO DIRECT NOISE LEVELS WHICH IMPROVE WORKING CONDITIONS OF THE CORRECTIONAL OFFICERS.*

☐ **Identifying An Unfilled Need Statement**

The basic need of target customers is . . . .

. . . .

Virtually all competing . . . . address this basic
(PRODUCTS OR SERVICES)

need fairly well. Other needs that are relatively important include . . . .

. . . .

MARKET ANALYSIS MARKET ANALYSIS

The various .... currently available address
(PRODUCTS OR SERVICES)

these needs by ....

....

Some customers have a need for ....

....

This need is not being well met by existing alternatives. Furthermore for some
buyers it is an important enough need that they would buy a new product largely
on the basis of how well it filled this need.

☐ **Increasingly Demanding Buyers Statement**

The basic need that buyers are looking for is ....

....

But because of the many competitive alternatives, buyers are demanding that
other needs be satisfied as well. Common demands from buyers now include ....

....

In addition some buyers are beginning not only to request, but to insist upon ...

....

☐ **Variable Needs Statement**

Even within the market segment that we are targeting, customer needs vary significantly from one buyer to the next. Companies are currently dealing with this
broad range of wants by (offering a highly customized approach, offering a broad range

of product or service options, specializing in servicing a narrow portion of the market segment, offering add-on features or services).

☐ **Changing Needs Statement**

Historically, buyers in this market have been overwhelmingly concerned with the following need . . . . Recently however, because of the following changes in the marketplace . . . ., many buyers have become increasingly concerned about . . . .

This need is not being adequately addressed by current solutions that are available. But our company intends to directly address this need and use it as leverage to quickly build market share.

EXPERT ADVICE

Customer Needs

At first thought, this section may seem trivial, but the more you think about it the more important it may appear. For example people buy cars for transportation, right? Wrong. People may use cars for transportation but they serve many other needs. Someone spending a lot of money for a name-brand luxury car is buying for a need other than just transportation. Someone buying a sports car with a big engine, powerful enough to more than double any legal speed limit, is buying for a need other than just transportation. These "softer" needs are more difficult to identify and discuss, but don't underestimate their importance. By identifying a strong unfilled customer need, you may be able to create a new market niche, position your product or service uniquely, or develop a distinctive marketing campaign.

Customer Buying Decisions

Describe the steps and the thought process that buyers go through in making purchasing decisions. Include rational as well as emotional elements of their decision-making process and identify all participants typically involved in making or influencing the decision.

Select and edit the <u>one</u> statement that best applies.

☐ **Basic Customer Buying Decision Statement**

These are the typical steps that buyers will typically go through in considering purchasing the _SECURITY ACOUSTICAL CEILING_ . The single most important

(PRODUCT OR SERVICE)

factor in determining a buyer's decision is _THAT THE CEILING MUST COMPLY WITH THE SPECIFICATIONS GENERATED BY THE OWNER._ Other important factors ~~are~~ is _PRICE._ ~~and~~

☐ **The Impulse Purchase Statement**

The buying decision is an impulse purchase made instantly on-the-spot. Hence key purchasing factors include availability of product, prominence of display, any special display fixtures, signage, packaging, and a low impulse price point.

☐ **Planned Purchase Statement**

The buying decision is made in advance of the actual purchase time. The buyer makes a conscious decision to purchase the product or service. Importantly, the buyer either (does or does not) decide in advance of visiting or calling the purchasing establishment what specific brand or model or type to purchase. Because this is a planned purchase, display and ready, easy availability of the .... (PRODUCT OR SERVICE) .... are less important factors. Absolute low price also tends to be less crucial. What is most important is reaching and influencing the potential buyer before the purchase decision is made.

☐ Presentation Purchase Statement

The buying decision is almost always made (at an in-person or during a telephone) sales presentation. The personal touch appears to be essential for moving buyers to action for this

.... (PRODUCT OR SERVICE) .... because ....

....

To support the sales presentation (advertising, product recognition, incentives) **are** (very important, somewhat important, of uncertain importance, not important) in closing the sale.

☐ Buying the Company Statement

Buyers in this market tend to put much weight on the company rather than just on the particular merits of the product or service being offered. While this tends to favor more established

EXPERT ADVICE

Customer Buying Decisions

Many business plans either skip this section or include it in customer needs. However, I think it is important, especially for internal business planning, to make a clear distinction between underlying buyer needs and the actual buying process itself. By clearly identifying the buyer's process of making the purchase decision, you will probably gain much insight in how to affect, influence, and change that purchasing decision.

It may be difficult to identify how buyers make decisions. You could take surveys of potential buyers. But this takes time and energy and might even produce misleading results. For example on a survey, buyers might tell you that they buy because of quality or by carefully comparing features, when in reality they buy because of price.

MARKET ANALYSIS MARKET ANALYSIS

companies, it can work to the advantage of a newer company that carefully hones a very specific and favorable image for itself.

☐ **Rational/Emotional Decision Statement**

Buyers tend (or don't) tend to make a careful decision based primarily upon an examination of the .... (PRODUCT OR SERVICE) merits. Instead emotional factors come into play including ....

☐ **Competitive Comparisons Statement**

Buyers tend to (very carefully, somewhat carefully, very casually, not at all) examine .... (PRODUCT OR SERVICE) .... features and benefits before making a purchasing decision.

☐ **The Herd Mentality Statement**

The buyer's perspective of the .... (PRODUCT'S OR SERVICE'S) relative success or lack of success for other buyers plays an important role in the decision-making process. Buyers in this market feel very nervous about adopting a .... (PRODUCT OR SERVICE) that they do not feel has been widely adopted. At the same time, they are more likely to buy a product just because others have already purchased the product. For many buyers their feeling about the .... (PRODUCT'S OR SERVICE'S) relative acceptance and success plays a more important role in their decision to buy it than their own careful examination of its actual merits.

MARKET ANALYSIS MARKET ANALYSIS

☐ **Special Closing Incentives Statement**

Buyers are increasingly expecting to get a "special incentive" to make the final buying decision. And the more special incentives are offered, the more buyers seem to expect them. Special incentives that buyers seem to respond best to include . . . .

. . . .

☐ **Corporate Buying Decisions Statement**

Corporate buyers of our product seem to respond best to the following sales pattern: first, having a chance to read printed literature; second, being called to action by a phone call; third, being shown the specifics of the product or service during a personal presentation; fourth, being carefully followed up with over a period of several (days, weeks) as the decision to purchase is considered and often discussed with other people.

☐ **Multiple Decision-Makers Statement**

At corporations the (president, buyer, sales manager, controller, purchasing agent) is usually the primary decision-maker, and crucial for moving the decision ahead. However other people, such as . . . .

. . . .

are often able to influence the decision-making process or veto the decision to buy.

☐ **Couples Making Decisions Statement**

When we sell to married couples both the husband and the wife play a role in the decision-making. Usually the (husband or wife) plays the key decision-making role, but the other spouse must at least acquiesce for the purchase decision to move ahead. Nonetheless, we have found it is highly desirable to be able to make the sales presentation when both spouses are home.

☐ **Buying Display Space Statement**

While in this industry, retailers do not technically require slotting fees, they seldom will buy a product without a heavy commitment to buy co-op advertising—of which the manufacturer must pay 100%. Co-op launch funds can be as high as $ . . . . . for a single product at a major account.
(\$)

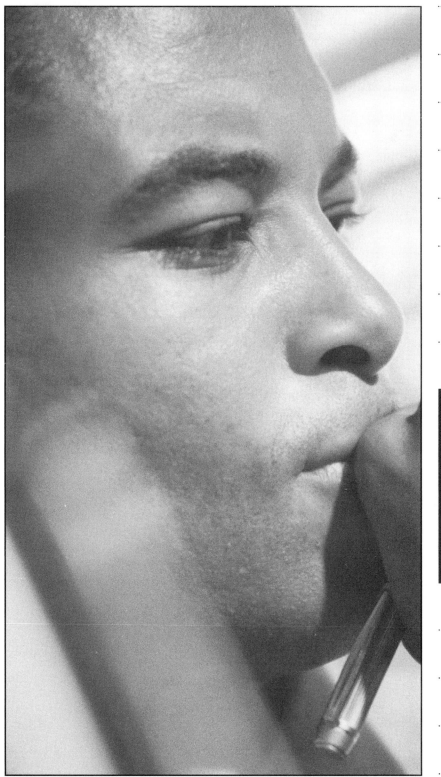

CHAPTER 10

Competitive Analysis

Industry Overview

Present a concise overall picture of the industry. Useful information may include industry structure, degree of competitiveness, level of profitability, and other important characteristics.

Select and edit the <u>one or more</u> statements that best apply.

☐ **Basic Industry Overview Statement**

Total sales in this industry nationwide are $ . . . . Companies in this industry
_($)
range in size from $ . . . . . in sales to $ . . . . . in sales. The industry is (dominated
_($)   _($)
by one company: . . . . , dominated by a few large players, primarily
_(NAME OF COMPANY)
composed of mid-sized firms ranging in size from $ . . . . . to $ . . . . . , composed
_($)   _($)
largely of smaller firms under $ . . . . . who account for the vast majority of sales).
_($)
Companies compete with one another generally (across the globe, across the
nation, within particular regions such as . . . . , within particular metropoli-
_(REGION)
tan areas, locally, within a particular city or town). **Companies within this indus-**
try are best categorized by (their size, the market segment they serve, the type of
customer they serve, by their sales method, their production method, their types
of product, their types of services, their specialization, their relative pricing/qual-
ity). **Hence the industry can be divided into the following categories:**

1. . . . .
            _(CATEGORY OR SEGMENT 1)   _(SIZE OF SEGMENT 1)
2. . . . .
            _(CATEGORY OR SEGMENT 2)   _(SIZE OF SEGMENT 2)
3. . . . .
            _(CATEGORY OR SEGMENT 3)   _(SIZE OF SEGMENT 3)

COMPETITIVE ANALYSIS COMPETITIVE ANALYSIS

Important characteristics of each category are . . . .

. . . .

☐ Number and Size of Competitors Statement

Across the country there are ..4.. companies in ~~this industry. In~~
(#)
the market that we will be competing, ...
(DESCRIBE MARKET SEGMENT OR
. . . . there are . . . . . companies. They range in
GEOGRAPHICAL LOCATION,)   (#)
size from . . . . . . to . . . . However, most firms are in the
(SIZE)   (SIZE)
. . . . size range. Some of the firms focus exclusively on this
(SIZE)
type of . . . . , while for others it
(PRODUCT OR SERVICE)
is just one part of their business.

☐ Companies Grouped by Category Statement

There are several different kinds of competitors in this industry.
The major determining difference in this industry is (sales
method, production method, marketing method, target segment, size of company, specialization, etc.). Companies that are
similar in this regard generally tend to compete much more
directly and compete in more similar ways than companies that
are not similar in this regard.

☐ Industry Segments Statement

This industry can be broken into the following segments:

EXPERT ADVICE

Industry Overview

Don't spend a lot of time researching a lot of facts about the overall industry. A brief summary of the basic facts is useful for giving the reader some context. What's more important is the structure and characteristics of the industry. If industry segmentation is clear or an important part of the structure of this industry, be sure to note that. I find that the degree of competition can be a particularly important factor.

If the industry is extremely competitive for example, with participants quickly matching one another's features or products or constantly trying to undercut one another's prices, then this should have a significant impact on your business strategy and tactics. The ease of entry into the industry and rate at which firms exit the industry are also often important, bellweather characteristics.

1. . . . .
   (DESCRIBE SEGMENT 1)   (SIZE OR NUMBER OF COMPANIES)
2. . . . .
   (DESCRIBE SEGMENT 2)   (SIZE OR NUMBER OF COMPANIES)
3. . . . .
   (DESCRIBE SEGMENT 3)   (SIZE OR NUMBER OF COMPANIES)

. . . . is characterized by . . . .
            (SEGMENT 1)

. . . .

. . . . is characterized by . . . .
            (SEGMENT 2)

. . . .

. . . . is characterized by . . . .
            (SEGMENT 3)

. . . .

☐ **Description of Industry Participants Statement**

The . . . . industry can be thought of as firms that offer the
         (NAME)

following . . . . In addition some firms in
              (LIST COMMON TYPES OF PRODUCTS OR SERVICES)

this industry also offer . . . . Most
                              (LIST LESS COMMON TYPES OF PRODUCTS OR SERVICES)

firms are (owner operated, professionally managed, publicly held, subsidiaries or

divisions of larger corporations). Most firms have been in business (for many

years, for at least ten years, for just a few years). The most common sales and mar-

keting methods that companies use are . . . .

. . . .

Customers tend to (be highly loyal to one company, switch companies often, be

open-minded to trying new companies, stay with one product or service).

COMPETITIVE ANALYSIS COMPETITIVE ANALYSIS

☐ **Common Consumer Service Industry Structure Statement**

Competition is highly limited by locality. Customers are reluctant to use service providers based in distant locations and even tend to do business with a service business that specifically focuses on their (city, town, region, metro area). As a result, in our target market .... (SPECIFY), there are only ..... (#) direct competitors. Because these companies are private, exact sales information is not available, but based on their number of (employees, service trucks, etc.) I would estimate that no one competitor dominates, and that the market share of each firm ranges between ..... % (%) and ..... %. (%)

☐ **Common Business Service Industry Structure Statement**

Competitors tend to focus on (specific cities or regions, industries, functions, sizes of companies, etc.). Because of the tendency to specialize, the degree of competition varies widely from one selling situation to the next. Competition tends to be most intense for larger volume accounts ....

....

And competition tends to be less intense for potentially smaller volume accounts

....

☐ **Hyper-Competitive Statement**

The industry can be best characterized as hyper-competitive. There are many firms competing more or less directly for the same customers. Competing companies .... (PRODUCTS OR SERVICES) are highly similar, yet, without a clear difference from one to the next. Profit margins tend to be relatively thin and market shares within the industry tend to fluctuate from one year to the next.

☐ Mild Competition Statement

Competition in this industry is rather mild. There are only a few direct competitors. Customers do not switch firms very often and do not tend to carefully comparison shop before making buying decisions. Market shares tend to be relatively stable. Competitors do not make aggressive marketing moves such as running predatory or comparative advertising campaigns. There is little competition on price, and price incentives or promotions are rare.

☐ Business Is Transaction Oriented Statement

Ongoing relationships are not important in this industry. This doesn't mean that relationships don't matter at all, but instead, customers tend to put more weight on their perception of the supplier's ability to meet their needs today, as opposed to whether or not they previously did business with the company. As a result there is relatively little customer loyalty in this industry. Multiple competitors tend to either serve the same customers simultaneously, or they tend to find that their customers are often switching from one firm to the next.

☐ Relationships Are Important Statement

Customers do not switch suppliers often and tend to be relatively satisfied with current vendors. The strength of the relationship between customer and seller plays just as important a role as any other factor such as features, pricing, etc.

COMPETITIVE ANALYSIS COMPETITIVE ANALYSIS

Customers tend not to seriously consider unsolicited overtures from new vendors, and it takes a strong reason for them to specifically request a presentation from a new vendor.

☐ **Industry Dominated by Few Key Players Statement**

While there are many different firms competing in this industry, competition is dominated by (one, two, three, etc.) firms. Together these firms have a market share of ..... %. These firms are by far the most visible in the industry and their
_(%)
moves tend to determine industry direction and the nature of the competition. The larger firms tend to have much broader ....
_(PRODUCT OR SERVICE)
lines, while the smaller firms tend to be more specialized.

☐ **Structure in Our Target Market Statement**

The general market that we are serving .... is of course
_(SPECIFY)
a huge and complex industry about which there are large amounts of information available from many sources. But because we are specifically targeting a very limited part of this market, we will limit the discussion to this market segment. The .... is characterized by ....
_(SPECIFY SEGMENT) _{(LEVEL OF COM-}
.... It (is or is not) dominated by (one, two, three, etc.) firms. The
_{PETITION)}
type of firms that we are going to compete most directly with are characterized by

....

....

☐ **The Power Is Held by Statement**

In this industry, power is really held by the (manufacturers, wholesalers, retailers, customers, end-users, suppliers, etc.). They tend to be much larger firms and each of them wields considerable power by controlling access to . . . .

. . . .

On the other hand, the firms that they (buy from, sell to, etc.) tend to be much smaller and hence lack market power. The concentration of this power has considerable impact on the industry. For example . . . .

. . . .

☐ **Cyclical Statement**

This industry tends to be highly cyclical. Sales generally fall and rise in parallel to the basic (national, world, or specific industry) economic cycles. At the low point of the cycle not only sales, but also prices, and of course, profits, fall significantly. At the high point of the cycle sales rise, prices rise, profits soar, and capacity is strained until the industry invests in more plants and equipment.

☐ **Seasonality Statement**

The industry has consistent seasonal swings. First quarter tends to be . . . . . of (%) sales; second quarter tends to be . . . . . % of sales; third quarter . . . . . % of sales; (%) (%) fourth quarter . . . . . % of sales. Industry profits are overwhelmingly concentrated (%) in the . . . . quarter. Seasonality in this industry has the following important (QUARTER) implications . . . .

. . . .

☐ **Financial Outlook Statement**

The profit levels in this industry are (high, low, mixed, in the range of . . . . . % of
$_{(\%)}$
sales). Profits are (fairly consistent from one firm to the next, highly inconsistent
from one firm to the next, overwhelmingly concentrated at the larger firms).
Firms that have higher profit margins tend to share the following characteristics

. . . .

. . . .

Firms in this industry tend to be (cash rich, have excellent access to capital, have
moderate debt, have high levels of debt).

☐ **A Tough, but Growing Industry Statement**

While the rapid growth of this industry has attracted many new firms from start-
ups to large established corporations, many firms have experienced huge losses.
Some have withdrawn from the field, others continue to struggle along, others
have been acquired by more successful firms, and still others have fallen into
bankruptcy or even liquidation. Problems that have created the most problems for
companies in this industry include . . . .

. . . .

☐ **A Highly Lucrative Industry Statement**

Historically, this industry has been highly lucrative with high margins, below average competition, steadily rising sales, and solid financial performances. What has limited entrance to this industry is (the need for specialized training, most people do not want to operate a business of this type, significant investment requirements, the difficulty of getting customers to switch from existing companies, how well-entrenched existing firms are).

☐ **Ease of Entry Statement**

Ease of entry in this industry can be characterized as . . . .
(DESCRIBE)
Many firms (successfully or unsuccessfully try to) enter this field each year. Firms that have been most successfully entering this field have tended to. . . . .

. . . .

Firms that have not been successful trying to enter this field have tended to . . . .

. . . .

☐ **Ownership Statement**

Most firms in this industry are (sole proprietorships, partnerships, closely-held corporations, publicly held corporations, subsidiaries of publicly held corporations). Ownership patterns have been (relatively steady, shifting toward more ownership by publicly held corporations). Debt loads in the industry tend to be (relatively marginal, low, average, moderately high, high, in the range of . . . . . % of
(%)
total capitalization).

Nature of Competition

Evaluating and summarizing not just who competes, but how they compete, is a very important part of preparing a successful plan for your business. You want to identify not all the ways that firms compete—but the methods of competition that competitors give the most effort to and what methods of competition tend to be most successful. For example, is price emphasized more than anything else in advertising, and do the lowest-priced products or services have the largest market share? Or is a certain qualitative feature emphasized again and again?

Select and edit the <u>one</u> statement that best applies.

☐ **Basic Competition Statement**

Competition in this industry focuses largely on (price, quality, features, performance, specialization, expertise, reliability, technology, customer relationships, marketing, advertising, sales, publicity, distribution, serving particular market niches, appealing to particular consumers). This is emphasized in advertising, in press releases, and in sales pitches. While companies compete on other dimensions as well, this is the primary direction that most competitive effort goes into. Apparently the management at most

EXPERT ADVICE

Nature of Competition

Here the key is finding the one or very few ways that companies focus most of their competitive effort—not just listing every way in which companies compete. What does top management focus on? What does ad copy focus on? What do companies spend a lot of time or money on? What do companies emphasize in sales pitches or on their packaging? What do they focus on when they compare their products to their competitors?

companies feel that this factor is most important in consumer buying decisions. Important secondary focuses of competition are . . . .

. . . .

☐ Features Are King Statement

Competitive effort largely focuses on features. New features are regularly added and are very highly trumpeted in press releases, in advertising, and in sale pitches.

☐ Quality Counts Statement

Quality is a major focus on the competitive battle in this industry. Quality is usually meant to mean . . . .

. . . .

Quality is conveyed to potential buyers by . . . .

. . . .

Price is seldom a competitive factor, and firms that compete on price risk undermining their quality image.

☐ Price Is the Bottom Line Statement

Most competitors focus overwhelmingly on price. Price is emphasized again and again in advertising and even included in some store's taglines. As a result, companies work very hard to drive their costs down. They try to squeeze the last penny out of vendors. And they work hard to cut their overhead and other costs of doing business.

COMPETITIVE ANALYSIS COMPETITIVE ANALYSIS

☐ **Customer-Focused Statement**

Competition in this industry is customer-focused. Companies go out of their way to respond very quickly to serving the unique requests and desires of individual customers. They remain flexible and adaptive to their customers needs and usually create a strong amount of loyalty with customers that they serve.

☐ **Quality of Service Statement**

Competition focuses on the quality of service. Price is seldom emphasized and tends not to vary much between most firms. Instead firms try to emphasize to their customers how their service is better than that of their competitors. For example, they might mention in their advertising or sales pitch (number of years in service, levels of training, licenses, certificates, size of company, availability, quality of parts, guarantees, etc.).

☐ **Sales-Driven Statement**

While there is some differences between the competing .... (PRODUCTS OR .... SERVICES) , the heart of competition is the sales process. Usually, the more effective salesperson will get the sale. As a result, companies spend a huge amount of their senior management time focused on improving their sales process and a high percentage of their budgets on sales costs. Companies are particularly cautious about losing salespeople to competing firms and quick to hire talented salespeople with industry experience.

☐ **Product-Driven Statement**

This industry is product driven. New products are introduced at the rate of ..... New products tend to account for about ..... % of total sales. The life
(#)   (#)
cycle of products is typically short, such as ....

A very large percentage of new products ..... % quickly fail and are withdrawn
(#)
from the market.

☐ **Product Upgrades Statement**

Products tend to be upgraded on average approximately every ....
(MONTHS/YEARS)
Major products tend to be upgraded more frequently, such as every .... Product upgrades (usually, often, usually not, seldom)
(MONTHS/YEARS)
represent substantial changes. They are (usually, often, usually not, seldom) accompanied by much marketing attention.

☐ **Positioning Statement**

The competitive battle in this market is waged in the mind of potential consumers. Most buyers are pre-sold on one brand of product or another before they actually buy it. As a result, advertising and other kinds of marketing are particularly important.

☐ **Spoils to the Winner Statement**

People tend to buy .... in this industry just
(PRODUCTS AND SERVICES)
because they are the market leader. This makes competing difficult for small companies—except for those firms with very specialized products or services. As a

result, firms spend huge amounts of money and effort when they feel they have a chance of taking over the leadership position for any key . . . . (PRODUCT OR

. . . .
SERVICE) .

☐ Trade Emphasis Statement

Competition focuses primarily on selling to retailers or wholesalers, because the task of selling to end consumers is seen as largely outside the control of the manufacturer. This is particularly true because products in this industry are low priced impulse products.

☐ Relationship-Driven Statement

Companies strive not only to build relationships with their current customers, but also to emphasize to new customers how strong and beneficial a long-term relationship with them will be. The emphasis is on selling not a particular product or service, but the whole company. Often extra intangibles such as . . . .

. . . .

are emphasized to show that the value of the whole relationship is greater than the sum of the actual . . . . that are being sold.
(PRODUCTS OR SERVICES)

☐ Local Proximity Statement

In this industry local proximity is a major competitive factor. Firms not only emphasize that they are conveniently located, but they go beyond this to infer that there is extra goodwill that accompanies their ties to the local community. Advertising statements such as (local ownership, based in . . . . ,
(LOCATION)

a local business, etc.) show how much importance is placed on closeness to the community.

☐ **Technology-Driven Statement**

C̶ ̶ ̶ ̶ ̶ ̶ ̶ ̶ ̶ ̶ ̶ ̶ ̶ ̶ ̶ Firms invest great of effort in

THEIR POSITION AS THE INDUSTRY LEADER. ENVIRONMENTAL INTERIORS PROMOTES THE VOLUMN OF CEILINGS THEY HAVE FURNISHED TO DATE. THEY ALSO INVEST TIME INTO DEVELOPING ACCESSORIES THAT CAN BE SOLD WITH THEIR CEILING SYSTEMS. EXAMPLES ARE LIGHT FIXTURES AND ACCESS DOORS.

☐ **Mixed Nature of Competition Statement**

Different companies focus their competitive energies in many different ways in this industry. Some (ONE) firms, for example, give their primary competitive focus to

Examples of these firms are

COMPETITIVE ANALYSIS COMPETITIVE ANALYSIS

ANOTHER FIRM FOCUSES ON EASE OF INSTALLATION.
TRUSSBILT HAS A CEILING PLANK THAT'S PROFILE
ALLOWS IT TO SNAP TO AN ADJACENT PLANK
WITHOUT MECHANICAL FASTENER. THIS SAVES
TIME BUT COSTS MORE.

AEROTECH AND WILSECURE
THE OTHER FIRMS FOCUS ON PROVIDING FULL
SERVICE (MATERIAL AND INSTALLATION) LIKE
THE INDUSTRY LEADER BUT COST COMPETITIVE.

Changes in the Industry

Summarize major pertinent changes that are shaping the industry. Describe what the impact of these changes are on the different players in the industry including, if applicable, suppliers, your competitors, dealers, wholesalers, retailers, and consumers.

Select and edit the <u>one or more</u> statements that best apply.

☐ **Basic Industry Changes Statement**

A Current changes taking place in this industry are (consolidation, the entrance of

IS A SHIFT IN MORE FOR DEMAND A "LIGHT GAUGE" SECURITY
CEILING IN-LIEU-OF AND IN ADDITION TO THE HEAVY
GAUGE PLANK SYSTEMS. THE LIGHT GAUGE SYSTEMS
ARE MORE ECONOMICAL THAN PRICE COMPETITIVE. FOR THE PLANK SYSTEMS
BUT PROVIDE LESS DURABILITY. THOSE FIRMS
THAT DO NOT SELL BOTH SYSTEMS WILL BE
AT A DISADVANTAGE ON THOSE PROJECTS THAT
REQUIRE BOTH. CONTRACTORS WILL NOT WANT TO BUY
FROM TWO SUPPLIERS / SUBCONTRACTORS.

Implications of these changes include . . . .

COMPETITIVE ANALYSIS COMPETITIVE ANALYSIS

☐ **Growth Statement**

The industry is currently experiencing a period of (rapid growth, moderate growth, average growth, flat sales, declining sales, uncertainty, volatility) caused by . . . .

. . . .

In the years ahead this trend is expected to (accelerate, continue, abate, slow down) because of . . . .

. . . .

The current (growth, stability, decline) in the industry has had the following implications . . . .

. . . .

☐ **Consolidation Statement**

The industry is going through a period of consolidation as (larger firms are acquiring smaller firms, larger firms are expanding and smaller firms are going out of business, a few dominant players are increasing their control of the industry). This consolidation has had the following implications . . . .

. . . .

☐ **Major Corporations Entering the Industry Statement**

The fast growth of this marketplace has attracted major corporate players, several of whom have already launched products,

EXPERT ADVICE

Changes in the Industry

Changes can be just as important—if not more important—than the underlying structure and nature of the industry. Especially for a new or less established company, changes may affect you the most. Not being wedded to the old ways of doing business, you may be better able to design your company to take advantage of the changes going on in the industry. On the other hand, other kinds of changes, such as a trend toward industry consolidation, make it even more difficult for a small, new firm to succeed, especially without a clearly distinctive product or service.

When you examine trends currently underway, you should discuss where you think the trend may lead. If it's not clear where a trend may lead, you may want to describe two or more different possible scenarios for the industry.

and several of whom are expected to do so shortly. They are launching their products with major advertising and promotional expenditures and using the clout of their national sales forces to roll out their products. As a result, it is becoming a much more difficult climate for smaller players, especially less established ones, to launch products that are not specialized or aimed at narrow market segments.

☐ **Shift to Fewer Vendors Statement**

To improve their operating efficiencies, customers have been cutting their lists of vendors and consolidating their purchasing to a few larger suppliers and wholesalers. They have also become increasingly demanding of their suppliers, for example insisting that all vendors use Electronic Data Interchange, requiring their suppliers to always be in stock of critical items, and enforcing strict shipping requirements.

☐ **Power Shift Statement**

Power in this industry is shifting to the (manufacturers, wholesalers, retailers, customers, end-users, suppliers, etc.). They are growing in size and clout and have the ability to become increasingly demanding of the companies with which they deal. Implications of this trend are . . . .

. . . .

☐ **Outsourcing Statement**

Industry participants are outsourcing more and more of their work. Functions that are most likely to be outsourced include . . . .

COMPETITIVE ANALYSIS COMPETITIVE ANALYSIS

Possible impact of this change is . . . .

. . . .

☐ **Strategic Alliances Statement**

As this industry continues to grow and become increasingly complex, companies are forming strategic alliances. Common strategic alliances are between firms that

. . . . This trend means that . . . .
  (DESCRIBE RELATIONSHIP)

. . . .

☐ **Bundling/Unbundling Statement**

. . . . in this industry are increasingly being
  (PRODUCTS OR SERVICES)

(bundled, unbundled). This makes it (easier, more difficult) for firms to compete who can't offer all of the bundled goods.

☐ **Shift to One-Stop Shopping Statement**

More and more customers are looking for one single source. This gives a huge advantage to firms that offer an extremely broad array of . . . .
  (PRODUCTS OR

. . . . , but a disadvantage to those that don't. Depending on how
SERVICES)

much this trend continues, the likely result will be . . . .

. . . .

☐ **Product Substitute Creating Change Statement**

The continuing inroads of . . . . .con-
(THE PRODUCT OR SERVICE SUBSTITUTE)

tinues to shake this industry and can be expected to continue to do so for some

time to come. Most firms are reacting to this challenge by . . . .

. . . .

Other firms are . . . .

. . . .

Still others are . . . .

. . . .

Additional implications of this change include . . . .

. . . .

Primary Competitors

Here you should focus on the companies that you compete with—not their particular products or services. Direct your competitive analysis to those few firms that you compete most directly with. Focus in less depth on firms that you compete with less directly.

Select and edit the <u>one</u> statement that best applies.

☐ **Basic Competing Company Statement** (repeat for each competitor)

Analysis Name: . . . .

Location: . . . .

Sales: . . . . .
_($)

Profitability: . . . .

Number of employees: . . . . .
_(#)

Years in business: . . . . .
_(#)

Strategy: . . . .

. . . .

Competitive strengths: . . . .

. . . .

Competitive weaknesses: . . . .

. . . .

Other pertinent info: . . . .

. . . .

EXPERT ADVICE

Primary Competitors

Deciding which competitors to list is an important first step. You may want to rank them, categorize them into distinctive groups, or perhaps just list the one, two, or three most important. Generally I recommend that you make a distinction between those firms that you compete most directly with, versus those firms that you compete less directly with. In addition to listing the basic characteristics of your competitors, you may want to add characteristics that are particularly pertinent for your situation.

Look for factors that are possible strengths or weaknesses of each firm, or that may be predictive of their future plans, or how they might react to your competitive moves. Try to determine and succinctly summarize the strategy of each competitor.

COMPETITIVE ANALYSIS COMPETITIVE ANALYSIS

itor)

#2 IS AEROTECH
by PRICE AND THEIR KNOWLEDGE OF THE
INDUSTRY AND THEIR CONTACTS. ESTIMATED
SALES ARE 1 MILLION. THEIR WEAKNESS IS
THAT THEY DO NOT OFFER A LIGHT GAUGE SYSTEM
WHICH NARROWS THEIR SALES OPPORTUNITIES.

#3 IS WILSOURE
by BEING A FULL SERVICE PROVIDER IN A NICHE
MARKET FOR THE CITY OF NEW YORK. ESTIMATED
SALES ARE 1 MILLION. THEIR WEAKNESS IS
PRICE OUT SIDE OF NEW YORK AND THEIR LACK
OF KNOWLEDGE AND CONTACTS IN THE INDUSTRY

Sales strength:

COMPETITIVE ANALYSIS COMPETITIVE ANALYSIS

Advertising strength: . . . .

. . . .

Use of promotions: . . . .

. . . .

#1 Strength: . . . .

#1 Weakness: . . . .

Other key point: . . . .

. . . .

☐ **Principle Competitor Strategy Statement (Repeat for each principle competitor)**

Our (#1, #2, #3, etc.) competitor is . . . . (NAME) . . . . They compete

largely by (p

advertising,

ing custome

bility in . . . .

being partic

focusing on

market nich

. . . .

Their major

. . . .

They have s

. . . .

#1 IS ENVIRONMENTAL INTERIORS
by WORKING WITH ARCHITECTS ON NEW PROJECTS AND
GETTING THE CEILING LINES AND ACCESSORIES LISTED
IN THE SPECIFICATIONS, WHEN THEY WANT A JOB
THEY WILL BACKDOOR THEIR REPRESENTATIVES AND
SELL A JOB DIRECT FOR A MORE COMPETITIVE PRICE
PAYING THEIR REPS ONE HALF OR LESS THEIR NORMAL
COMMISSION RATES. ESTIMATED SALES IS 2 MILLION

...sed,

...s FROM

PREVIOUS
~~OVER~~ ~~NEXT~~ PAGE

COMPETITIVE ANALYSIS COMPETITIVE ANALYSIS

Competitive Products/Services

Focus your competitive comparison on those few products or services that you compete with most directly. Focus in less depth on products or services that you compete with less directly.

> THE CEILING SYSTEMS SOLD BY ENVIRONMENTAL INTERIORS COMPETES WITH US DIRECTLY. THEY ARE POSITIONED AS BEING THE MARKET LEADER. THEIR MAJOR COMPETITIVE STRENGTHS ARE BRAND NAME RECOGNITION AND PROVIDING FULL SERVICE. THEIR WEAKNESS IS PRICE BECAUSE OF THEIR SALES STRUCTURE (REPS) AND OVERHEAD (LARGE COMPANY).

Price: ....
(\$)

Target Buyers: ....

....

Primary positioning: ....

....

Features/attributes most emphasized in ads/sales pitches or packaging:

1. ....

2. ....

3. ....

4. ....

5. ....

Sales methods: ....

....

Advertising budget: ....

Advertising themes: ....

....

Promotional/incentive programs: ....

....

Competitive strengths: ....

....

Competitive weaknesses: ....

....

Other pertinent info: ....

....

Expert Advice

Competitive Products/Services

It is more important to go into a lot of depth examining your most direct competitors, rather than trying to give equal time and attention to all competing products or services. Give particular attention to the market leaders and try to identify why they have been successful. It is also often useful to identify why secondary products or services have been less successful. Go beyond the product or service itself to examine other aspects of the competitive process that may be critical. For example, does the particular sales method or advertising approach seem to be a major success factor? Try to determine how your competitors are positioning their products. Are they targeting a particular market niche? Do they seem to succeed in this positioning?

COMPETITIVE ANALYSIS COMPETITIVE ANALYSIS

☐ **Competitive Product/Service Matrix Statement**
(Repeat for each principle competitive product/service.)

Product/service: ....

....

Price: .....
(\$)

Estimated Sales: ....

Sales trend: ....

....

Target customers: ....

....

Main features: ....

....

Secondary features: ....

....

#1 selling point: ....

#2 selling point: ....

#3 selling point: ....

#4 selling point: ....

Relative quality: ....

....

Relative reputation: ....

....

COMPETITIVE ANALYSIS COMPETITIVE ANALYSIS

Loyalty of customers: ....

....

Advertising support: ....

....

#1 Strength: ....

#1 Weakness: ....

☐ **Principle Competitive Product/Service Positioning Statement**
(Repeat for each principle competitive product/service.)

The .... competes with us (head-on, directly,
(NAME PRODUCT OR SERVICE)

directly for some customers, indirectly). **It is positioned as** (having outstanding
quality, being the low price option, having the best engineering, being the most
technically advanced, being specialized for ....

................................,,

being a highly customized solution, providing a high level of service, offering the
best personalized service, serving the following market niche ....

................................,,

being a recognized brand name, being the market leader, being the most innovative product, being the most professional, being the best option for customers who
................................).

Customers appear to (accept, agree with, not agree with, not be aware of, not care
about, not give much attention to, disagree) **with the company's intended positioning of it's** .... (Instead customer's view this
(PRODUCT OR SERVICE)

product or service as . . . .

. . . .).

The major competitive strength of this . . . . is . . . . . .
                       (PRODUCT OR SERVICE)

. . . .

Its major weakness is . . . .

. . . .

☐ **Basic Unfilled Needs Statement**

Based upon an evaluation of the market, buyers needs and current competitive offerings, we feel there is an unfilled need for a . . . .
                                            (PRODUCT OR SERVICE)
that . . . .

. . . .

This . . . . would be particularly desired by buyers who
           (PRODUCT OR SERVICE)

. . . .

Current offerings, such as . . . .

. . . .

partially meet the needs of such buyers, but a new . . . .
                                          (PRODUCT OR SERVICE)
that addresses their needs more directly would clearly appeal to some buyers of current options.

Opportunities

Compare markets, customer needs, and customer characteristics with competitive offerings to help determine market opportunities. Include all major opportunities that you think might exist, not just those you are most likely to pursue. This will help open your mind to new opportunities and make your plan more complete for future reference and for showing to outside investors or advisors.

Select and edit the <u>one</u> statement that best applies.

☐ **Basic Unfilled Needs Statement**

Based upon an evaluation of the market, buyers needs and current competitive offerings, we feel there is an unfilled need for a . . . .
(PRODUCT OR SERVICE)
that . . . .

. . . .

This . . . . would be particularly desired by buyers who
(PRODUCT OR SERVICE)

. . . .

Current offerings, such as . . . .

. . . .

partially meet the needs of such buyers, but a new (product or service) that addresses their needs more directly would clearly appeal to some buyers of current options.

☐ **Filling a Need Better Statement**

While there are many different .... attributes that
(PRODUCT OR SERVICE)
matter to buyers, ... is particularly important
(DESCRIBE FEATURE/ATTRIBUTE)
to them. While competing offerings include this feature, we believe there is significant room for improvement in it—and more importantly that such improvement would have a very strong attraction for buyers.

☐ **Finding a Niche Statement**

Most buyers needs appear to be fairly well served by current (product or service
offerings that are generally directed toward the needs of the largest portion of the
market which is most concerned with ....
....

However, some buyers who are more concerned with ....
....

are not being well-served by current product offerings). We believe there is a terrific opportunity for a .... that meets the needs of
(SERVICE OR PRODUCT)
these buyers directly.

☐ **Serving a New/Different Market Statement**

While the competition is well-established in, and gives a lot of focus to, current
major markets for this product, they are much less aggressively pursuing the
.... market. This market offers terrific potential
(ENTER EMERGING MARKET)
because it has significant growth potential, and the competition is not well-
entrenched here. Furthermore, this market differs from the other markets in the

COMPETITIVE ANALYSIS COMPETITIVE ANALYSIS

following important ways . . . .

. . . .

While this market may not be the largest, it appears a very solid opportunity for a less established competitor.

☐ **Opportunities in Competitor's Weaknesses Statement**

An examination of the competitive offerings finds several weaknesses. The most important weakness is . . . .

. . . .

This weakness is particularly important because it is of major concern to many buyers. Other weaknesses include . . . .

. . . .

A . . . . that was able to overcome
(PRODUCT OR SERVICE)
some of these weaknesses, for example by . . . .

. . . . ,

would rapidly gain a solid market position.

☐ **A New Competitive Focus Statement**

Many industry participants are well-entrenched with solid market positions. The nature of the competition is overwhelmingly focused on . . . .

. . . .

While this focus is relevant for the needs of most buyers, it tends to overlook and downplay other important needs of buyers

EXPERT ADVICE

Opportunities

In a perfect world you hope you are going to discover a strong consumer need not being addressed by any current competitor. This would be wonderful because it would mean, at least initially, that you would not be directly competing with any one. However, in the real world these situations are rare. And all too often I find that budding entrepreneurs who really think they have "discovered" a spectacular new consumer need either have a product or service idea that people aren't willing to pay for, or have an idea that someone else is already using. Generally you are more likely to find a path to success with an already existing product or service idea. Your degree of success will often be determined by how successfully you differentiate the same basic product or service from the competition.

such as ....

....

So a new .... that focuses on ....
(PRODUCT OR SERVICE)

....

will clearly stand out from the competition and quickly get the attention of buyers.

☐ **One Competitive Edge Statement**

After reviewing the currently successful .... in this
(PRODUCTS OR SERVICES)

marketplace, it is apparent that all of them do a relatively good job of addressing

the following basic needs of buyers.

SECURITY CEILINGS

THEY PROVIDE A DURABLE CEILING SYSTEM THAT
PROTECTS THE MECHANICALS OF THE BUILDING AND NOISE
REDUCTION CHARACTERISTICS. A NEW FIRM WOULD HAVE
TO PROVIDE A CEILING SYSTEM THAT MET THOSE NEEDS
AS WELL AS PROVIDE FULL SERVICE. BUT TO SUCCEED
THE ~~PRODUCTS~~ CEILINGS AND INSTALLATION MUST BE LOW PRICED.
~~WITH~~ TO EXPAND ON THE FULL SERVICE POSITION
WE COULD PROVIDE SOFFIT ENCLOSURES AND DETENTION
                                        FURNITURE.

option would be to ....

....

COMPETITIVE ANALYSIS COMPETITIVE ANALYSIS

The advantages of this option would be . . . .

. . . .

The disadvantages of this option would be . . . .

. . . .

This option (would or would not) **match our capabilities well because** . . . .

. . . .

A second option would be to . . . .

. . . .

The advantages of this option would be . . . .

. . . .

The disadvantages of this option would be . . . .

. . . .

This option (would or would not) **match our capabilities well because** . . . .

. . . .

A third option would be to . . . .

. . . .

The advantages of this option would be . . . .

. . . .

The disadvantages of this option would be . . . .

. . . .

This option (would or would not) **match our capabilities well because** . . . .

. . . .

Threats and Risks

Identify the most significant risks the business faces. You may want to include competitive threats, possible adverse market changes, major challenges from new products/services, competition reaction to your moves, changes in the industry and changes from outside the industry—such as the introduction of a product or service substitute. If you are raising money from outside sources, especially for equity investment, not adequately disclosing possible risks may be grounds for a lawsuit if the business does not succeed.

Select and edit the <u>one or more</u> statements that best apply.

☐ **Basic Threats Statement**

Threats that pose significant risks to our business include . . . .

. . . .

The implications of these threats is . . . .

. . . .

The likelihood of these threats materializing is . . . .

. . . .

We could respond to such threats by . . . .

. . . .

☐ **Start-Up Risks Statement**

The business faces the normal risks faced by any business, the uncertainty inherent in a (start-up, new, young) business, the risks common to firms in this

COMPETITIVE ANALYSIS COMPETITIVE ANALYSIS

industry (such as . . . .

. . . . ,

most notably . . . .

. . . . ,

of particular concern . . . .

. . . .),

and the following risks peculiar to this company . . . .

. . . .

☐ Larger, More Established Competitors Statement

The company faces the risk of competing with much larger, better entrenched competitors. These firms have established and commanding market shares, large advertising budgets, large sales forces, established relationships with customers, and tremendous financial resources. We hope to offset this risk by .

. . . .

☐ Breaking into an Established Marketplace Statement

While our competitive analysis shows that our . . . . (PRODUCT OR . . . . out performs competing offerings, there is still a SERVICE) risk that (buyers will be reluctant to adopt a new product, buyers will not consider a new vendor, that market acceptance may take longer than anticipated). So to help accelerate and increase

Expert Advice

Threats and Risks

Every business faces lots of threats and risks. So focus on the most important threats—those most likely to happen and/or those that could do the most damage. The nature of threats will vary widely from one business situation to the next.

However, new business people particularly, tend to underestimate possible competitive reaction to either their market entrance or business strategy. The fewer direct competitors that you face, the more chance a competing business will respond to your business initiatives. If there is one lawn mowing business in town and they charge $40 to mow a lawn and you come along and start charging $20, the established business is probably going to react. On the other hand if there are fifty lawn moving businesses in town, there is less likely to be a competitive reaction.

the likelihood of a successful launch we are (launching a major marketing program as described in the marketing section, making a generous one-time product offer as described in the promotion section, developing an aggressive sales program as described in the sales section).

☐ No Proven Market Statement

Because we are launching a new type of ....(PRODUCT OR SERVICE)........ , there are no guarantees that a market exists for it. We believe however that as shown in our customer needs section of this plan that (there is significant demand to make this product/service viable, there is great demand for this product/service, that our new offering will better serve customers' needs than existing alternatives). We have done (customer surveys, focus groups with potential buyers, informal discussions with key buyers, extensive market research, test marketing, comparisons with other similar markets) that confirm our belief that our offering will succeed in the marketplace.

☐ Turbulent, Fast Changing Market Statement

The marketplace that we are targeting is very turbulent and fast changing. We believe that our ....(PRODUCTS OR SERVICES)............ will meet the needs of buyers in the market for the foreseeable future, but this market has been characterized by short life cycles of product and rapid product obsolescence. We plan to be prepare for market changes by...

....

COMPETITIVE ANALYSIS COMPETITIVE ANALYSIS

☐ **New Products/Services Statement**

While we do not have current knowledge of such plans, it is possible that a competitor could launch a new . . . . that would even more
(PRODUCT OR SERVICE)
directly compete with us than current offerings do. The kind of offering that would be most threatening for us would be . . . .

. . . .

The competitors that would be most likely to launched such a product are . . . . . .

. . . .

We would be particularly threatened by such a . . . . launch
(PRODUCT OR SERVICE)
because . . . .

☐ **Changes in Features/Attributes Statement**

Possible changes or additional features with competitors' offerings comprise a potential threat. The competitors we are most concerned about in this regard are

. . . .

. . . .

Most threatening would be the following potential changes . . . .

. . . .

These would be threatening because . . . .

. . . .

☐ **Competitive Reaction Statement**

It is possible that one or more existing competitors will react to our entrance into this market. Because of their established market positions, a strong competitive reaction could be a formidable threat. The competitive reactions that would be most threatening would be . . . .

. . . .

However, because of our relatively small anticipated market share, we feel a swift competitive response is extremely unlikely, and there is a good chance that the competition may not directly respond at all. If a competitive response does occur, it is most likely to be in the form of a . . . .

. . . .

The time frame for different possible competitive reactions we estimate as follows

. . . .

. . . .

☐ **Competitive Reaction Unlikely but Possible Statement**

Because we are a small firm, we do not anticipate a meaningful or prompt reaction to our market entrance from our larger and more established competitors. However, we have developed contingency plans for certain reactions that competitors may make. If competitors lower their prices, we will (match, better, beat by . 10 . %) their move. We plan to watch for other competitive moves such as
(%)
(special offers, incentives, new advertising initiatives, product upgrades, service changes, etc.) and we plan to react swiftly to any competitive move. Reacting to

competitive moves will in the short run hurt our profit margins, but will in the long run preserve our market share.

> TYPE IN AFTER "THEIR MOVE BY 10%".
>
> SECONDLY, WE RUN THE RISK OF A NON COMPETE LAW SUIT BY WILDECK WHERE THE FOUNDER OF SECURITY CEILINGS WAS PREVIOUSLY EMPLOYEED. THE LIKELIHOOD OF THIS THREAT IS MINIMAL BASED ON THE LEGAL ADVISE GIVEN BY ATTORNEYS KEVIN KEANO AND CHARLES COUSLAND. WE WOULD RESPOND TO THEIR CEASE AND DESIST LETTER WITH A VOID CONTRACT DEFENSE.

...een known ...sitions are ...sure more ...e building ...might be in ...titors.

...us in a way ...nay.......

It is possible that given the rough nature of competition in this business, that a competitor may even attack our .... by
(PRODUCT OR SERVICE OR COMPANY)
name in their advertisements.

☐ Product Substitutes Statement

Alternatives to the .... are a potential threat. A few
(PRODUCT OR SERVICE)
buyers have been shifting some of their budgets to ....

....

While the amount of money being funneled into substitutes now is quite small, the substitution trend could accelerate in the future.

☐ Changing Industry Conditions Statement

Changes in the industry could lead to potential problems. The current trend that is most immediately threatening is ....

....

The potentially negative implications of this trend are ....

....

Trends that are not particularly threatening now, but may become more so in the future, include ....

....

Implications to be concerned are ....

....

☐ Business Cycle Risk Statement

Sales in this industry tend to go up and down with the general business cycle. While there is no guarantee of how far our sales might decline in a general business downturn, we believe that we will have the capability to withstand a (minor, moderate, substantial, large) business downturn. As our profit and loss projections show, even in our weakest sales projection, with sales off ..... % from the _(%) likely scenario, we still project (breaking even, a profit of ..... %, a loss of only _(%) ..... %).
_(%)

COMPETITIVE ANALYSIS COMPETITIVE ANALYSIS

☐ **Legal Risks Statement**

We face possible legal risks from (government agencies, changing legislation, competitors who might claim ....

....,,

customers that might claim ....

....,,

suppliers that might ....

....).

We intend to minimize this risk by ....

....

☐ **Insurance Coverage Statement**

To limit some of the risks facing the firm we (have, intend to) purchase(d) a wide variety of insurance policies including workers compensation insurance (as required by law), key-person life insurance, product liability insurance, equipment insurance, property insurance, loss of receivables information insurance, business disruption insurance, employment liability insurance, non-owned motor vehicle insurance, and...

....

CHAPTER 11

Strategy

STRATEGYSTRATEGYSTRATEGYSTRATEGY

Key Competitive Capabilities

List and describe your firm's major competitive capabilities. Explain why these capabilities are important and how much advantage they are likely to give your firm.

Select and edit <u>all</u> the statements that best apply.

☐ **Basic Competitive Capabilities Statement**

In comparison to our primary competitors, we possess key competitive capabilities that will go a long way to ensuring the success of our business. Particularly important are the following key capabilities . . . .

. . . .

☐ **Advantages in Particular Functional Areas Statement**

We have a strong competitive advantage in our superior ability in (sales, marketing, production, engineering, service, etc.). Important differences between our capabilities and those of our main competitors are . . . .

. . . .

☐ **Advantage of Key Personnel Statement**

We are fortunate to have several highly experienced and talented people in key positions. The expertise and experience that they bring to us really sets us off from the competition. Of particular note is their background in . . . .

. . . .

STRATEGYSTRATEGYSTRATEGYSTRATEGY

This gives us the capability to ....

....

☐ **Product/Service Advantage Statement**

Our key competitive advantage lies in our (product(s), service(s), product concept, service concept). We have a major advantage in our (design, technology, packaging, cost, capability, quality, ease of use, flexibility, etc.).

☐ **Better Positioned for New Trends Statement**

We are better positioned than our main competitors to take advantage of new trends in (the market, market segmentation, buyer's needs, customer preferences, the nature of the competition, changes in the industry). The particular trend that will benefit us is ....

....

This will benefit us because ....

....

☐ **More Customer Responsive Statement**

We have an advantage in our customer-responsive approach to doing business. Other firms give lip service to the importance of their customers, but leave a lot of room to be desired in how far

EXPERT ADVICE

Key Competitive Capabilities

I know what you're probably thinking . . . "The competition has been in business for years, they have a large loyal customer base, they have lots of money, good products or services, and a solid reputation. Competitive analysis is easy—they have all the strengths and I have all the weaknesses!" Having started twelve businesses, I can tell you that any business, even a new business, always has important strengths. A new business, for example, isn't tied into the existing way of business and can more easily adopt a new strategy or new positioning approach for its products or services. A small, privately owned company has natural advantages when competing with large public corporations in that it can be much more flexible and responsive to changes in the market or the needs of particular customers.

STRATEGYSTRATEGYSTRATEGYSTRATEGY

they go to serving their customers. But we (are, are planning on) going the extra mile in serving and responding to our customers.

☐ **Technology Edge Statement**

We have a clear advantage in our technology. This advantage derives from ......

....

This contrasts with our competitors who are ....

....

☐ **Innovation Edge Statement**

Being a (new, young, forward-looking) company, we are in a position to adopt new and innovative ideas. Unlike our highly established competitors, we are also uniquely well-suited to benefit from change in the industry. Some specific new approaches that give us a competitive advantage are ....

....

☐ **A More Professional Approach Statement**

Our advantage lies in the more professional approach that we bring to this industry. Our management approach and the style of our company sharply contrasts with our main competitors. Examples of this are ....

....

STRATEGYSTRATEGYSTRATEGYSTRATEGY

☐ **More Employee Centered Statement**

Because superior employees and superior employee performance means such a difference in this industry, our fresh approach to human resources will mean a significant advantage over our competition. Not just another department, human resources for us is one of the most important pillars of our firm. We intend to go out of our way, every day, to see that our employees needs are served. By doing so, we expect to realize a competitive advantage in almost any work where a human being is involved.

☐ **More Aggressive Approach Statement**

Our aggressive business approach will be a significant competitive advantage. Other firms in the industry tend not to focus very much on their competitors, seldom make directly competitive moves, and do not maximize their potential. On the other hand, our firm is much more competitively minded and determined to push hard for all the market share that we can possibly get.

☐ **Tightly Focused Advantage Statement**

Our specialized focus is a significant advantage. Our main competitors are (in many markets, targeting several market segments, offering many different products, offering many types of services, shifting their focus frequently, etc.). But we are going to target our focus on . . . .

. . . .

STRATEGYSTRATEGYSTRATEGYSTRATEGY

This will allow us to better . . . .

. . . .

☐ **Advantages of Being a New Business Statement**

Being a new entrant into this field has obvious disadvantages, but it also has advantages. We can design our business from scratch and position our business to take advantage of recent changes in the marketplace and our knowledge of the current positioning of the other competitors. It allows us to create a totally fresh approach to business that is more appropriate to today's markets and the needs of today's customers.

☐ **Advantages of Being Locally Owned Statement**

Being a locally owned and operated firm gives us several strong advantages. We can stay much more closely attuned to the needs of our local market and customers. We can respond much more quickly to the demands of these customers. And we can respond rapidly to competitor's moves as well.

☐ **Advantage of Being a Very Small Company Statement**

Being a very small company with few employees gives us several advantages. Our cost structure is lower than the competition. Our firm can be much more responsive to customers and changes in the marketplace. And we have that extra determination to succeed that comes from being a very small firm. In addition . . . .

. . . .

STRATEGYSTRATEGYSTRATEGYSTRATEGY

☐ **Reputation Advantage Statement**

We have a major competitive advantage in our reputation as (a leader in our market segment, a specialist in . . . . , an easy company to do business with, a high-quality provider, a low-cost provider, an innovative firm, a technological leader, offering superior service, etc.).

☐ **Advantages by Affiliation Statement**

Our affiliation with . . . .

. . . .

gives us a significant advantage. This affiliation allows us to . . . .

. . . .

☐ **Lower Cost Structure Statement**

A LOW ~~OVERHEAD~~ AND
↓ SALES COMMISSIONS TO PAY

A major advantage is that we have a lower cost structure. ~~We have no fancy offices,~~

WE HAVE A LOW OVERHEAD, ~~NO SALARY~~ ~~EMPLOYEES~~ PAY NO SALES
COMMISSIONS AND ~~CAN~~ OPERATE AS A "ONE MAN SHOW"
~~DUE DO~~ WHICH DOESN'T REQUIRE EMPLOYEES. THIS ALLOWS
US TO CHARGE LOWER PRICES WITHOUT SACRIFICING
QUALITY AND STILL EARN A GOOD PROFIT.

☐

STRATEGYSTRATEGYSTRATEGYSTRATEGY

seasonal, are less cyclical etc.). The implications of this are . . . .

. . . .

☐ **Well Suited to Take Advantage of Competitor's Weaknesses Statement**

We are well suited to take advantage of our main competitor's weakness in . . . . . .

. . . .

We are able to do this because . . . .

. . . .

☐ **Have Better Access to the Customers Statement**

A significant advantage is that we have better access to our customers than do our

key competitors. Customers are more aware of our . . . . ,
(PRODUCTS OR SERVICES)

more responsive to initiatives that we put forth, and open-minded to new

. . . . that we may offer. This is because . . . .
(PRODUCTS OR SERVICES)

. . . .

STRATEGYSTRATEGYSTRATEGYSTRATEGY

Key Competitive Weaknesses

List and describe the major weaknesses that your firm has versus your competitors. Explain the seriousness and depth of these weaknesses, and differentiate between weaknesses that definitely will be an issue, weaknesses that may likely be an issue, and weaknesses that are unlikely to be an issue. If you are using this plan to raise money, you want to emphasize here or elsewhere in the plan how you will overcome or mitigate major weaknesses.

Select and edit the <u>one or two</u> statements that best apply.

☐ **Basic Competitive Weaknesses Statement**

In comparison to our primary competitors we possess some competitive weaknesses that may limit the success of our business. These are the weaknesses . . .

. . . .

Of most concern is . . . .

. . . .

We intend to offset this weakness by . . . .

. . . .

☐ **Weaknesses in Particular Functional Areas Statement**

We have a competitive weakness in (sales, marketing, production, engineering, service, etc.). Important differences between our capabilities and those of our main competitors are . . . .

. . . .

STRATEGYSTRATEGYSTRATEGYSTRATEGY

We plan to narrow this competitive gap by . . . .

. . . .

☐ **Weakness in Key Positions Statement**

While we have many talented people in key positions, we are less competitive in
the . . . . The expertise and experience that is lacking in
(NAME POSITION)
this position . . . .

. . . .

We intend to overcome this weakness by . . . .

. . . .

☐ **Product/Service Weakness Statement**

We have a competitive weakness in the (design, technology, packaging, cost, capability, quality, etc.) of our (product, service, product concept, service concept).
Implications of this are . . . .

. . . .

We are going to strive to improve this by . . . .

. . . .

☐ **Not as Well Positioned for New Trends Statement**

We are not as well positioned as our main competitors to take advantage of new
trends in (the market, market segmentation, buyer's needs, customer preferences,
the nature of the competition, changes in the industry). The particular trend most

STRATEGYSTRATEGYSTRATEGYSTRATEGY

likely to harm us is . . . .

. . . .

This trend may adversely affect us because . . . .

. . . .

We can improve our ability to take advantage of this trend by .

. . . .

☐ Less Customer Responsive Statement

We have a weakness in our customer-responsiveness. In some instances other firms are doing a better job of going the extra mile in serving and responding to customers. Our shortcoming lies in . . . .

. . . .

We intend to improve this by . . . .

. . . .

☐ Technology Weakness Statement

We have a technological weakness in that . . . .

. . . .

This weakness derives from . . . .

. . . .

Key Competitive Weaknesses

It's hard to write about your firm's weaknesses because you are so to close to them. So for a few minutes think of yourself as an outside analyst or a business reporter. What weaknesses might they identify? Because a careful examination of your business (especially if it is a new business) could turn up almost unlimited weaknesses, you need to decide which are the most immediately or severely threatening weaknesses and focus on them in depth. Simply listing every functional area of your business and explaining how the competition is so much bigger or better will not help you. Instead you need to prioritize your focus.

You should also explain what steps you can take to offset or minimize potential weaknesses.

STRATEGYSTRATEGYSTRATEGYSTRATEGY

This contrasts with our competitors who are . . . .

. . . .

We intend to mitigate the impact of this weakness by . . . .

. . . .

☐ **Competitors Are Adopting New Innovative Ideas Statement**

We have a competitive weakness in that some of our competitors are adopting new, innovative ideas more quickly than us. The new approach to doing business that has made the most difference is . . . .

. . . .

We intend to shortly adopt some new, innovative ideas in our business including

. . . .

☐ **Less Professional Approach Statement**

In the past, our company has suffered from a less professional approach of doing business than some of our competitors. Examples of this include . . . .

. . . .

In order to become a more professionally run firm, we intend to take the following steps . . . .

. . . .

☐ **Less Employee-Centered Statement**

We have been at a competitive disadvantage to some of our competitors, because we have not matched their initiatives in human resources. Specifically they have been using a different business model that places much more emphasis on addressing the needs and concerns of employees. The implications for us have been ·

In the future we intend to give more emphasis to our management of human resources. Among the steps we plan on taking are ·

· ·

☐ Less Aggressive Approach Statement

Some other firms in this industry are competing much more aggressively than we are. Our past approach has not focused on the competition as much. We have not made aggressive competitive moves, we have not responded to competitors moves strongly, and in general we have not gotten too excited about changes in the marketplace or the industry. Implications of this approach are ·

· ·

In the future we intend to compete more aggressively. We intend to carefully track market shares of our key · , to follow our com-
(PRODUCTS OR SERVICES)
petitors more closely, to respond to our competitors initiatives, and to celebrate our gains in the marketplace.

☐ More Tightly Focused Competitors Statement

The narrow focus of some of our competitors gives them a competitive advantage. Because we are (in many markets, targeting several market segments, offering many different products, offering many types of services, shifting their focus frequently, etc.) we can not focus our effort as specifically as do some of our com-

STRATEGYSTRATEGYSTRATEGYSTRATEGY

petitors. The implications of this have been . . . .

. . . .

We intend to offset this disadvantage in the future by appointing product managers to focus on particular (products, services, markets, market niches, market segments, customer types, customers).

☐ **Disadvantages of Being a New Business Statement**

Being a new business competing largely against established firms has huge disadvantages for us. To significantly build sales, we must not just find new customers—we must take customers away from existing firms. Having (no, little) sales we have (no, little) income stream. Other disadvantages are . . . .

. . . .

To be taken seriously as a new firm, we intend to take the following steps (develop a very professional looking corporate logo and letterhead, obtain publicity in key publications serving our market, be visible at important trade shows, develop a polished company brochure, have a major grand opening celebration, etc.).

☐ PROMOTE THE FACT THAT THE FOUNDER HAS 7 YEARS EXPERIENCE IN THE PRODUCTS ‸BEING SOLD AND 15 YEARS IN THE CONSTRUCTION INDUSTRY, AND OFFER LOWER PRICES TO MAKE THE CUSTOMERS DISCUSSION TO BUY FROM US MORE ATTRACTIVE,

STRATEGYSTRATEGYSTRATEGYSTRATEGY

We hope to offset this by . . . .

. . . .

☐ **Disadvantage of Being a Very Small Company Statement**

Being a very small company with few employees creates several potential weaknesses. It means for example that all employees must wear several hats. At times we may not be able to give the attention to some aspects of our business that larger firms do. We also do not have deep expertise in all functions. Other potential weaknesses are . . . .

. . . .

We hope to mitigate these weaknesses by . . . .

. . . .

☐ **Reputation Weakness Statement**

We have a competitive weakness in that our competitors have much more established reputations. In addition to being recognized as established companies, other firms are each recognized for their own special reason. These include recognition as (market leaders, proven specialists in . . . ., an easy

(SPECIALTY)

company to do business with, a high-quality provider, a low-cost provider, an innovative firm, a technological leader, offering superior service, etc.). To further establish our reputation we intend to . . . .

. . . .

STRATEGYSTRATEGYSTRATEGYSTRATEGY

☐ **Lack of Affiliations Statement**

Our competitor's affiliation with . . . . give them a competitive advantage. This affiliation allows them to . . . . We intend to offset this advantage by . . . .

☐ **Higher Cost Structure Statement**

In comparison to some of our competitors, our cost structure is a disadvantage. Because of our higher costs of . . . . , our costs are
(SPECIFY HIGHER COSTS)
higher than our competition. We intend to work around this disadvantage by emphasizing our . . . .

☐ **Financial Strength Statement**

Our financial position is a relative weakness. Our competitors have (no debt, have less debt, have more equity capital, have better access to money, have a higher profit margin, have a secondary revenue stream, have more diversification, have a stronger balance sheet, own their own buildings, own their own equipment, are less seasonal, are less cyclical etc.). The implications of this are . . . .

We intend to limit the weakness of our relative financial position by . . . .

STRATEGYSTRATEGYSTRATEGYSTRATEGY

☐ **Well Suited to Take Advantage of Competitor's Weaknesses Statement**

Some of our competitors are well suited to take advantage of our important weakness in . . . .

. . . .

We intend to counter this by . . . .

. . . .

☐ **Less Access to Customers Statement**

Our competitors have better access to customers than we do. Customers are more aware of their offerings, more responsive to initiatives that they make, and more open-minded to new . . . . that they may offer. This
(PRODUCTS OR SERVICES)
is because they are (more established than us, have had longer relationships with customers, have on-going relationships with these customers, are seen as a less risky alternative, have a better reputation for . . . .

. . . . ,

are viewed as more likely to be successful, are seen as more prestigious, etc.). Implications of this are . . . .

. . . .

We intend to mitigate this weakness by . . . .

. . . .

STRATEGYSTRATEGYSTRATEGYSTRATEGY

Strategy

Your strategy is the unique formula for success that forms the foundation of your business plan, as well as governing day-to-day operations. This strategy is not a definition or summary of pertinent markets, but instead, it is an account of the one or two key factors that distinguish your firm from your competitors, and is most expected to contribute to your firm's long-term success. If you are creating a highly detailed plan for an existing business, you may want to also list secondary strategies—but this is certainly not expected in a plan to raise money and your two strategies need to compliment one another so that you are not sending your business in two different directions.

Select and edit the <u>one or at most two</u> statements that best apply.

☐ **Basic Strategy Statement**

Our strategy will be to . . . .

. . . .

Key elements of this strategy are . . . .

. . . .

This strategy will be particularly effective in meeting the following customer needs . . . .

. . . .

STRATEGYSTRATEGYSTRATEGYSTRATEGY

This strategy will clearly distinguish us from the competition, help us get attention from customers, and quickly build our sales. This strategy takes advantage of our competitive strengths because . . . .

. . . .

☐ **Outstanding in One Function Statement**

Our strategy is to build a (sales, marketing, production, engineering, service, etc.) driven organization. While our company will become recognized as highly competent in all areas of its business, we intend to be recognized as the clear leader in the (sales, marketing, production, engineering, service, etc.) function. We intend to go all-out in . . . . to insure our success. We will continue
(FUNCTION)
to hire top people in this area, be sure that senior management is actively involved and supportive of it, and when necessary cut expenses in other areas first. We believe that truly outstanding excellence in this area will clearly distinguish us from other firms in the industry and will provide the best opportunity for building and maintaining a leadership position. This strategy takes advantage of our competitive strengths because . . . .

. . . .

☐ **Product/Service Based Strategy Statement**

Our strategy is based around the highly (distinctive, unique, superior, differentiated, customized, personalized) . . . . that we offer.
(PRODUCT OR SERVICE)

STRATEGYSTRATEGYSTRATEGYSTRATEGY

Our strategic advantage lies in our (design, technology, packaging, cost, capability, quality, etc.). We intend to maximize the benefit of this strategy by . . . .
. . . .
. . . .

☐ **The Best, Personalized Service Statement**

Our strategy will be to offer the best, most highly personalized service in the marketplace we serve. Especially being a very small, owner-operated company, we intend to use this to our advantage to be absolutely certain that every one of our customers receives excellent service. We will go out of our way to make sure that our customers know that they truly matter to us. We intend to be very flexible in the way we provide service and to do whatever we can to accommodate our customer's needs. Employees who deal with customers will be carefully trained and will be given wide latitude for insuring that customers are always satisfied.

☐ **Niche Market Focus Statement**

Our strategy is to focus 100% of our efforts on the . . . .
(MARKET NICHE)
By focusing all of our effort and energy on this particular niche, we expect to quickly develop and maintain a leadership position. While other firms try to be all things to all people, we believe that our singular focus will give us significant advantages. Most of the firms serving this niche now also serve much larger markets and give only secondary attention to the . . . . On the
(MARKET NICHE)
other hand, our firm will give our total focus to this niche; our key executives will

STRATEGYSTRATEGYSTRATEGYSTRATEGY

stay in personal touch with customers in this niche; and we will be able to respond to changes in this market much faster than our competitors.

☐ New Market Focus Statement

Our strategy is to focus on the . . . . for
(NEW MARKET)

this . . . . While the other markets
(PRODUCT OR SERVICE)

for this product are already fairly well developed and the competitors fairly well established, we believe that we will have a significant advantage by being the first company to aggressively develop this (new market). This strategy plays well to our competitive strengths and weaknesses because, being a new firm, we would be at a disadvantage competing in already established markets for this . . . . But because
(PRODUCT OR SERVICE)

the established firms are focusing a lot of attention on the currently larger markets for this product, we may at least initially have an advantage by focusing intently on the new market.

☐ Specialized Product/Service Strategy Statement

Our strategy is to have a specialized focus (one, two, very few, a highly limited number, one related line of, etc.) . . . .
(PRODUCTS

. . . . By concentrating all of our energy and
OR SERVICES)

resources we believe we will be able to be highly competitive.

EXPERT ADVICE

Strategy

If you only had time to create one part of your business plan, this is the part I would do. Strategy is the heart and soul of your business plan—and of your business itself. However, developing a really great strategy is much more difficult than it first appears. There are all kinds of traps you can fall into—believe me, I've fallen into them all! The most common mistake is basing your strategy on having the "best products" or offering the "best service." In a highly competitive marketplace, it is usually difficult for buyers to determine what is the "best" product or service. Furthermore, buyers care more about which product or service best fits their needs.

Generally you'll be much better off with a strategy that focuses on uniqueness or a distinctive product or service positioning.

STRATEGYSTRATEGYSTRATEGYSTRATEGY

Particular benefits from this specialized focus are . . . .

. . . .

☐ Product Proliferation Strategy Statement

Our strategy is to build a broad line of . . . . to meet
(PRODUCTS OR SERVICES)
the full range of our customers' needs. The market trend is toward one-stop shopping. Currently customers are increasingly giving a larger share of their business
to vendors who provide multiple . . . . And vendors
(PRODUCTS OR SERVICES)
who have the broadest product lines have the most advantage in working with customers. This strategy is also one of the fastest and strongest ways that we can differentiate our company from the competition.

☐ Premium Producer/Service Provider Statement

Our strategy is to be the premier . . . . in
(PRODUCT PRODUCER, SERVICE PROVIDER)
every way possible. We intend to deliver premium quality . . . .
(PRODUCTS OR SER-
VICES) . . . . and to run our business in a first class manner throughout.
Absolutely everything about our business will be top notch, and our marketing
strategy will be to communicate our premium quality to all possible customers.

☐ Low Price/Low Cost Strategy Statement

Our strategy is to compete on price and be the value leader in our field. Given the
high level of competition in our industry and the increased difficulty of potential
consumers to clearly differentiate among the offerings of different firms, we are
convinced that more and more purchase decisions will be based primarily on

STRATEGYSTRATEGYSTRATEGYSTRATEGY

price. We intend to be the low price leader. And we intend to be able to do so while
still realizing above average profit margins, without sacrificing quality. To do this,
we intend to have a low cost focus throughout our operation. In addition to keeping costs down, we intend to ~~streamline our focus to have a relatively narrow line~~
SELL OUR PRODUCTS DIRECT, NOT WITH MANUFACTURES REPS.
THIS WILL ENSURE AN AGRESSIVE AND SUCCESSFUL SALES EFFORT.
~~of~~ . . . . ~~. Also we intend to leave out many of the fea-~~
(PRODUCTS OR SERVICES)
~~tures and options that raise the cost of doing business but add only marginal value~~
~~to consumers.~~ This is a natural strategy for us because we do not have an established brand identity, and it would be difficult for us to develop a reputation that
allowed us to command a superior price.

☐ Name Brand Strategy Statement

Our strategy is to build a brand identity. The brand will stand for . . . .

. . . .

Our . . . . plan and our marketing plan will all support
(PRODUCT OR SERVICE)
this name brand strategy. By developing a name brand we will be able to charge
premium prices for our . . . . and at the same time
(PRODUCT OR SERVICE)
develop a stronger identity with customers than by simply developing a premium
product, but without branding it.

☐ Generic Alternative Strategy Statement

We will not spend any effort at all developing a brand identity. Instead we will focus
on lowering our costs and delivering our . . . . at the
(PRODUCT OR SERVICE)
lowest possible price. This strategy will be particularly important given our mar-

ket analysis, which shows a large portion of customers make their buying decisions based overwhelmingly on price.

☐ Market Share Leader Statement

Our strategy is to be the market share leader. We shall monitor our competitors closely. We shall match, if not beat, all major moves by competitors. We shall move quickly to restore any losses in market share such as by increasing advertising, upgrading our ....(PRODUCTS OR SERVICES)........................., using promotional incentives, or lowering price. This strategy may involve short-term sacrifice of profits at times, but we believe the long-term potential of this market more than makes up for this potential risk. We are particularly well suited for this strategy because ...

. . . .

☐ Industry Innovator Statement

Our strategy is to adopt innovative and leading-edge techniques to all aspects of running our business. Being a younger, smaller company than our competitors, we will have a natural advantage of being able to become recognized as the industry innovator. We have much less invested than our competitors in the past way of doing business, so we have little to lose and much to gain by doing business differently. We want to particularly be recognized as using innovative ideas to directly benefit our customers, such as new policies on pricing and service. But we also want to try innovative techniques for running our business better internally. Because so many of the firms in our industry are seen by customers as doing busi-

STRATEGYSTRATEGYSTRATEGYSTRATEGY

ness "the same old way" and taking their customers for granted, we expect to quickly develop a highly favorable reputation as an industry innovator.

☐ **Leading Response to One Particular Trend Statement**

Our strategy will be built around the new trend (in our market, in our market segment, in our area, in our industry, among our customers) to . . . .

. . . .

We will respond to this trend by . . . .

. . . .

By being one of the first companies to take these steps, we will be seen as a progressive leader, on the cutting edge of change, looking for new ways to serve customers, and do business better. Implications of this will be . . . .

. . . .

☐ **Most Professional Statement**

We intend to be a stand-out in our market as the most professionally operated firm. Especially in a field filled with small mom-and-pop operators who run their businesses in a casual way, we intend to bring a new level of professionalism to this field. We are going to plan our business very carefully; have rigorous hiring and training programs; have specific policies and standards for serving customers; and carefully monitor the quality of our service. We are also going to carefully communicate and market to our customers the key differences and advantages in doing business with us, as opposed to with the competition. We will be sure that

STRATEGYSTRATEGYSTRATEGYSTRATEGY

our target customers know that choosing us as a supplier is the safe choice for consistent, high quality service.

☐ **Numbers Driven Strategy Statement**

Our strategy is manage our business more aggressively and systematically than our competitors by rigorously focusing on the numbers. We will operate with highly specific sales, cost, and profit targets for our company as a whole, and for each department. As much as possible, we will have very specific goals for individuals, too. We will share important cost and sales information with employees. And more importantly we will share profits. Sales people will work according to closely monitored goals, production will be managed according to a tightly managed budget, and everyone will help us minimize overhead. As much as possible we will urge employees at all levels to play an active role in boosting sales, lowering costs, and ultimately increasing profits. By carefully managing the business with an extra focus on the numbers, we intend to become the most profitable business of our size in this market.

☐ **Balance Between Stakeholders Statement**

The key difference between us and our competitors is that we are going to give equal focus to specifically aiming to give just as much attention to serving our customers and our employees, as we do to reaching profit goals. By striving to serve all three equally, we believe that we will also ultimately best serve the interests of each group individually. We intend to go way out of our way to take care of

STRATEGYSTRATEGYSTRATEGYSTRATEGY

our customers. This may mean that we don't always make a profit on that customer today—but ultimately we will more than make up for it by repeat business from the customer and goodwill throughout the industry. We also intend to go out of our way to take care of our employees. Not just in terms of offering good compensation and benefits, but also in seeing that they have a strong say in how the company is run. Customers and employees are more than crucial to our business. They are our business—and we fully intend to recognize each group as such!

☐ **New Standard of Customer Service Statement**

We are going to set a new standard of customer service. We are going to go well beyond the definitions of old customer service and take customer service to a new level. In addition to just plain treating customers well and being responsive to their needs, we are going to provide additional services to customers. Initially these new services are going to include . . . .

. . . .

☐ **Superior People in Key Positions Statement**

Our strategy is to insure that we have absolutely outstanding performers in the few key positions whose performance will go a long way to determining the overall performance of the firm. Because so much of one's success in this industry is determined by the abilities of a few people in key positions, this strategy is highly appropriate for this situation. The positions we will focus on are . . . .

. . . .

STRATEGYSTRATEGYSTRATEGYSTRATEGY

☐ Preferred Provider to Corporations Statement

We will be seen as a premium service provider for larger corporations in our area. While there are many firms in this area providing . . . . , most (SERVICE) are poorly suited or positioned for providing these services to corporations. But because of our experience, our professionalism and particularly because of our exclusive dedication to this market, we will quickly become recognized as the preferred provider for corporations. Every aspect of our operation, from our logo to how our phones are answered, will be designed to appeal to the corporations that comprise our target market.

☐ Technological Leader Statement

Our strategy is to be on the cutting edge of technology in our industry. When a company wants leading edge solutions, we intend to be the first name to come to mind. The impressive past technological achievements of some of our key personnel make this a realistic goal. In addition, we will focus on creating an environment suitable for fostering technical advances. Our key development people will be sheltered from the day to day concerns of production issues. And our whole corporate culture will celebrate our technical prowess.

☐ Leadership Position Statement

Our strategy is to be the undisputed industry leader in (quality, service, personalized service, customization, workmanship, marketing, technology, support, instal-

STRATEGY STRATEGY STRATEGY STRATEGY

lation, new products, design, fashion, distribution, etc.) To achieve this we will .

....

This will clearly set us off from the competition because ....

....

We are well suited to pursue this strategy because ....

....

☐ Affiliation/Alliance/Partnership Strategy Statement

We will pursue (affiliations, alliances, partnerships, strategic relationships, etc.) with companies that ....

....

This will give us the advantage of ....

....

☐ Product Feature Emphasis Strategy Statement

We will focus on providing .... that feature
                              (PRODUCTS OR SERVICES)
.... Although this focus will limit us to only part of
(DESCRIBE THE PARTICULAR FEATURE)
the market, this focus will quickly differentiate us from our competitors. Focusing

all of our resources on .... with this feature, we will
                         (PRODUCTS OR SERVICES)
be able to outperform our competition in this area. This strategy matches our

competitive capabilities because ....

....

STRATEGYSTRATEGYSTRATEGYSTRATEGY

☐ Strategy by Company/Customer Type Statement

Our strategy is to target as customers, companies that (are in a particular industry, are a particular size, are at a particular state of progress in this area, have a particular need, are in a particular geographical area, etc.). While we have the capability to service a broader range of firms, we are much more likely to succeed by focusing on a narrower range of prospects and by serving them extremely well. By limiting ourselves to companies that meet our criteria, we will quickly expertise in working for these type of corporations, we will develop a word of mouth reputation more quickly, and most of all we will gain an advantage in developing a reputation as a specialist.

☐ Web-Based Focus Statement

Our strategy is to base our business on the World Wide Web. While some competitors are beginning to include the Web in their business operations, none have made a whole-hearted effort to make it the center of their business. We intend to do just that. Not only will this differentiate us from our competition, but it will do so in a very positive way. We will immediately be positioned as a high-tech, leading-edge provider. The experience of several of our key employees in development work on the Web makes this a solid strategic choice for us.

☐ Custom Solutions Focus Statement

Our strategy is to become known as the premier source for customized solutions to difficult problems. By becoming known as the firm that can solve the most difficult and unique problems, firms will be more confident in hiring us for even moderately difficult situations and willing to pay a premium for the extra security in hiring the best. The expertise of our employees makes us particularly well-suited to pursue this strategy.

☐ Marketing-Driven Strategy Statement

Our strategy is to focus on our marketing. The . . . .
(PRODUCTS, SERVICES)
offered by competing companies are similar enough so that customers do not readily distinguish between them based on performance or features. Instead, competition is becoming increasingly focused on marketing and in particular (the sales process, advertising, product positioning, promotions). This is generally how customers and buying decisions are influenced. We will focus our marketing efforts on . . . .

. . . .

We are well suited for this strategy because . . . .

. . . .

More detail is provided in the Marketing Section of this business plan.

☐ Aggressive Sales Strategy Statement

We are going to be a sales-driven organization. We will insure that our sales effort is second to none. We are going to go all out to hire and retain top salespeople. We will give extra effort to insure that salespeople are motivated and enthusiastic and will aggressively sell new accounts. We will basically design and run the rest of the business around the sales organization, because the strength of our sales team is what is going to lead this company to success. We are well suited for

STRATEGYSTRATEGYSTRATEGYSTRATEGY

this strategy because . . . .
. . . .

☐ **Customer Service Focus Statement**

Customer service is what we're all about. We're going to make sure that our customer service is so good that it really stands out from the competition and gives
us a competitive advantage. Clearly customers care about customer service. And
none of our competitors are offering consistently superior customer service. To
insure that we are more responsive to our customers we will (assign a service
manager for each account, offer toll free support, create a customized service plan
for each customer, offer one-hour response time, offer on-site service, give a wide
variety of service options, offer 24-hour support, guarantee absolute satisfaction)

☐ **Limited Customer Strategy Statement**

Our strategy is to limit our customers to those relatively few who meet all of the
following criteria . . . .
. . . .

By limiting our customer base, we will be able to design, build, and optimize our
entire organization to serving the highly specific needs of these customers better
than any competitor. And more importantly we will not get distracted away from
the customers that matter. We will be able to give these customers the attention
they want, and we will be able to be highly responsive to their needs.

STRATEGYSTRATEGYSTRATEGYSTRATEGY

Implementing Strategy

It's one thing to have a great strategy. It's another to really integrate your strategy into your way of doing business. Beyond the basic ground covered in other parts of this plan, this section gives you a chance to explain specific steps you are going to take to be sure your strategy is really adhered to. If it seems too obvious or is thoroughly covered in other parts of this business plan, you may want to skip this section.

Select and edit the <u>one or two</u> statements that best apply.

☐ **Basic Steps to Implementing Strategy Statement**

We will focus very narrowly on (one, two, very few, a highly limited number, one related line of, etc.) . . . . By concentrating all of our
(PRODUCTS OR SERVICES)
energy and resources we believe we will be able to be highly competitive. Particular benefits from a narrow focus are . . . .

. . . .

☐ **Implementation Focuses on Statement**

Successful implementation of our strategy needs to focus overwhelmingly on (our products, our services, our engineering, our development, our new products, our marketing, our production, our advertising, our sales program, etc.). While we shall be diligent in all aspects of implementing our strategy, we will give extra emphasis to this dimension. Particularly important to successful implementation

STRATEGYSTRATEGYSTRATEGYSTRATEGY

is insuring that . . . .

. . . .

☐ **Strategy Implementation Timetable Statement**

Because this new strategy represents significant changes in our current way of doing business we shall implement it gradually over a period of time, in the following stages:

Stage 1: . . . .
(DESCRIBE STAGE 1)   (TARGET DATE)

Stage 2: . . . .
(DESCRIBE STAGE 2)   (TARGET DATE)

Stage 3: . . . .
(DESCRIBE STAGE 3)   (TARGET DATE)

☐ **Getting the Company Behind the Strategy Statement**

In order to insure our success, we are going to put the full effort of the company behind this strategy. We are going to be sure that senior employees have a chance to discuss the strategy and offer their feedback if they have not already done so. And we are going to be sure that employees at all levels are aware of the basics of our strategy and keep it in mind as they perform their work. We will launch our new strategy with an all company meeting. When we do our monthly profit and loss and budget reviews, we are also going to spend some time measuring how well our strategy is being implemented. Perhaps most of all we intend to survey our customers to get their input on how well our strategy is serving their needs.

STRATEGYSTRATEGYSTRATEGYSTRATEGY

☐ **Tying Compensation into Strategy Statement**

All too often a great strategy fails to get implemented because people don't really get behind it. Too often employees give first emphasis to increasing sales or profits in the short-term because they feel (either rightly or wrongly) that this is overwhelmingly how their performance is being judged. We are going to change this. We are going to make a significant part of compensation dependent upon how the individual helps the company implement and focus on its strategy. We will take into consideration the employee's contribution to executing the company's strategy in determining (management salary reviews, all salary reviews, performance bonuses, profit-sharing distribution, employee awards).

☐ **Implementation in a Changing Market Statement**

Because we are competing in a marketplace and industry where fast and dramatic change is the norm and not the exception, we will evaluate the success and effectiveness of all aspects of our strategy on an on-going basis. It is likely that minor aspects of our strategy or product positioning will change frequently, and it is likely that we will make significant changes in strategic direction from time to time. To promise that our strategy will be static or that it will ideally suit fast changing market conditions

EXPERT ADVICE

Implementing Strategy

For many years the big complaint about the major strategic consulting firms was that they would come up with a great strategy and impress the CEO and the board of directors. But the consulting firm would go on to their next assignment, the CEO would move back to focusing on quarterly earnings, and the strategy would be forgotten about. Even at a small firm it is often easier to create a great strategy than to implement it because it's hard to get people to change their way of doing things. Even at a new firm, it can be hard to get people to follow strategy, because the key people have lots of experience at other firms that probably pursed different strategies. So to get people committed to strategy—you've got to continually remind people about it.

STRATEGYSTRATEGYSTRATEGYSTRATEGY

would not be appropriate. Similarly we are going to take a pragmatic approach to implementing our strategy for particular products, services, marketing programs, etc. At the same time it is the rapidly changing dynamics of our marketplace that make strategy extremely important, and we fully intend to give the strategic process and its implementation the importance that it deserves.

☐ **For New Firms Only Statement**

Being a new firm, we have a big advantage in implementing strategy in that we can start with a clean slate. We can be sure that every new hire is keenly aware of our strategy, from their first job interview, and knows how it should affect their work.

☐ **For Firms Changing Strategy Statement**

One of our biggest challenges of implementing this new strategy is going to be getting people to change the old way of doing things. Old habits die hard—and we need to have patience and put extra effort into explaining to the people involved why we are changing strategy, why the change in strategy is beneficial, why their role in implementing the new strategy is important, and how they can help us implement it. Implementing this strategy can not just be a one-shot effort, but something that we continually need to remind people about on an on-going basis.

CHAPTER 12

Products/
Services

PRODUCTS/SERVICESPRODUCTS/SERVICES

Product/Service Description

First give a brief overall description of your products/services. Then go into more depth on particular attributes and features that are important to buyers or differentiate your offerings from those of your competitors. If you haven't yet launched your product or service, describe the products or services you plan on launching.

Select and edit the <u>one or more</u> statements that best apply.

☐ **Basic Product/Service Description Statement**

Our current . . . . can be described as . . . .
        (PRODUCT OR SERVICE)

. . . .

The basic purpose it serves for buyers is to . . . .

. . . .

We first introduced this . . . . in . . . .
                    (PRODUCT OR SERVICE)

. . . .

Since then we have made the following changes . . . .

. . . .

☐ **Description for Multiple Products/Services Statement**

Our current . . . . can be summarized as . . . .
                (PRODUCT OR SERVICE)

. . . .

Their overall purpose for buyers can be summarized as . . . .

. . . .

Our most successful offering is . . . .

PRODUCTS/SERVICESPRODUCTS/SERVICES

It can be described as ....

Our second most successful offering is ....

It can be described as ....

☐ **Description for Multiple Product/Service Lines Statement**

Our current product offerings consist of basically (two, three, four, etc.) different lines. The most successful line is ....

The principle .... in this line are .
(PRODUCT OR SERVICE)

The next most successful line is ....

The principle .... in this line are .
(PRODUCT OR SERVICE)

The third most successful line is ....

The principle .... in this line are .
(PRODUCT OR SERVICE)

EXPERT ADVICE

Product/Service Description

Your actual product or service should support your product positioning strategy, your business strategy, and the needs of your target customers. If it doesn't, then it may be time to redesign it so that it does. Or you could change your strategy, positioning, or target market. With the product or service description, you should start with a very brief, easily understood statement of what your product or service is, and/or what it does. You want readers to be able to understand in an instant the essence of your product or service. Then describe in more detail important characteristics that are unique or are substantially different than the competition's.

PRODUCTS/SERVICESPRODUCTS/SERVICES

☐ **List of Products/Services Statement**

These are the principle products we offer ranked in descending order by sales volume:

1. . . . . $ . . . .
    (PRODUCT OR SERVICE)   (OPTIONAL QUICK DESCRIPTION)   (SALES)

2. . . . . $ . . . .
    (PRODUCT OR SERVICE)   (OPTIONAL QUICK DESCRIPTION)   (SALES)

3. . . . . $ . . . .
    (PRODUCT OR SERVICE)   (OPTIONAL QUICK DESCRIPTION)   (SALES)

4. . . . . $ . . . .
    (PRODUCT OR SERVICE)   (OPTIONAL QUICK DESCRIPTION)   (SALES)

5. . . . . $ . . . .
    (PRODUCT OR SERVICE)   (OPTIONAL QUICK DESCRIPTION)   (SALES)

☐ **Description of Development Progress Statement**

Currently we have (one, two, three, etc.) products/services in development. At the time of the writing of this plan the . . . . is (almost
(FIRST PRODUCT/SERVICE)
ready to ship, almost ready to launch, nearing completion, ... % complete, ...
(%)   (%)
% finalized, at prototype, in the research stage, carefully planned out, at the alpha/beta test stage, in testing, ready to go to test market, etc.). Development is progressing well and we hope to (finalize, ship, launch, take to market) this . . . . in . . . . The major steps left to be
(PRODUCT OR SERVICE)   (ESTIMATE TIME)
accomplished are . . . .

. . . .

The other products are at the following stages of development . . . .

. . . .

PRODUCTS/SERVICESPRODUCTS/SERVICES

☐ **Basic Product or Service with Many Options Statement**

Essentially we provide just (one, two, three, etc.) . . . . but
(PRODUCTS OR SERVICES)

we offer many different (variants, features, options, etc.). The basic product

. . . .
(DESCRIBE BASIC PRODUCT)

The most common (variants, features, options, etc.) are. . . . .

. . . .

☐ **Product/Service Philosophy Statement**

Our underlying philosophy in (developing, making, creating, designing, buying,

selling, renting, providing, delivering) OUR METAL SECURITY ACOUSTICAL CEILING SYSTEMS has been
(PRODUCTS OR SERVICES)

to DO IT DESIGN THEM TO BE THE MOST ECONOMICAL TO FABRICATE.

. . . .

Important objectives are to MAINTAIN THE QUALITY AND PROFILE

AS DESCRIBED IN THE ARCHITECT'S SPECIFICATIONS.

We insure that we achieve these objectives by REVIEWING AND UNDERSTANDING ANALYZING

THE SPECIFICATIONS AND FINDING THE LIMITS TO WHICH OUR PRODUCTS

MUST PERFORM TO.

☐ **Products and Related Services Statement**

We offer a range of . . . . as well as provide related ser-
(DESCRIBE PRODUCTS)

vices. We try to serve as many needs as possible for our customers in terms of

. . . . Our prin-
(DESCRIBE THE TYPES OF CUSTOMER NEEDS YOU SATISFY)

ciple products are. . . . .

. . . .

PRODUCTS/SERVICESPRODUCTS/SERVICES

The services we provide are . . . .

. . . .

☐ **Typical Local Service Business Description Statement**

We are a local service business providing . . . . We offer the
(TYPE OF SERVICE)

following specific service options . . . .

. . . .

Our customers are primarily from the areas of . . . .

. . . .

But we also get some customers from . . . .

. . . .

We have been in business for . . . .

. . . .

years. Over the last few years (our customer base has changed, our business has
grown considerably, our mix of services has shifted to . . . .

. . . . ,

we have changed . . . .

. . . ., etc.).

☐ **A Broad Range of Services Statement**

We offer a broad range of services to our customers. We serve (companies ranging
in size from . . . . to . . . . companies primarily in the following
(SIZE)   (SIZE)

industries . . . .

PRODUCTS/SERVICESPRODUCTS/SERVICES

. . . . ,

people who are . . . .

. . . . ,

customers that seek . . . .

. . . . ,

etc.). The common element of all of our services is that . . . .

. . . .

Following is a summary and description of our primary services . . . .

. . . .

☐ **Service Described in Terms of Goals Statement**

The goal of our service is to help . . . . to better . . . .
(PEOPLE, COMPANIES)

. . . .

They engage our services because . . . .

. . . .

We provide help by doing the following . . . .

. . . .

Typical situations that we have (expect to) work in are . . . .

. . . .

☐ **Highly Customized Solutions Statement**

We provide highly customized solutions for companies that need . . . .

. . . .

PRODUCTS/SERVICESPRODUCTS/SERVICES

Companies engage us because of our expertise in . . . .

. . . .

Recent projects have included . . . .

. . . .

The average assignment requires about . . . .

days to complete. Some customers we work with on a one-shot project basis, and

other customers we work with on an ongoing basis.

☐ General Provider with a Specialty Statement

We are a general provider of . . . . for the
(PRODUCTS OR SERVICES)

. . . . We cover a broad range of needs from . . .
(DESCRIBE MARKETPLACE)

. . . .

to . . . .

. . . .

We have also developed a specialty in . . . .

. . . .

☐ Major Features Statement

Important features of our . . . . are . . . .
(PRODUCT OR SERVICE)

. . . .

These features serve the needs of buyers by . . . .

. . . .

An important unique feature of our . . . . is . . . .
(PRODUCT OR SERVICE)

PRODUCTS/SERVICESPRODUCTS/SERVICES

This is important to buyers because . . . .

. . . .

Other unique features of our . . . . are . . . .
(PRODUCT OR SERVICE)

. . . .

☐ **What Buyers Find Appealing Statement**

What buyers have found particularly appealing about our . . . .
(PRODUCT OR SERVICE)

is . . . .

. . . .

This allows buyers to . . . .

. . . .

The advantage of this is that . . . .

. . . .

☐ **Unique Aspects of Product/Service Statement**

What is particularly unique about our . . . . is its .
(PRODUCT OR SERVICE)

. . . .

This is important to customers because . . . .

. . . .

☐ **Product Selection Criteria Statement**

Product selection plays an important role in defining our business. We select
products with great care using the following criteria . . . .

PRODUCTS/SERVICESPRODUCTS/SERVICES

We are particularly careful to select products that will . . . .

On the other hand we avoid products that . . . .

Overall we strive for a mix of products that . . . .

. . . .

☐ Pricing Statement

Our . . . . has a (standard, suggested retail, estimat-
(PRODUCT OR SERVICE)
ed street) price of $ . . . . Typically we (offer discounts, rebates, incentives, vol-
($)
ume savings, offer specials, hold sales, etc.) to make the average selling price . . .

. . . .

Our pricing can be considered to be (high, above average, slightly above average,
average, slightly below average, below average, low) in comparison to our main
competitors.

☐ Revenue Break-Out Statement

Our revenue break out by (product, product line, service or service line) is . . . . . .

. . . .

Product/Service: Unit Sales: Revenue: Percent of Total:

1. . . . .

. . . .

PRODUCTS/SERVICESPRODUCTS/SERVICES

2. ....

....

3. ....

....

4. ....

....

5. ....

....

6. ....

....

☐ **Summary Listings of Products/Services Statement**

We offer the following ....(PRODUCTS OR SERVICES)...........................

....

Name: ....

....

Brief description: ....

....

Key features: ....

....

Sales: ....

....

PRODUCTS/SERVICESPRODUCTS/SERVICES

Price: ....

....

☐ **Rewards/Honors/Achievements Statement**

We have received the following (awards, achievements, honors) for our

.... This honor was awarded for
(PRODUCTS OR SERVICES)

....
(CRITERIA FOR PRIZE)

☐ **Favorable Media Reviews/Attention Statement**

Our .... have received (glowing, positive, encour-
(PRODUCTS OR SERVICES)

aging, wonderful, excellent) reviews in the following media ....

....

Of particular note is an article that appeared in .... that described
(PUBLICATION)

our .... as ....
(NAME PRODUCT OR SERVICE)

....

PRODUCTS/SERVICES PRODUCTS/SERVICES

Positioning of Products/Services

In many business plans, the positioning of products or services will be adequately covered in the strategy section and you won't need to address positioning as a separate issue. But if positioning was not already covered, or if you want to discuss it in more depth, here is the place to do it.

Select and edit the <u>one or two</u> statements that best apply.

☐ **Basic Positioning Statement**

Our ·········· (PRODUCTS OR SERVICES) ·········· will be positioned in the marketplace as ···

They will be targeted at buyers who have a need for a ·········· (PRODUCT OR SERVICE) ·········· that ··································

···

These are the particular (attributes, features, components, aspects) of our offerings that will be important for positioning our ·········· (PRODUCTS OR SERVICES) ··········

···

☐ **Outstanding Quality Positioning Statement**

We will position our ·········· (PRODUCTS OR SERVICES) ·········· as the quality leaders. We see quality in this market as largely being defined as ··························

···

Our ·········· (PRODUCTS OR SERVICES) ·········· will be seen as offering higher quality than

PRODUCTS/SERVICESPRODUCTS/SERVICES

EXPERT ADVICE

Positioning of Products/Services

It should be emphasized that the process of positioning should first focus on how your products or services are perceived by potential customers. Actual product or service differences or advantages should receive secondary focus in your discussion of positioning. In fact, in some cases there are no real differences between competing products, except in the minds of the users. An example would be when a company sells a food product through supermarkets both as a store or generic brand, and also at a higher price as the food company's own, nationally advertised brand. Another example would be when two cola drink companies sell essentially the same product.

competing lines because of . . . .

. . . .

☐ **Low Price Positioning Statement**

We will position our *METAL SECURITY ACCOUSTICAL CEILING SYSTEMS* . . . . . as
(PRODUCTS OR SERVICES)
the low price alternative. We will let buyers know that they
can buy our . *CEILING SYSTEMS* . . . . with confi-
(PRODUCT OR SERVICE)
dence and that it ~~matches the most important features of~~
MEETS SPECIFICATION
~~competing~~ . . . . , but our cen-
(PRODUCTS OR SERVICES)
tral positioning will be price point.

☐ **Best Engineered Positioning Statement**

We will position our . . . . as
(PRODUCTS OR SERVICES)
offering the best engineering. We will particularly emphasize our (reliability, high performance, performance in highly demanding situations, durability, etc.). This positioning is
well suited to our capabilities because . . . .

. . . .

☐ **The Most Technically Advanced Products or Services Statement**

We will position our . . . . as
(PRODUCTS OR SERVICES)
the most technically advanced offerings available today. We
will particularly emphasize the (performance, certain fea-

PRODUCTS/SERVICESPRODUCTS/SERVICES

tures, certain capabilities, state-of-the-art capabilities, etc.) **of**

our . . . .
(PRODUCTS OR SERVICES)

☐ **Providing Specialized Products/Services Statement**

We will position our products as highly specialized solutions for (the market seg-

ment . . . .

. . . .,

buyers who demand . . . .

. . . .,

consumers who desire . . . .

. . . .).

We will target this part of the market exclusively and develop a reputation as a

leading provider in this market niche.

☐ **Highly Customized Solutions Statement**

We will position ourselves as providing highly customized solutions to customers

with particularly demanding or specific requirements. We will be highly flexible

and responsive in adapting our . . . . to the needs of
(PRODUCTS OR SERVICES)

these buyers. The types of buyers we are most likely to benefit from our approach

will be . . . .

. . . .

PRODUCTS/SERVICES PRODUCTS/SERVICES

☐ Products with a High Level of Service Statement

We will position ourselves as providing a unusually high level of service in combination with our product offerings. While the quality of our products will compare favorably with our competition, it is our extraordinarily high commitment to service that will really distinguish us from the competition.

☐ The Best Personalized Service Statement

We will position our service as the best and personalized available. Taking advantage of the small size of our company, our devotion to excellence, and our close attention to customer's needs, we are going to build a reputation for the highest quality, personalized service unparalleled in our marketplace.

☐ Serving a Niche Market Statement

Our .... (PRODUCTS OR SERVICES) will be 100% focused on the .... (MARKET NICHE) .... Each of our .... (PRODUCTS OR SERVICES) .... will be (optimized for this market, designed specifically for the needs of this market, tailored for this market, marketed as the best solution for this market, positioned as ideal for buyers who want ....

....)

☐ Brand Name Positioning Statement

Our .... (PRODUCTS OR SERVICES) will be positioned as a brand name, high quality solutions for the needs of buyers in this marketplace. Our brand will quickly assure buyers that they are getting a .... (PRODUCT OR SERVICE) that will

PRODUCTS/SERVICESPRODUCTS/SERVICES

This brand name will be carefully cultivated through a comprehensive marketing program.

☐ **Market Leader Positioning Statement**

Because of our high market share, we are in the unique position to present our
. . . . as the market leaders. While there are certain
(PRODUCTS OR SERVICES)
particular attributes and features that we will emphasize in marketing from time
to time, we are first and foremost going to position our . . . .
(PRODUCTS OR SERVICES)
as the market leaders that they are. Many buyers have shown their preference to
go with the . . . . that they believe is the market
(PRODUCTS OR SERVICES)
leader even when it commands a slightly higher price—so we believe that this is
a particularly powerful positioning strategy.

☐ **Most Innovative Positioning Statement**

Our . . . . will be positioned as the most innovative
(PRODUCTS OR SERVICES)
solutions in the marketplace. Some of the types of innovations that we will ini-
tially emphasize are . . . .
. . . .

Being a younger, smaller company than our competitors we have a natural advantage of being able to be recognized as the industry innovator.

PRODUCTS/SERVICESPRODUCTS/SERVICES

☐ **Most Professional Positioning Statement**

We intend to have our .... (PRODUCTS OR SERVICES) .... stand out in the marketplace as the most professionally delivered solutions available today. Especially in a field filled with mom-and-pop operators who run their businesses in a casual manner, we intend to position our .... (PRODUCTS OR SERVICES) .... as the professional alternative. Not only will we offer more consistent and higher quality solutions—but our marketing strategy will clearly communicate these differences to our potential customers.

☐ **Positioned for Certain Company/Customer Type Statement**

We will position our .... (PRODUCTS OR SERVICES) .... as designed for companies that (are in a particular industry, are a particular size, are at a particular state of progress in the area, have a particular need, are in a particular geographical area, etc.). While without too much effort our .... (PRODUCTS OR SERVICES) .... could be sold to a broader range of firms, we want to clearly position our .... (PRODUCTS OR SERVICES) .... for this narrower range of prospects. By doing so we will position our .... (PRODUCTS OR SERVICES) .... as specialized solutions.

☐ **Positioned for Certain Consumers Statement**

We will position our .... (PRODUCTS OR SERVICES) .... for consumers who (are in the age group of ....,
have the following lifestyle characteristics ....
....,

are male or are female, have an income in the range of . . . .

work in the . . . .

profession, live in . . . .,

partake in the following type of activities . . . .

. . . ., etc.)

☐ **Positioned by Affiliation Statement**

Our . . . . .will be positioned by our affiliation
           (PRODUCTS OR SERVICES)

with . . . .

We will reflect this affiliation in our (product or service name, in our packaging,

in our advertising, in our literature, in our sales calls, in cross promotions with

the affiliated organization, etc.).

☐ **Multiple Positioning Strategies Statement**

Each of our . . . . lines will be positioned distinctly to
               (PRODUCT OR SERVICE)

allow us to capture as much of the market as possible and minimize the degree to

which our lines compete with one another. Each line will be positioned as follows

. . . . : . . . .
        (PRODUCT OR SERVICE LINE #1)   (POSITIONING)

. . . . : . . . .
        (PRODUCT OR SERVICE LINE #2)   (POSITIONING)

. . . . : . . . .
        (PRODUCT OR SERVICE LINE #3)   (POSITIONING)

PRODUCTS/SERVICESPRODUCTS/SERVICES

Competitive Evaluation Of Products/Services

Especially for plans for a new business, I would skip this section—it's hard to evaluate products or services that don't yet exist. If you do include this section, give your first focus to the most important competitive differences. Then if you want to get into more detail, work your way through the less important competitive differences, going into less depth as you get further away from the major issues.

Select and edit the <u>one or more</u> statements that best apply.

☐ **Basic Competitive Evaluation Statement**

Overall in comparison to the offerings of other firms, our . . . . are (excellent, above average, slightly above
(PRODUCTS OR SERVICES)
average, average, slightly below average, well below average, weak). Our primary

. . . . strengths are . . . .
(PRODUCT OR SERVICE)

. . . .

Our primary . . . . weaknesses are . . . .
(PRODUCT OR SERVICE)

. . . .

The weakness that we should give first focus to improving is . . . .

. . . .

We can improve this aspect by . . . .

. . . .

PRODUCTS/SERVICESPRODUCTS/SERVICES

☐ **Quick Competitive Summary of Your Product/Service**

Statement

Either rank each entry from 1 being the lowest to 10 being the highest or rank each item: Excellent, good, above average, average, below average, weak.

This is a quick summary of how our . . . .
(PRODUCT OR SERVICE)

compares to our main competitors on key dimensions:

Product/service: ____

Market share   ____

Sales trend   ____

Profitability estimate   ____

Price   ____

Clarity of positioning   ____

Overall quality   ____

Overall value   ____

Reputation   ____

Distribution   ____

Packaging   ____

Sales force ability   ____

Advertising program   ____

Promotional program   ____

Customer service/support ____

Guarantee/warranty   ____

Feature #1 . . . .
(SPECIFY FEATURE)

EXPERT ADVICE

Competition Evaluation of Products/Services

This section is primarily designed for existing businesses, but may also be appropriate if you are preparing an extremely thorough plan for a new business. Note that this section focuses on how your existing (or planned) products/services compare to those of your competitors. This contrasts with the similarly titled section "Competitive Products/Services" in the Competitors section of the plan that focused just on the products/services of your competitors, not on your products/services. Existing businesses tend to give too much emphasis in planning to hitting sales and profit numbers by boosting and adjusting marketing plans and launching new products as opposed to trying to bridge any important qualitative gaps with competitors' products or services.

PRODUCTS/SERVICESPRODUCTS/SERVICES

Feature #2 ....
(SPECIFY FEATURE)

Feature #3 ....
(SPECIFY FEATURE)

Feature #4 ....
(SPECIFY FEATURE)

Rank each of the following product/service attributes relative to the competition. Ranking versus competition for this product/service (5=excellent, 4=above average, 3= average, 2=slightly below average, 1=weak).

Overall quality   ____

Competitive pricing   ____

Clear target market focus   ____

High level of service   ____

Most personalized service   ____

Name recognition   ____

Most innovative   ____

Most professional   ____

Engineering/design   ____

☐ **The Top Five Strengths Statement**

For our .... our top five competitive strengths are:
(PRODUCT OR SERVICE)

1. ....

2. ....

3. ....

4. ....

5. ....

PRODUCTS/SERVICESPRODUCTS/SERVICES

☐ **The Top Five Weaknesses Statement**

For our .... our five most serious competitive weak-
(PRODUCT OR SERVICE)

nesses are:

1. ....

2. ....

3. ....

4. ....

5. ....

☐ **Competitive Analysis for Our Best-Selling Products/Services Statement**

For each of our best-selling .... these are our main
(PRODUCTS OR SERVICES)

competitive strengths and weaknesses:

1. .... Main strength: ....
(PRODUCT/SERVICE)
                                        Main weakness: ....

2. .... Main strength: ....
(PRODUCT/SERVICE)
                                        Main weakness: ....

3. .... Main strength: ....
(PRODUCT/SERVICE)
                                        Main weakness: ....

4. .... Main strength: ....
(PRODUCT/SERVICE)
                                        Main weakness: ....

5. .... Main strength: ....
(PRODUCT/SERVICE)
                                        Main weakness: ....

PRODUCTS/SERVICESPRODUCTS/SERVICES

☐ **Increasing Competitiveness Statement**

In order to make our . . . . more competitive, we
(PRODUCTS OR SERVICES)

intend to . . . .

. . . .

By taking these steps, we should improve our competitive standing on this issue of

. . . .

from . . . .

. . . .

to . . . .

. . . .

we expect these changes will have a (huge, large, substantial, significant, slight,
marginal) improvement in our sales.

☐ **Addressing Weaknesses Statement**

The most serious competitive weaknesses we face are . . . . and
(WEAKNESS #1)

. . . . At this time, we are not going to address
(WEAKNESS #2)

. . . . because (it is less pressing, it would be too difficult to
(WEAKNESS #?)

focus on, it would be too expensive to change, the outcome of working on this

issue would be uncertain). **Instead we are going to focus on improving**

. . . . We intend to address this by . . . .
(WEAKNESS #?)

. . . .

PRODUCTS/SERVICESPRODUCTS/SERVICES

☐ **Competitive Gap Statement**

In comparison to competitive ....(PRODUCTS OR SERVICES).................... the most threatening competitive gap that we face today is....................................

....

We (will, will not, may) be able to narrow this gap in the foreseeable future. To do
this, we would have to ....

....

This appears that it (would, would not, be a worthwhile expenditure).

☐ **Competitive Comparison of Success of Positioning Statement**

Customers appear to (accept, agree with, disagree with, not accept, question, are
not sure about) how we are trying to position our product/service. Instead, our
customers perceive our ....(PRODUCT OR SERVICE).................... as being ....

....

Other companies (have been successful, have not been successful, have had mixed
results) in successfully positioning their ....(PRODUCT OR SERVICE).................... in the
mind's of customers. Companies that have been particularly successful are ......

....

They have succeeded at this by ....

....

In order to be more successful in positioning our ....(PRODUCT OR SERVICE).................... we
should ....

....

PRODUCTS/SERVICESPRODUCTS/SERVICES

Future Products/Services

Here discuss not just potential new products/services, but also changes that you might make to your current products/services. Go into detail only if your plans for future offerings are relatively firm.

Select and edit the <u>one or more</u> statements that best apply.

☐ **Basic Future Product/Service Description Statement**

We are (doing feasibility studies of, researching, planning, working on a prototype, nearing production on, getting ready to release, getting ready to deliver) . . . . **. The basic purpose it will serve is for**
(DESCRIBE NEW PRODUCT OR SERVICE)

buyers to . . . .

We plan to introduce this . . . . in . . . .
(PRODUCT OR SERVICE)

. . . .

We will first market it to . . . .

. . . .

The key differences with this future . . . . and our cur-
(PRODUCT OR SERVICE)

rent . . . . is . . . .
(PRODUCT OR SERVICE)

. . . .

The impact of this new . . . . on the company will be
(PRODUCT OR SERVICE)

. . . .

PRODUCTS/SERVICESPRODUCTS/SERVICES

☐ **Product/Service Improvement/Changes Statement**

We intend to (improve the quality, improve the functionality, improve the versa-tility, improve the packaging, upgrade the image, lower the price, increase the selection, expand the variety, etc.) of our . . . . We
(SERVICES OR PRODUCTS)
will do this by making the following changes . . . .

. . . .

An important implication of (this or these) change(s) is . . . .

. . . .

☐ **Major New Product/Service Statement**

We aim to launch a major new . . . . that will signifi-
(PRODUCT OR SERVICE)
cantly boost our revenues. By launching this new . . . . we
(PRODUCT OR SERVICE)
hope to achieve . . . .

. . . .

Important characteristics of this new product will be . . . .

. . . .

This new . . . . will differ from our current offerings in
(PRODUCT OR SERVICE)
that . . . .

. . . .

☐ **Product/Service Upgrades Statement**

We intend to (upgrade, revise, update) (all of our, our leading, our best-selling, our most popular) . . . . at least every . . . .
(PRODUCTS OR SERVICES)   (MONTHS OR YEARS)

PRODUCTS/SERVICESPRODUCTS/SERVICES

EXPERT ADVICE

Future Products/Services

Sooner or later most products or services need changes to remain competitive or may even need to be completely replaced by a more updated version. In some sectors of the high tech industry products become completely obsolete within a year. But even in non-tech industries, changes in the market force companies to re-evaluate continually their product or service mix to stay competitive. Even if you don't have any specific plans for new products or services, you should discuss here changes that you are considering, or may consider, for your existing offerings. And even if aren't currently giving any thought to product shifts or changes, you should at least give a timeframe for when you will consider new products or services or how you will determine to make product or service changes.

Upgrades will typically involve . . . .

. . . .

Upgrades are an important way to make our . . . . (PRODUCTS
. . . . appear current without the expense of an
OR SERVICES)
entirely new offering, to stay competitive with other firms, and to get the attention of potential buyers.

☐ Product/Service Launches Statement

We aim to launch . . . . major new products per
(ENTER NUMBER)
year. Common attributes of these . . . .
(PRODUCTS OR
. . . . will be . . . .
SERVICES)

. . . .

In order to achieve this number of new . . . .
(PRODUCT OR
. . . . launches it is particularly important that we
SERVICE)
(increase the staff, increase the advertising budget, add salespeople, move to a larger facility, obtain additional financing, increase our customer service staff).

☐ Improve Performance Statement

We will improve the performance of our . . . .
(PRODUCT/
. . . . as measured by . . . .
SERVICE)   (MEASUREMENT MEANS)
We will achieve this by . . . .

. . . .

PRODUCTS/SERVICESPRODUCTS/SERVICES

Currently on this criteria we (are on a par with, are slightly behind, are well behind, are slightly ahead of) our competitors. After these steps are taken we hope to significantly outperform our competitors in this area.

☐ **Competitive Feature Response Statement**

We will match every major feature that our principle competitors add to their .... within .... months. To do this, we
(PRODUCTS OR SERVICES)   (ENTER AMOUNT)
will monitor their offerings closely and respond promptly to any significant enhancements they make.

☐ **Competitive Price Response Statement**

We will match every price decrease or special offer that our competitors offer and we will seek to reduce our costs to offset any decrease in margin. We will not let our competitors use price as a tool to increase market share.

☐ **Shift Product/Service Mix Statement**

We intend to shift our product mix so that (..... % of our sales come from new
(%)
products; ..... % of our sales come from ....
(%)
....
product; ..... % of our sales come from service; ..... % of our sales come from
(%)   (%)
....
customers). By doing this, we will (increase our profit margins, have a stronger foothold in an important growing market, diversify our customer base, decrease our dependence upon our main product, better position ourselves for growth).

PRODUCTS/SERVICESPRODUCTS/SERVICES

☐ **Basic Change of Product/Service Statement**

We are planning to change our .... in the following
(PRODUCT OR SERVICE)

way ....

....

The basic purpose of this change will be to serve buyers better be ....

....

We anticipate making this change in .... We expect this change to have
(MONTH, YEAR)

the following impact ....

....

☐ **Change/Addition/Subtraction of Major Features Statement**

We are planning on (changing, adding, removing) ~~the following major feature(s)~~ *SERVICE OF* *THE INSTALLATION*

of our CEILING PRODUCTS IN JANUARY, 2001.
(PRODUCT OR SERVICE)

~~These features serve the needs of buyers by~~ *THIS SERVICE MEETS THE* GENERAL CONTRACTOR WHO *DOES* NOT KNOW HOW OR WANT TO INSTALL *THE CEILING SYSTEMS* THEM SELVES.

This (is or is not) important to buyers because IT MAKES THEIR JOBS EASIER, IF THEY CAN ISSUE ONE CONTRACT INSTEAD OF TWO.

We expect the impact of this change to be AN INCREASE IN SALES OF $500,000.

~~We anticipate making this change in~~ ....
(MONTH, DATE)

PRODUCTS/SERVICESPRODUCTS/SERVICES

☐ **No New Products/Services or Changes Currently Planned Statement**

At this time, we do not have plans for new .... or
(PRODUCTS OR SERVICES)
for significant changes to our current offerings. However, we do intend to be
responsive to changes in market conditions, customer demands, and competitive
offerings. We will closely monitor the marketplace and make plans for changes or
new .... should conditions so warrant.
(PRODUCTS OR SERVICES)

☐ **New Unique Aspects of Product/Service Statement**

ALSO

In the future we are going to add ..METAL.. ENCLOSURES FOR PLUMBING
.AND.. OTHER.. BUILDING.. MECHANICALS..
PRODUCT
This ~~feature~~ will be unique to our ...CEILING.. SYSTEMS...., and will help
(PRODUCT OR SERVICE)
further distinguish us from the competition. What is particularly unique with this *PRODUCT*
~~feature~~ is its ..EFFECTIVE.. MEANS.. OF.. PROVIDING.. PROTECTION.. AT..
.AN.. ECONOMICAL.. PRICE.
This is important to customers because ..IT.. GIVES.. THEM.. ONE.. MORE..
.OPTION.. TO.. MEET.. THEIR.. VARIOUS.. NEEDS.
WE EXPECT THE IMPACT OF THIS CHANGE TO BE AN INCREASE IN SALES OF $500,000.

☐ **Product Selection Criteria Shift Statement**

In the future, we plan on shifting our product selection criteria to ....
....
We will give added emphasis to ....
....

PRODUCTS/SERVICESPRODUCTS/SERVICES

Our overall product mix will . . . .

. . . .

☐ **Outside Vendor Selection/Management Change Statement**

The sourcing process from outside vendors will change in the following way . . . .

. . . .

We will change the criteria used in selecting vendors . . . .

. . . .

We will give more emphasis to . . . .

. . . .

☐ **Engineering/Design Process Change Statement**

We will change our (engineering, design) capabilities to . . . .

. . . .

We will seek to improve our ability to . . . .

. . . .

We will do this by . . . .

. . . .

☐ **Reputation Goal Statement**

We will strive further for (quality, high quality, superior quality, reliability, integri-
ty, high technology, speed, efficiency, low prices, unique products, dependable service, fashion trends, etc.) reputation. We will do this by . . . .

. . . .

PRODUCTS/SERVICESPRODUCTS/SERVICES

☐ **Pricing Changes Statement**

We will change our . . . . (standard, base, suggested
(PRODUCT OR SERVICE)
retail, estimated street) price from $ . . . . . to $ . . . . . . We will (increase volume
($)   ($)
discounts, increase dealer discounts, decrease volume discounts, decrease dealer
discounts, eliminate rebates, phase out promotional offers, cut back on sales,
change the base price) to make the average selling price . . . .

. . . .

We will shift our pricing to be (high, above average, slightly above average, average, slightly below average, below average, low) in comparison to our main competitors.

☐ **Pro Forma Revenue Breakout Statement**

We anticipate to have established our new . . . . in the
(PRODUCT OR SERVICE)
marketplace by . . . . By this point in time we expect the following sales
(MONTH, YEAR)
and revenue:

Product/Service:	Unit Sales:	Revenue:	Percent of Total:
1.	. . . .	. . . .	. . . .
2.	. . . .	. . . .	. . . .
3.	. . . .	. . . .	. . . .
4.	. . . .	. . . .	. . . .
5.	. . . .	. . . .	. . . .
6.	. . . .	. . . .	. . . .

PRODUCTS/SERVICESPRODUCTS/SERVICES

☐ **Summary Listings of New Products/Services Statement**

We will offer the following new . . . .
(PRODUCTS OR SERVICES)

Name: . . . .

. . . .

Brief description: . . . .

. . . .

Key features: . . . .

. . . .

Sales: . . . .

Price: . . . . .
(\$)

☐ **Detailed Future Product/Service Listings Statement**

same as template for evaluating competitive products

1. . . . . :
(PRODUCT/SERVICE)

Pro forma unit sales: . . . . .
(#)

Pro forma dollar sales: . . . .
(\$)

Pro forma sales trend: -

Pro forma profitability: . . . .

Price: . . . . .
(\$)

Target Buyers: . . . .

. . . .

Primary positioning versus competitive offerings: . . . .

. . . .

PRODUCTS/SERVICESPRODUCTS/SERVICES

Features/attributes to be most emphasized in ads/sales pitches or packaging:

1. ....

2. ....

3. ....

4. ....

5. ....

Sales methods: ....

....

Advertising budget: ....
(\$)

Advertising themes: ....

....

Promotional/incentive programs: ....

....

Competitive strengths: ....

....

Competitive weaknesses: ....

....

Other pertinent info: ....

....

Principle competitive offerings: ....

....

CHAPTER 13

Sales and
Marketing

Marketing Strategy

Your marketing strategy is your program for getting customers to buy your products or services. State the underlying principles or commonalties of all of your marketing efforts. Explain how your marketing program will support your company strategy, and your positioning plan for your products or services. Discuss any particular message that you want your marketing to send to customers. You many also want to identify the key differences between your marketing program and those of your competitors.

Select and edit the <u>one or two</u> statements that best apply.

☐ **Basic Marketing Strategy Statement**

Our basic marketing strategy is to . . . .
. . . .

Our marketing efforts will emphasize . . . .
. . . .

The message that we want to send to customers is that . . . .
. . . .

We will primarily direct our marketing toward . . . .
(DESCRIBE MARKET OR TYPES OF BUYERS
. . . . We will (exclusively, largely, primarily, equally) **rely upon** (our
TARGETED)
sales effort, our advertising, our direct mail, our promotion and incentive offers,
etc.) to drive sales ahead. Key differences between our **marketing program** and

those of our principal competitors is ....

....

☐ **Consistent Image Statement**

We will closely integrate all of our marketing and sales efforts to project a consistent image of our company and a consistent positioning of our .... (PRODUCTS OR SERVICES) .... The image we will present is ....

....

We will emphasize .... (THIS IMAGE) .... in our sales approach by ....

....

We will emphasize .... (THIS IMAGE) .... in our advertising by ....

....

We will emphasize .... (THIS IMAGE) .... in our support materials by ....

....

☐ **Change Image Statement**

A major role of our marketing is to change our image. In the past our .... (COMPANY, PRODUCTS, SERVICES) .... have been perceived as ....

EXPERT ADVICE

Marketing Strategy

In any business plan—for raising money or for internal planning—it is important to show coherence and consistency in all of your marketing and sales efforts. By having a clearly defined marketing strategy you will insure that all of your marketing and sales efforts work together. Be sure that your marketing strategy is appropriate for your overall business strategy. For example, if your overall business strategy is to emphasize quality, then you don't want to base your marketing strategy on discount coupons or customer rebates. Also, be sure that your marketing effort is appropriate for your financial resources, not just a scaled down version of a big national competitor's program. Smaller companies with smaller budgets need to focus on leading the customer to action—not building image.

We want to change how we are perceived in our marketplace. We want to be seen as . . . .

. . . .

We will accomplish this by . . . .

. . . .

☐ **Marketing Message Statement**

The marketing message that we want to send is . . . .

. . . .

We particularly want to emphasize . . . .

. . . .

This differs from the messages of our key competitors who are generally emphasizing . . . .

. . . .

in their marketing.

☐ **Supporting Company Strategy Statement**

Our marketing program will support our overall company strategy by emphasizing . . . .

. . . .

This will be reflected in all of our marketing including in our sales efforts, in our

SALES AND MARKETING SALES AND MARKETING

advertising, and in our literature. For example . . . .

. . . .

☐ **Positioning Objectives Statement**

A major goal of our marketing is to position . . . .
(OUR PRODUCTS, SERVICES,

. . . . as . . . .
COMPANY)

. . . .

We want to convince our potential customers to think of us as . . . .

. . . .

We aim to accomplish this by . . . .

. . . .

☐ **Sales Objectives Statement**

Our marketing objective is to increase sales to $ . . . . . by . . . . We want to
($) (DATE)
increase our customer base to . . . .

. . . .

We want to increase our share of the market to . . . .

. . . .

We want to increase sales (in a certain market segment, of a certain product type,
internationally, etc.) to . . . . . % of total sales. We want to shift our sales mix to the
(%)
higher margin . . . . such as . . . .
(PRODUCTS OR SERVICES)

. . . .

SALES AND MARKETING SALES AND MARKETING

☐ **Target Markets Statement**

The primary target market for our marketing effort will be . . . .

. . . .

The marketing programs we will direct toward this market is . . . .

. . . .

Secondary target markets are . . . .

. . . .

Marketing programs in these markets will include . . . .

. . . .

☐ **Sales Focused Marketing Effort Statement**

Our marketing strategy will be based around an aggressive sales effort. In person sales presentations will be the core of our selling effort. Other marketing activities including advertising and publicity will be geared to getting potential customers to agree to meet with our salespeople.

☐ **Advertising Focused Marketing Effort Statement**

Our marketing strategy will be focused around advertising in (the yellow pages, industry publications, local newspapers, the major metro paper, the World Wide Web, etc.). Our selling effort will consist of responding to inquiries that are generated by this advertising.

SALES AND MARKETING SALES AND MARKETING

☐ **Database Focused Marketing Effort Statement**

Our marketing effort will focus on a limited number of qualified leads that we carefully track. Our information on these leads will be stored in our database. We will market to these leads using a variety of one-to-one type contact including (mailings, phone calls, e-mails, faxes, etc.). We will add to our qualified lead list by

....

☐ **Guerrilla, Low-Cost Approach Statement**

We will take a guerrilla approach in our marketing, avoiding traditional market-ing methods such as expensive ~~advertising campaigns~~ TRADE SHOWS, and instead rely on ~~lower~~ AGGRESIVE SALES EFFORT. ~~cost, more creative approaches.~~ We shall be very ~~pragmatic and quickly drop any~~ SELLECTIVE WHEN DECIDING ~~marketing method that does not work and replace it with new ones.~~ TO ADVERTISE IN TRADE MAGAZINES, WE ARE LISTED ON THE INTERNET UNDER THE DIRECTORY FOR CONNECTIONS.COM,

☐ **Overall Marketing Direction Statement**

The overall direction of our marketing is to (support the company's strategy, sup-port the positioning of the company's products or services, rapidly open new accounts, acquire new customers, insure that we achieve our sales goals, increase the visibility of our company in the marketplace, differentiate us from our com-petition). We shall achieve this by a cohesive marketing program that emphasizes (our company's unique strengths, our product's unique advantages, our service's unique benefits, an aggressive sales effort, the comparative benefits of doing busi-ness with our company). Specifically we will ....

....

SALES AND MARKETING SALES AND MARKETING

☐ **Marketing Program Components Statement**

Our marketing program will have (2, 3, 4, 5, etc.) major components. Each component will (have it's own specific goal, will be designed to compliment and support the other marketing components, be directed at a specific target market, will support of overall marketing strategy of . . . .).

Program 1. . . . .
(DESCRIBE)
. . . .

Program 2. . . . .
(DESCRIBE)
. . . .

Program 3. . . . .
(DESCRIBE)
. . . .

☐ **Revamp Company Image Statement**

We will revamp the company's image to appear just as competitive and capable as much larger firms. We will redo the company's logo, letterhead, signage, and packaging, and have a consistent look for all company communications. We will also develop a new central design theme for our advertising that echoes our new image.

☐ **World Wide Web Strategy Statement**

The World Wide Web will be a core component of our marketing strategy. We will develop a major Web site that we will promote aggressively. We will accept orders on the site, and we will provide constantly updated information for our customers.

EXPERT ADVICE

Sales Tactics

Selling directly to customers is a much more assured way of getting sales than running advertising, doing publicity, or any other alternative. If direct selling will work for your product or service, then I'd give it a huge effort. In fact, for a small new business, you may want to initially put all of your effort into developing a super sales program, and not even think about advertising or publicity until a later point in time. For some products, and especially for consumer services, making cold calls to prospective customers may not prove effective and you may need to run advertising or promotional programs to get prospects to call you. But remember, selling is still very important.

Sales Tactics

Describe the different methods and/or sales channels that you are using, or plan to use, to sell your product or service. Detail any aspect of the sales approach that is particularly important for success. Point out any aspects of your sales tactics that are different than your competitors.

Select and edit the <u>one or more</u> statements that best apply.

☐ **Basic Sales Tactics Statement**

Our **primary sales method is** (face-to-face selling, outbound telephone sales, inbound telephone sales, our national sales force, independent sales reps, distributors, wholesalers, through retailers, etc.). **A particularly important aspect of our sales process is** (generating leads, selecting salespeople, training salespeople, finding independent sales reps, selecting distributors, getting retail shelf space, etc.). **We address this by** . . . .

. . . .

Our sales tactics differ from our principle competitors in that . . . .

. . . .

SALES AND MARKETING SALES AND MARKETING

☐ **A Variety of Sales Methods Statement**

We are going to use a variety of sales methods to reach our target markets as effectively as we can. Our sales methods will vary depending upon the type and size of customer we are targeting.

1. . . . .
   (SALES METHOD #1)

   . . . .
   (TYPE AND SIZE OF CUSTOMER TARGETED)   (EXPECTED % OF TOTAL SALES)

2. . . . .
   (SALES METHOD #2)

   . . . .
   (TYPE AND SIZE OF CUSTOMER TARGETED)   (EXPECTED % OF TOTAL SALES)

3. . . . .
   (SALES METHOD #3)

   . . . .
   (TYPE AND SIZE OF CUSTOMER TARGETED)   (EXPECTED % OF TOTAL SALES)

☐ **Inbound Telephone Sales Statement**

Our sales effort is limited to responding to prospects that telephone our business. At this point the customer is seriously interested in buying a . . . .
(PRODUCT OR
. . . . of the type we are offering but they have not yet decided from
SERVICE)
which company they will make the purchase. Many prospective customers will call only two or three prospective providers. Hence there is a high conversion rate of turning inquiries into sales. What drives our sales effort is getting the phone to ring in the first place, which is the goal of our advertising program. In responding to prospective customers on the phone, we have found that it is particularly important to emphasize our (low price, high quality, high service level, years in business, reliability, guarantee, free quotations, fast response, etc.). By emphasizing this competitive advantage we have found we are more likely to land the sale.

SALES AND MARKETING SALES AND MARKETING

☐ **Inbound Telephone Leads/Face-to-Face Closing Statement**

Our sales process begins when the potential customer responds to our advertising by telephoning us for more information. We have found that rather than providing more information over the phone, our best chance of closing the sale is to arrange an appointment to visit the prospect in person. We have found it is fairly easy to persuade potential customers to agree to see a representative of our company in person. The most difficult part of the sales process, however, is closing the sale. Closing the sale requires not only knowledge of the . . . . (PRODUCT OR SERVICE) but also strong sales skills. We have found that the unique advantages of our . . . . (PRODUCT OR SERVICE) that are important to emphasize in sales calls are . . . .

☐ **Finding Leads/Telephone Cold Calling/Face-to-Face Closing Statement**

There are basically three core elements to our sales process—all critical for its success. The first is finding good leads. We ~~generally find leads by~~ HAVE CONTRACTED THE SERVICES OF W.F. DODGE TO SCAN THE ENTIRE COUNTRY FOR CONSTRUCTION PROJECTS THAT POSSES METAL SECURITY ACOUSTICAL CEILING SYSTEMS;

~~Other sources for leads include~~ THIS SERVICE NOT ONLY PROVIDES THE LEAD, IT ALSO PROVIDES THE CONSTRUCTION DOCUMENTS AND BIDDERS LIST, WE CALL THE CONTRACTORS ON THE BIDDERS LIST AND INITIATE DIALOG WHICH BUILDS A RELATIONSHIP FOR THE BIDDING ON THAT SPECIFIC PROJECT. OUR TARGET MARKET IS VERY WELL DEFINED AND EASY TO CONTACT. THESE ARE BONA FIDE LEADS WHICH MAKE THE SALES EFFORT HIGHLY SUCCESSFUL, THE THIRD CORE ELEMENT IS THE OPPORTUNITIES GIVEN TO US BY OUR NATIONAL CONTACTS FOR PROJECTS THAT ARE "PRIVATE". THESE LEADS ARE FOLLOWED BY THE INDEPENDANT REPS WHO HAVE FOUND THEM. THEY ARE LOCAL TO THE PROJECT AND HAVE STRONG RELATIONSHIPS

. . . .
(ENTER NUMBER) of prospects to arrange one appointment. The biggest challenges in cold calling are just to get the decision-maker on the phone and then to get them to really listen to the sales pitch. Salespeople require patience and skill to get past gatekeepers such as receptionists, secretaries, and assistants, or increasingly often, voice mail. The third core element, the face-to-face appointment is important also because less than (half, a quarter, 10%, etc.) of all appointments turn into sales. It is during the face-to-face presentations that we really emphasize our unique benefits such as . . . .

. . . .

☐ Face-to-Face Selling Statement

In-person selling is critical for successfully selling our . . . .
(PRODUCT OR
. . . . We have found that selling over the phone, no matter how good a
SERVICE)
presentation you make, is much less effective than in person selling. Key elements in a successful presentation include . . . .

. . . .

☐ National Sales Force Statement

Our sales are largely handled by our national sales force. It (consists of, will consist of, will be expanded to) . . . .

. . . .

salespeople and . . . .

. . . .

support staff. The salespeople will be based in . . . .

. . . .

Our national sales force focuses its efforts on (all accounts, our top . . . . .accounts, only the largest national accounts, current customers, ... markets).

☐ **Independent Sales Reps (Sometimes Called Manufacturer's Reps) Statement**

Independent sales reps are an important part of our sales effort. We (have, will have, intend to have, plan to grow to having) . . . .

. . . .

sales reps covering the following sales territories . . . .

. . . .

The standard commission rate is . . . . Exceptions to the standard commission
_(RATE)
rate are . . . .

. . . .

By employing independent reps, we are able to have a highly experienced and talented sales force with established access to important accounts. We minimize our overhead because the cost of independent reps goes up and down with our sales volume.

☐ **Distributors Statement**

We rely on distributors to get our product to market. We (have, plan to have, are in talks with) . . . .

. . . .

distributors covering the following (territories, markets, regions, countries): . . . . The advantages of distributors are many. For one,
(TERRITORIES)
they have their own established sales forces and regular access to key customers. They have a large number of established accounts and customers do not have to go through all of the paperwork of setting up a new vendor to buy our product. Also, we do not have to collect payment from each account we deal with—only from the distributors.

☐ **Retailers Statement**

Our products are sold through retailers. The overwhelming challenge in our sales effort is to get stocked on retailer's shelves. We intend to sell to retailers by (a national sales force, independent sales reps, telephone marketing, direct mail, by distributors, through wholesalers, by trade shows, an affiliation with . . . .

. . . . ,

by a combination of . . . .

. . . .).

We will support this sales effort with (trade advertising, a targeted trade show presence, direct mail, consumer advertising, special offers to open accounts, co-operative advertising programs, free samples). Key elements in successfully selling to retailers are . . . .

. . . .

☐ **World Wide Web Statement**

We use the World Wide Web to sell our . . . . and to
(PRODUCT OR SERVICE)
attract new customers. We publicize our Web site (in our literature, in our advertising, with references in the major search engines, with links to related Web sites,
by advertising our Web site in . . . .
. . . .).

☐ **Key Account Focus Statement**

Because so much of the market is concentrated at a few major accounts, the core
of our sales effort is selling these few companies. While we are certainly pleased to
get orders from midsized and smaller accounts, we focus our effort overwhelmingly on the key accounts. Being a relatively small company with limited
resources, we would rather focus all of our effort on covering a few accounts
really well, rather than covering many accounts less thoroughly. Also, the
smaller accounts often tend to eventually buy many of the same
. . . . as the larger accounts even without any sales effort.
(PRODUCTS OR SERVICES)

☐ **Sales Tactics Are Very Important Statement**

In our business, sales tactics are crucial. Often customers will buy a
. . . . that is not the best solution on the market for
(PRODUCT OR SERVICE)
them, because of superior selling tactics of the selling company.

SALES AND MARKETING SALES AND MARKETING

☐ **Sales Tactics Are Not Crucial Statement**

In our business sales tactics are not crucial. Usually customers will compare the competitive .... carefully, and then analyze and
                    (PRODUCTS OR SERVICES)
select the best solution for their needs. It is important to have an adequate sales program. But basically the competition is driven by the nature of the products or services, not by the ability or nature of the sales tactics.

☐ **Exploring Unique Needs/Benefits Statement**

An important part of our sales process is uncovering the key concerns and needs of the buyer—which often differ from one customer to the next. Because of this, it is important to have bright and engaging salespeople who can think on their feet and who are also effective in establishing a rapport with their customers.

☐ **Strategic Partnership Statement**

We have developed a strategic partnership with (company, organization, association) to sell our .... They will (sell our product or
                        (PRODUCTS OR SERVICES)
service, sell our product or service to their members, provide us with prospect lists, recommend our product or service). **In exchange we will** (give them ..... %
                                                                                                            (%)
of the net receipts, allow them the discounted price of .... , pay them
                                                          (PRICE)
.....). **This is an** (exclusive, non-exclusive, written, verbal) agreement and its
  ($)
term is (..... years, ... months, open-ended, indefinite).
            (#)   (#)

SALES AND MARKETING SALES AND MARKETING

☐ **Owner or President Does Most Sales Statement**

The (owner or president) of the company will do most of the sales work. This is an important competitive element because customers prefer to deal with the (owner or president) and (he or she) is able to be sure that the company will do everything possible to land the sale and to keep the customer happy.

☐ **New Markets Statement**

We plan on selling into the following new markets . . . .

. . . .

We (will or will not) use our existing sales programs to service these markets. The sales methods we will use are . . . .

. . . .

☐ **Sales Collateral, Support Statement**

We will support our sales effort with the following collateral (brochures, flyers, video's, computer slide shows, computer presentations, data sheets, specification sheets, testimonial sheets, reprints of press articles, free samples, mock-ups, demonstrations).

☐ **Sales Terms Statement**

We will sell (on a cash basis only, for cash, checks with proper identification, and credit cards, for credit, for credit after references are checked). Our terms will be (payment in advance, half down and half upon completion, net 30, net 60, net 90, 2% 10–net 30).

Advertising

Describe your advertising message or theme that you want to deliver. State the advertising vehicles that you will use and why you believe they are the best choice for delivering your message to your target audience. You may want to group and describe your advertising programs by product/service line, by target market, or by selected media.

Select and edit the <u>one or more</u> statements that best apply.

☐ **Basic Advertising Statement**

The message or theme that our advertising will deliver is . . .

. . . .

The primary advertising vehicle(s) that we will use is (are) (the local newspaper, the metro newspaper, newspaper inserts, shopper newspapers, flyers delivered to homes, ads on bulletin boards, the World Wide Web, local cable television, television, radio, billboards, signs, etc.). **Secondary advertising vehicles that we will use are** . . . .

. . . .

Our advertising program can best be broken out by (target market, trade/consumer, individual products or services,

EXPERT ADVICE

Advertising

Test! Test! Test! So many times I've run advertisements eagerly anticipating sales that never materialized. There are so many variables in advertising that there is no expert or ad agency that can guarantee great results every time. The media, the size of the ad, the placement, the ad copy, the ad design, the offer, the day of the week, even the weather—any one of these variables could make or break your advertising results. One of the best ways to research advertising without spending money is to closely watch where your competitors repeatedly advertise. If (and that's a big if!) they are tracking results, then that advertising vehicle is probably working for them.

Avoid announcements or image advertising that basically says who you are and where you are. Instead include a call for action in your ads.

SALES AND MARKETING SALES AND MARKETING

product/service line, selected media) **as follows** . . . .

. . . .

☐ **Unique Selling Proposition Statement**

While our . . . . has several strong, unique competitive
(PRODUCT OR SERVICE)
advantages, we will focus on just one in our advertising in order to more clearly
distinguish ourselves from the competition in a meaningful way and rather than
confuse consumers with multiple messages. The benefit we will focus on is . . . . .

. . . .

We have developed the following unique selling proposition (short catchy phrase
that captures this competitive advantage in just a few words that customers can
easily remember) **that will be an important focus of all our advertising:** . . . .

. . . .

☐ **Using Advertising to Position Products/Services Statement**

Our advertising will be designed to position our . . . . **as**
(PRODUCT OR SERVICE)
(the leading product or service, the quality leader, the most technically advanced,
the most reliable, the low cost alternative, the one-stop solution, the most personalized, the most customized, the best for the . . . .
market, specifically designed for customers who . . . .

. . . . **,**

affiliated with . . . .

. . . . **,**

SALES AND MARKETING SALES AND MARKETING

the brand name in the market). **We will accomplish this positioning by** . . . .

. . . .

☐ **Advertising Competitive Advantages Statement**

Our advertising will stress these following competitive advantages . . . .

. . . .

The ads will communicate these advantages by . . . .

. . . .

☐ **Target Market for Advertising Statement**

Our advertising will be focused at . . . . **We partic-**

(DESCRIBE TARGET MARKET)

ularly want to reach potential buyers who . . . .

. . . .

The message we want to be sure to communicate to these buyers is . . . .

. . . .

☐ **Trade Advertising Statement**

We will use trade advertising to reach (buyers, decision-makers, executives, retailers, wholesalers, dealers, etc.). **The objective of our trade advertising will be to**
(stock up retailers, stock up wholesalers, increase our stocking levels, introduce
new products, increase the acceptance of our products, position our firm) **as** . . . .

. . . .

Our   trade   advertising   will   be   focused   in   the   following   media

. . . .

(LIST MEDIA)

☐ **Business-to-Business Advertising Statement**

To reach business customers, we will advertise in the business media. Specific advertising vehicles are (industry publications, industry directories, business-to-business phone books, business magazines, business sections of newspapers, local business periodicals, national business newspapers, business television shows, business radio shows, radio news programs, television news programs, etc.). Our advertising campaign to businesses will emphasize . . . .

. . . .

☐ **Advertising to Support Sales Effort Statement**

The purpose of our advertising is to support our sales efforts. It will do this by increasing awareness of our . . . . This in turn
(COMPANY, PRODUCT, SERVICE)
will make it easier for salespeople to (get appointments with buyers, get through to decision makers, get their phone calls returned, close sales, achieve their sales goals).

☐ **Ad Agency Statement**

We will (hire, engage, continue to use) an advertising agency . . . .
(NAME AGENCY IF ALREADY
. . . . to (develop our creative message, write our advertising copy, produce our
DECIDED)
finished ads). We will work closely with them and monitor every step of the process. In selecting an ad agency, we will particularly look for . . . .

. . . .

SALES AND MARKETING SALES AND MARKETING

☐ **Freelancers/Outside Firms/Ad Agencies/Graphic Houses Statement**

We will hire (freelancers, outside firms, ad agencies, graphic houses, copywriters) to help us with the following aspects of our advertising (market research, market surveys, concept, copywriting, production, typesetting, recording, taping). **Other** aspects of our advertising we will do in-house: (market research, market surveys, concept, copywriting, production, typesetting, recording, taping). **Our criteria in** choosing outside firms will be . . . .

. . . .

☐ **Metro/Daily Newspaper Advertising Statement**

We will advertise in the major metropolitan newspaper, ... **We will**
(NAME PAPER)
advertise in the (sports, lifestyle, main, local, business, food, real estate, classified, auto, etc.) **section of the paper. We will buy** (the full run of the paper, in our local region/zone) **in the following zones** . . . .

. . . .

which cover the following areas . . . .

. . . .

We will advertise in the (Sunday or daily, morning, afternoon, evening) **edition.**

☐ **Local/Weekly Newspaper Advertising Statement**

We will advertise in the following local newspapers . . . .

. . . .

This will allow us to zero in on the specific market(s) that we are trying to target.

It will also help position our firm as being closer to the local community than firms that advertise in more broadly circulated media.

☐ Shopper Advertising Statement

We will advertise in the local shopper(s), or free newspaper(s), that is (are) distributed in the following areas . . . .

. . . .

Advertising in shoppers (instead of, in addition to) **regular newspapers gives us the advantage of** (lower cost per thousand, saturation coverage of every household in the market—not just to paid subscribers, a better environment for the promotion-oriented advertising we plan on using).

☐ Magazine Advertising Statement

We will advertise in the following magazine(s). This will us allow to target an audience . . . . It will also help position our

(DESCRIBE AUDIENCE)

. . . . **as** . . . .

(PRODUCTS OR SERVICES)

. . . .

☐ Radio Advertising Statement

We will advertise on the following type of radio stations (talk radio, news radio, easy listening, contemporary, country, urban, classic, etc.). **We will advertise in the following day parts** (morning drive time, evening drive time, lunchtime, midday, evening, late night, overnight). **We will use** (prerecorded spots, live reads, prerecorded spots with live intro's, sponsorships, on-site broadcasting, special promotions).

☐ **Local Cable Or Traditional Television Advertising Statement**

We will advertise on (cable, local, national, national cable) **television** (on the following systems, in the following communities, in the following markets, on the following networks, in markets) **that** . . . .

. . . .

We will advertise on the following channels . . . .

. . . .

We will advertise during the . . . . **We will advertise on**
(DAYS OR DAY PARTS)
the following shows . . . .

. . . .

Our ads will feature (video text, a talking head, our product or service in use, our business establishment, satisfied customers, our major selling benefits, special pricing, promotions).

☐ **Yellow Pages/Industrial Directory Advertising Statement**

We will advertise in the . . . . (Yellow Pages,
(SPECIFY TOWN OR REGION OR INDUSTRY IF APPROPRIATE)
phone directory, trade directory, industrial directory). **We will place ad(s) in the following category(ies)** . . . .

. . . .

SALES AND MARKETING SALES AND MARKETING

☐ **Direct Mail Advertising Statement**

We will use direct mail advertising to reach potential customers. We will target our mailings to .... We will get our lists of names
(SPECIFY TARGET AUDIENCE)
from (magazine subscribers, associations, phone directories, our own customer lists, mailing list brokers, etc.). **We will mail** (simple postcards, sales letters, a black and white brochure, a first class four color flyer, catalogs, discount/special offer coupons, etc.).

☐ **Low-Cost Ad Alternatives Statement**

We will employ the following low-cost advertising techniques (notices on billboards, handing out coupons, delivering leaflets door-to-door, putting flyers on car windshields, handing out business cards, cross promotions with other businesses, leaving flyers at other businesses, discount toward next purchase coupons, signs on customer premises, car/truck advertising, transit advertising signs, *AND DIRECT MAILING TO SPECIFIC ARCHITECTS IN THE* World Wide Web links, chat group on-line discussions, advertisements in invoices *CORRECTIONS MARKET.* or statements sent to customers, advertising on the outside of envelopes, advertisements on the back of business cards).

☐ **Ad Breakout by Product/Service Statement**

We will use the following ad media for the following products ....

....

1. ....
     (PRODUCT 1)   (AD MEDIA)   (% OF TOTAL AD BUDGET)
2. ....
     (PRODUCT 2)   (AD MEDIA)   (% OF TOTAL AD BUDGET)

SALES AND MARKETING SALES AND MARKETING

3. . . . .
       (PRODUCT 3)   (AD MEDIA)   (% OF TOTAL AD BUDGET)

☐ **Advertising Frequency Statement**

We will run our advertising (daily, weekly, monthly, continuously, using a see-saw approach alternating between heavy and light schedules, in quarterly blitzes to concentrate our impact once per quarter, exclusively during our peak season of .

. . . .).

☐ **Advertising Schedule Statement**

This is our advertising schedule:

1. . . . .
   (DATE)   (MEDIA)   (SIZE OF PRINT AD OR NUMBER OF RADIO/TV SPOTS)   (COST)

2. . . . .
   (DATE)   (MEDIA)   (SIZE OF PRINT AD OR NUMBER OF RADIO/TV SPOTS)   (COST)

3. . . . .
   (DATE)   (MEDIA)   (SIZE OF PRINT AD OR NUMBER OF RADIO/TV SPOTS)   (COST)

4. . . . .
   (DATE)   (MEDIA)   (SIZE OF PRINT AD OR NUMBER OF RADIO/TV SPOTS)   (COST)

EXPERT ADVICE

Promotions/Incentives

Before you start a business, promotions and incentives may sound foolish. "Why bother to pass out discount coupons or to spend money giving customers rebates?" Well the answer is that it can be very expensive to lure customers with advertising—especially advertising that doesn't have strong calls to action. Remember that often you need not only to interest a new prospect in your product or service, but you must also lure them away from either the company they are currently doing business with, or a competing product or service they are considering.

Some promotion programs you can even run without buying advertising. For example, you can hand out coupons on the street corner, place them on car windshields, deliver them to nearby homes, or drop them off at prospective businesses.

Promotions/Incentives

Describe any promotions or incentives that you will use to increase the sales of your product or service. Describe the duration and frequency of the promotions, the target audience, and how information of the promotion will be delivered to target customers.

Select and edit the <u>one or more</u> statements that best apply.

☐ **Basic Promotion/Incentive Statement**

We will use the following promotions and incentives to increase sales of our . . . . (PRODUCT OR SERVICE) . . . . : (sales, rebates, special events, exclusive offerings, discounts, frequent buyer cards, new customer offers, giveaways, free trials, guaranteed results, trades, cross promotions, gifts, free samples, contests, charity tie-ins). **The promotions will typically be held** (daily, weekly, monthly, quarterly, once per season, annually, when sales are slow, when inventory is high, etc.). **And they will usually last for about** (. . . . . days, ... weeks, ... months). **We will**
(DAYS)   (WEEKS)   (MONTHS)
announce these promotions by . . . .
. . . .

SALES AND MARKETING SALES AND MARKETING

☐ **Sales Promotions Statement**

We will run sales to help build our business. Discounts off our everyday pricing will typically range from .... to .... Sales will be run (every .... days, every
(\$)   (\$)   (DAYS)
.... weeks, seasonally, when sales are slow, when inventory is high, to tie in
(WEEKS)
with special events or product or service offerings). **Sales will last for**
(....... days, ... weeks, ... months). **We will promote our sales**
  (DAYS)   (WEEKS)   (MONTHS)
with (signs, handing out coupons or flyers, in-store flyers, mailings to current customers, mailings to target customers, newspaper advertising, radio advertising, etc.).

☐ **Rebates Statement**

We will offer rebates to (consumers, dealers, retailers, wholesalers) **to spur our sales. Rebates will be featured** (in our advertising, on our packaging, in direct mail to dealers, by our salespeople, in our trade advertising, at point-of-purchase, by our dealers' salespeople). **Rebates will be** (instantly redeemable at point of purchase, mailed in for redemption). **Rebates will typically be for $** .... **. Other con-**
                                                                    (\$)
ditions that apply are ....

....

We will offer rebates (once per year, every season, when sales are slow, to launch new products, when a product is becoming obsolete, when a competitor is gaining on us).

SALES AND MARKETING SALES AND MARKETING

☐ **Coupons Statement**

We will widely distribute coupons to promote our business. Coupons will offer (discounts, free gift with purchase, free trial, buy one get one free, buy one today get next purchase free). **We will distribute coupons** (by handing them out on the street, by delivering them door to door, at trade shows, in stores, in our newspaper ads, in co-op coupon books).

☐ **Frequent Buyer Program Statement**

We will use a frequent buyer program to build and retain a loyal customer base. Customers will be given a frequent buyer card that will be (marked, entered into the computer) **after each purchase. After** (2, 3, 4, 5, etc.) purchases they will (get a free purchase, get a ..... % discount, get a free gift, get a reward check). **We will** also use this program to get names, addresses and phone numbers of our customers and to track their purchase histories. This will help us tailor our marketing for customers with specific buying habits.

☐ **Giveaways/Gifts Statement**

We will use giveaways to (attract new customers, to build loyalty with current customers, to get more people to try our product or service, to get more people to visit our business establishment). **We will give away** (free samples, novelty items, ...).

We will promote this give away by . . . .
. . . .

SALES AND MARKETING SALES AND MARKETING

☐ **New Customer Offers Statement**

To get new customers we will offer (incentive pricing, discounts, freebies, free product samples, free service trials, money-back guarantees, extra advertising allowances). **We will promote this by** (our sales force, by calling on target prospects, by direct mail, through our advertising, by advertising in the following media . . . .).

Our new customer promotions will be (an ongoing offer, a limited time offer, offered to introduce new products or services, designed to help launch our business, offered on a seasonal basis, offered every . . . . months).
(MONTHS)

☐ **Grand Opening Sale/Celebration Statement**

To create awareness for our new business we will have a big grand opening celebration. The celebration will last for (. . . . . . . days, ... weeks, ...
(DAYS) (WEEKS) (MONTHS)
months). **During the celebration we will give away** (balloons, cookies, ice cream, coffee, doughnuts, raffle tickets for a free trip to . . . . , chances to win a . . . . , product samples). **We will offer** (special pricing, deep discounts, free gifts with purchase, free estimates, reduced service fees, extended warranties, rebates, etc.). **The grand opening will be promoted by** (signs, mailings, press releases, media interviews, newspaper advertising, radio advertising, direct mail, handouts, etc.).

☐ **World Wide Web Statement**

We will promote our business with a World Wide Web site. On the site we will offer (product information, service information, basic information about our business, suggestions on how to use our product/service more effectively, a wide range of information of interest to potential customers including . . . .

. . . . ,

links to related sites, discount coupons or rebates that may be printed out, information on how to reach us, pictures of our product or service). **We will promote our Web site** (on all our literature, by listing our Web address everywhere our street address is listed such as on business cards and on our stationary, in our advertising, in major search engines on the Web, by getting free links with related Web sites, by advertising on the Web).

☐ **Contests Statement**

We will hold contests to (draw attention to our business, help build awareness of our business, get names of prospects to follow up on, get free publicity for our business, create a sense of fun and excitement about our business). **A typical contest will be** (guess how many jelly beans in the jar, guess how big our sales are, drop your business card in the box, guess how fast our product can . . . .

. . . . ,

enter your name and address on the form) **for a chance to win a** (free product, free service, free trial service, all expense paid trip to . . . .

. . . . ,

a color TV, etc.).

☐ **Free Estimates/Evaluations/Trials/Tests Statement**

We will offer free (estimates, evaluations, trials, tests) **without any obligation. We will use this free offer as an opportunity to** (familiarize the prospect with our business, emphasize our competitive advantages, try to close the sale, offer special incentives such as . . . .

. . . . ,

to try to make the sale).

EXPERT ADVICE

Publicity

The best thing about publicity is that it is free! Better yet, customers are much more likely to respond to publicity about your business than advertising. Publicity isn't just for big or specialized businesses—any business can get publicity. If you sell life insurance for example, you could write an article for the local newspaper or appear on a local radio show explaining what level of life insurance coverage is appropriate for people in different situations. Publicity is free and any business can get it—but it can sometimes take a lot of time and effort. This is why you need to have a clear publicity plan to focus on the media that you will be most worthwhile for you, and perhaps more importantly, that you have a realistic chance of getting placement on.

Publicity

Describe the central focus or message of your publicity program(s). State the media vehicles that you will use and why you believe they are the best choice for delivering your message to your target audience. You may want to group and describe your publicity programs by product or /service line, by target market, or by selected media.

Select and edit the <u>one or more</u> statements that best apply.

☐ **Basic Publicity Statement**

The central message that our publicity will deliver is . . . . . .

. . . .

The primary publicity vehicle(s) that we will target is (are) (the local newspaper, the metro newspaper, trade publications, business periodicals, specialty magazines, the World Wide Web, local cable television, television, radio, signs, etc.). Secondary publicity vehicles that we will target are . .

. . . .

We will pitch the media by (mailing press packets, faxing press releases, sending pitch letters, making phone calls, arranging interviews).

SALES AND MARKETING SALES AND MARKETING

☐ **General Awareness Publicity Statement**

The main purpose of our publicity is to increase the general awareness of our

. . . . Our publicity is also intended to emphasize
(PRODUCT AND SERVICES)

our competitive advantages and to inform customers and potential customers of

new developments concerning our . . . . and our
(PRODUCTS OR SERVICES)

business.

☐ **Emphasis of Publicity Campaign Statement**

Our publicity campaign will emphasize sending press releases, sending press
packets, sending product samples, sending video tapes, arranging media interviews, holding press conferences, issuing statements, seeking product reviews.

☐ **Type of Media Being Targeted Statement**

Our publicity effort will target the following media (major daily newspapers, local
newspapers, network radio stations, local radio stations, network television shows,
local television shows, wire services, national magazines, trade magazines, consumer magazines, newsletters).

☐ **Product/Service Focused Publicity Effort Statement**

Our publicity effort will focus primarily on publicizing our particular

. . . . as opposed to the company as a whole. For
(PRODUCTS OR SERVICES)

every new . . . . launch we will develop a specific pub-
(PRODUCT OR SERVICE)

licity campaign. We will also occasionally send out press releases heralding note-

worthy achievements or milestones of our . . . .
(PRODUCTS OR SERVICES)

SALES AND MARKETING SALES AND MARKETING

☐ **Publicity Effort Focus Statement**

Our publicity effort will primarily be focused as follows

1. ....
   (PRODUCT OR SERVICE 1)   (TARGET MEDIA)   (NUMBER OF PRESS KITS OR CONTACTS)

2. ....
   (PRODUCT OR SERVICE 2)   (TARGET MEDIA)   (NUMBER OF PRESS KITS OR CONTACTS)

3. ....
   (PRODUCT OR SERVICE 3)   (TARGET MEDIA)   (NUMBER OF PRESS KITS OR CONTACTS)

4. ....
   (PRODUCT OR SERVICE 4)   (TARGET MEDIA)   (NUMBER OF PRESS KITS OR CONTACTS)

☐ **Newsletter Statement**

We will produce and send a newsletter every (month, other month, quarter, etc.)
to promote our company and our .... We will send
(PRODUCTS OR SERVICES)
approximately ..... copies to (current customers, customers and prospects, deal-
(#)
ers, prospects, the following mailing lists ....
....).

In the newsletter we will highlight ....
....

☐ **Press Conference(s) Statement**

We plan on holding a press conference(s) to announce ....
....

It will be held in .... on .... We will mail invitations
(LOCATION)   (TENTATIVE DATE)
to members of the media and we expect ..... people to attend.
(#)

SALES AND MARKETING SALES AND MARKETING

☐ **PR Firm/Ad Agency Statement**

We will (hire, use) (a PR firm or an advertising agency) . . . .
NAME AGENCY IF ALREADY
. . . . (to handle our entire publicity effort, to develop and write our pub-
DECIDED
licity messages, to produce our press materials, to create our publicity packages,

to contact the media, to arrange interviews for use, to mail press releases). We will

work closely with them and monitor every step of the process.

☐ **Inhouse Publicity Personnel Statement**

Our publicity effort will be handled in house by . . . .

. . . . ,

who will consult with . . . .

. . . .

Clerical support will be provided as needed by . . . .

. . . .

Trade Shows

Describe the kind of events you will attend. Specify the events by name if you are fairly certain which events you will attend. Describe what you will do to promote your organization and your products or services both at these events and before the events take place.

Select and edit the <u>one or more</u> statements that best apply.

☐ **Basic Trade Show Statement**

We will (attend, have a booth at, have a table at, conduct a workshop at, speak at, sponsor) (trade shows, business-to-business shows, consumer shows, conventions, seminars). The shows we are planning to attend are ACA (American Construction
(SPECIFY SHOWS BY NAME OR
ASSOCIATION) IN DENVER AND CISCA (CEILINGS & INTERIOR SYSTEMS CONSTRUCTION
LOCATION OR INDUSTRY)
ASSOCIATION)

☐ **Objectives of Trade Shows Statement**

Our objective of attending these shows is to (open new accounts, get names of possible leads, build relationships with current customers, launch our business, launch new products or services, emphasize our unique . . . .

. . . . ,

portray our firm as a major player in the . . . .

. . . .

industry, seek independent sales reps, seek overseas distribution, seek distributors, meet with key accounts, provide demonstrations, solve problems for customers, check out competitor's offerings, seek new products or services, keep up industry contacts).

☐ **Type of Display Statement**

We will use (a table top, a booth, multiple booths, a meeting room, part of a booth, our distributor's booth). Our basic layout will be a (simple array of our products or literature about our services, a placard that . . . .

. . . . ,

a commercial table top display, a portable exhibit booth, a rented exhibit booth, a custom built booth, a commercially built booth).

☐ **Emphasis of Display/Presentation Statement**

We will emphasize our (new products, new services, our unique

. . . . ,

a special offer . . . .

. . . . ,

our new customer offer . . . .

. . . . ,

our catalogs, our flyers, our relationship with our distributor, a contest . . . . ,

a promotion . . . .).

EXPERT ADVICE

Trade Shows

Many companies, especially small product companies, have used trade shows as a highly effective and relatively inexpensive means to quickly building their business. But you can also be lured into spending a lot of money and having little to show for it. Just like with advertising, start small. Carefully research one or two of the best shows for you. Don't just go to a show because it's biggest in the industry. Instead choose shows because other small companies can tell you that they've had good results at these shows. At some trade shows a lot of orders are written. But many trade shows are not primarily order writing shows.

Instead, companies often use trade shows to preview their products or services and to help reinforce their other sales efforts.

☐ **Promotion of Trade Show Exhibit Statement**

We will promote our trade show exhibit by (buying the list of attendees from the show organizers and direct mailing to them in advance, advertising in trade publications, advertising in the trade show circular, having special show offers, having a special event, mailing invitations to key accounts, having a party at the time of the show, giving away . . . .

. . . .,

getting a good location on the exhibit floor, having a drawing at our booth).

☐ **Trade Show Follow-Up Statement**

We will make an effort to gather names of prospects at the show by (asking for business cards, having a drawing, buying the list of attendees, having a guest book). We will follow up attendees after the show (by phone, by phoning to arrange a face-to-face meeting, by e-mail, by fax, by mail, by sending a sample).

CHAPTER 14

Operations

OPERATIONSOPERATIONSOPERATIONS

Key Personnel

Investors and lenders make their decisions on the basis of people. They especially want to see people who have a proven track record or highly relevant experience. It all starts with the person in charge. You will need to assure everyone who may become involved with the venture that the person running the business knows what he or she is doing and has what it takes to make money. After making these points, go on to describe the other key people. Your management team should have experience in the most important functional areas of the business. Attach detailed resumes for all key personnel in an appendix. If you are running an existing business you know the key people well, but it may be useful to take an arm's length view of their abilities by summarizing them in writing. Are the right people in the right positions? Should major or minor responsibilities be reassigned?

Select and edit the <u>one or more</u> statements that best apply.

☐ **Basic Management Team Statement**

Our management team includes .... individuals whose combined back-
(# OF)
grounds represent ....

....

years of professional experience in the .... The President,
(RELEVANT FIELD)
........................, has an excellent reputation in the field, and is particular-
(NAME)
ly well-known for .... (He/she) will be directly
(PRIOR SUCCESSFUL ACTIVITY)
involved in all aspects of the business on a daily basis, including management of

the .... and .... areas of the
(FUNCTIONAL AREA)   (FUNCTIONAL AREA)

OPERATIONSOPERATIONSOPERATIONS

company. The ....(TITLE).............., ...(NAME).............., will work closely with the President and will concentrate primarily on the ....(FUNCTIONAL AREA)............. (He/She) was chosen for this position due to (his/her) demonstrated expertise in ....(AREA OF EXPERTISE)............. A third key manager, ...(NAME)............., will serve as ....(TITLE)............. and have primary responsibility for ....(FUNCTIONAL AREA)............. Resumes of all key members of the management team follow.

☐ Management And Personnel Structure Statement

The Company will be managed by the ....(# OF)....... founding partners, whose individual areas of expertise cover all of the functional aspects of the business. ....(PRESIDENT'S NAME)............. will serve as the President of the Company, and will be responsible for ....(FUNCTIONAL AREAS)............. ....(NAME)............. will be the ....(TITLE)............. of the Company, in charge of ....(FUNCTIONAL AREA)............. The ....(TITLE)............. of the Company will be ....(NAME)............., overseeing ....(FUNCTIONAL AREA)............. These key positions will be supported by a full-time staff consisting of ....(# OF)....... employees, working in the areas of ....(FUNCTIONAL AREA)............., ...(FUNCTIONAL AREA)............., and ....(FUNCTIONAL AREA)............. In addition, part-time staff and independent contractors will be

EXPERT ADVICE

Key Personnel

The level of detail you go into here should be determined by how complex and large a business you are planning, and how clearly the past experience of the key personnel matches their responsibilities assigned in the plan. If, for example, you will be the only key employee and you have previously managed a similar business, a couple of sentences may be sufficient. If on the other hand you are planning a larger business, you should go into detail for each key position. Don't worry if you have not yet hired for all key positions. Simply outline the responsibilities of any unfilled key position and briefly describe the qualifications you are seeking in candidates to fill the position. Generally you should include resumes of key people at the end of the plan. Investors and bankers may first consider who the key people are before evaluating any other aspect of the plan.

OPERATIONSOPERATIONSOPERATIONS

utilized to accomplish several operational functions, including .... (FUNCTIONAL

.............., ... , and ....
AREA)   (FUNCTIONAL AREA)   (FUNCTIONAL AREA)

☐ **Only One Key Employee Statement**

The key employee is ...., who founded the business, owns the
(NAME)

business and has the title of .... has
(TITLE)   (NAME)

worked in this industry for .... years at a variety of companies.
(YEARS)

.... is particularly strong in the areas of (management, prod-
(NAME)

uct development, servicing customers, finance, accounting, engineering, market-

ing, sales, etc.). At .... he/she had experience in ...
(PREVIOUS COMPANY #1)

....

At .... he/she had experience in ....
(PREVIOUS COMPANY #2)

....

Areas that .... is weaker in are ....
(NAME)

....

In these areas assistance will be provided by (an outside accounting firm, an out-

side law firm, consultants, part-time employees, a new hire).

☐ **Three Key Employees Statement**

The company has three employees who can considered to be key.

.... is responsible for management, finances, accounting and
(NAME)

other administration issues. (He or she) has previously held the following relevant

positions ....

OPERATIONSOPERATIONSOPERATIONS

.... will be responsible for ....
(NAME)   (PRODUCTS OR SERVICES)
(He or she) has previously held the following relevant positions ....

....

.... will be responsible for sales, marketing, and customer rela-
(NAME)
tions. (He or she) has previously held the following relevant positions ....

....

☐ **President/CEO: Existing Business Statement**

.... is the President and principal shareholder of the company.
(NAME)
(He/she) has ...... years experience in the .... indus-
(# OF)   (RELEVANT FIELD)
try, and was .... for .... where
(JOB TITLE)   (PREVIOUS EMPLOYER)
he gained valuable experience in .... He formed
(FUNCTIONAL AREA)
.... in ......, and the company has had an average
(COMPANY NAME)   (YEAR)
annual growth rate of ..... % over the past ..... years, attributable to
(%)   (#)
.... and the excellent management team the
(REASON FOR GROWTH)
President has put in place. .... owns ..... % of the stock in
(NAME)   (%)
.... and acts as .... of the
(COMPANY NAME)   (BOARD POSITION TITLE)
Board of Directors.

☐ **President/CEO: New Business Statement**

The principal owner, DOUG PRAHST , has been involved in the
(NAME)

CONSTRUCTION .... industry since 1985. He/she attended THE UNIVERSITY
(NAME OF INDUSTRY)   (YEAR)

OF WISCONSIN, MILWAUKEE , and studied ARCHITECTURE , and then attended
(COLLEGE)   (MAJOR)
IS CURRENTLY ATTENDING

OPERATIONSOPERATIONSOPERATIONS

KELLER GRADUATE SCHOOL OF MANAGEMENT, where he ~~received a~~ WILL RECEIVE AN MBA degree
(GRADUATE SCHOOL)   (ADVANCED DEGREE)

in BUSINESS in 2000. In 1992, he began working for
(DISCIPLINE)   (YEAR)   (YEAR)

WILDECK, INC. as a PROJECT MANAGER. DOUG 's
(PREVIOUS EMPLOYER)   (POSITION)   (NAME)

expertise is focused in the area of PROJECT COORDINATION, which is central
(AREA OF EXPERTISE)

to the operations of the proposed business. He has an excellent reputation
throughout the industry and brings tremendous strength and experience to the
new enterprise.

AREAS THAT DOUG IS WEAKER IN ARE ACCOUNTING
AND LAW. ASSISTANCE WILL BE PROVIDED IN
THESE AREAS BY DAVID SMRECEK, ACCOUNTANT, OF
SMRECEK & CO. AND CHARLES COUSLAND, ATTORNEY, OF
BODE, CARROLL, McCOY & HOEFLE.

.... will have primary responsibility for the company's sales and
(NAME)

marketing activities, including management of the field sales organization and the
customer service department. (He/she) has an extensive background in all aspects
of sales and marketing management, with ..... years with ....
(#)   (PREVIOUS

.... as .... and .... years with
EMPLOYER)   (JOB TITLE)   (#)

OPERATIONSOPERATIONSOPERATIONS

.................(PREVIOUS EMPLOYER)............. as ....(JOB TITLE)........... . This much relevant experience in the ....(RELEVANT FIELD)........... industry insures his/her will perform well in this position.

☐ Vice President Production Statement

..............(NAME)............'s ......(#).. years of direct experience in operations and production management in the ....(RELEVANT INDUSTRY).......... field is a tremendous asset to this company. (He/she) is thoroughly familiar with all aspects of the production process, from the start-up and bidding phases through completion. In (his/her) past positions with ....(PREVIOUS EMPLOYER)........... and ....(PREVIOUS EMPLOYERS)........, ...(NAME)............ was also able to develop new and improved processes in the area of customer service and customer satisfaction.

☐ Vice President Human Resources Statement

................(NAME)............. began (his/her) career in human resources in ......(YEAR).. with ....(PREVIOUS EMPLOYER)............, where (he/she) was involved in incentive and employee benefit plans and the development of equal opportunity/diversity programs. In our organization, (he/she) will handle a similarly wide range of HR functions, as well as employee recruitment and hiring.

☐ Management Compensation and Incentives Statement

The compensation and incentive plan offered to key personnel is designed to give these individuals a significant stake in the company's success as a way of encouraging top performance and retaining them in their positions. In addition to

OPERATIONSOPERATIONSOPERATIONS

salaries, compensation for key personnel will include (stock options, profit sharing set at ..... % of pre-tax earnings, bonuses based on ....
(%)
....).

☐ **Board of Directors Statement**

Members of the board of directors have been selected for their ability to bring specialized skills and experience to the company. In addition to the .... princi-
(# OF)
pals involved in daily operations, these directors will include
................, whose expertise lies in the area of ....,
(NAME)   (AREA OF EXPERTISE)
.... , who will be counted on for ....,
(NAME)   (AREA OF EXPERTISE)
and ...., who is extremely knowledgeable in the area of
(NAME)
.... These non-management directors (will/will not)
(AREA OF EXPERTISE)
be compensated for their participation at a per diem rate ....
($ DAILY RATE)

OPERATIONSOPERATIONSOPERATIONS

Organizational Structure

This section explains the reporting structure in your firm and how work is divided between different people. If you have a formal organization chart, you should include the chart at the end of the business plan. For a very small business with a half-dozen or fewer employees (or for a less complex business plan) you may prefer to skip this section and include relevant information when discussing key personnel.

Select and edit the <u>one</u> statement that best applies.

☐ **Basic Organizational Structure Statement**

The company is divided into . . . .

. . . .

(departments, work groups, units, divisions, informal areas of focus). These are the key areas and their respective responsibilities . . . .

. . . .

(Note if an organizational chart is included at the end of the business plan.)

☐ **Organizational Structure Statement**

1. Executive. Consisting of the President, ... ,
(NAME)
and . . . .

EXPERT ADVICE

Organizational Structure

This section is designed to show how responsibilities and lines of command will be established. You may choose to cover this ground in the previous section, Key Personnel or skip it altogether if you are starting a very small business. On the other hand, this section may prove particularly important for running your business if have several roughly similarly talented and experienced partners or key employees. This section then would give you a chance to clearly define the responsibilities of each key person so to help avoid disputes over responsibilities in the future.

OPERATIONSOPERATIONSOPERATIONS

support staff. Responsibilities include overall management, determining strategic direction, and . . . .

. . . .

2. Finance/Accounting. Headed by the (CFO, Vice President of Finance, Controller, Accounting Manager) and consisting of . . . .

. . . .

employees. Responsibilities include producing monthly financial statements, preparing cash flow forecasts, handling day-to-day banking relations, credit, collections, and . . . .

. . . .

3. Sales/Marketing. Headed by the (Vice President of Marketing, the Marketing Manager, the Sales Manager) and consisting of . . . .

. . . .

employees. Responsibilities include developing marketing strategy, developing advertising concepts, arranging for product and placement of advertising, arranging for publicity, directly selling to key accounts, management of independent commission sales reps who sell to smaller accounts, management of relationships with distributors.

4. (Manufacturing or Service). Headed by the (Vice President of Manufacturing, Vice President of Service, the Plant Manager, the Service Manager) and consisting of . . . .

. . . .

OPERATIONSOPERATIONSOPERATIONS

employees. **Responsible for** (manufacturing products or delivering services) including . . . .

. . . .

5. (Include other distinctive areas your company may have such as Engineering, Customer Service or Support, Human Resources, Operations, Shipping & Receiving, etc.)

☐ Informal Organizational Structure Statement

Our organizational structure is very informal, without written job descriptions of specific departments formally dividing responsibilities. This is partially because there are so few employees, partially because we are all willing to pitch in to do whatever it takes to get the job done, and partially because we sometimes are forced to shift all of our focus to work together on the most pressing priorities. As a matter of practice however, here is who takes the primary role in each of the major functional areas:

Finance: . . . .
(NAME)

Marketing and Sales: . . . .
(NAME)

Operations/Office: . . . .
(NAME)

. . . . : . . . .
(PRODUCT OR SERVICE)   (NAME)

OPERATIONSOPERATIONSOPERATIONS

☐ **Reliance on Outside Resources Statement**

Being a very small company with only .... employees, our selection and use
(#)
of outside contractors and service providers is an important part of our operation.

Here is a breakout of the key outsiders that will be supporting our business:

Accounting: ....
(FIRM OR INDIVIDUAL)

....
(RESPONSIBILITIES)

....

Legal: ....
(FIRM OR INDIVIDUAL)

....
(RESPONSIBILITIES)

Other: ....
(NAME IF AVAILABLE)

....
(RESPONSIBILITIES)

☐ **Planned Change in Organizational Structure Statement**

Until now our organization has been divided into .... groups:
(#)
.... We intend to reorganize into .... groups
(LIST EACH GROUP) (#)
.... Essentially the .... will be
(LIST GROUPS) (GROUP TO CHANGE)
(eliminated, merged into the group, broken into new groups). Accompanying this

change we will be (hiring a new manager, hiring new people, eliminating posi-

tions). We are making this change because ....

....

OPERATIONSOPERATIONSOPERATIONS

Human Resources Plan

It would be appropriate to discuss here specific issues such as which positions need to be created and filled, your procedures for hiring employees, your policies on reviewing employees, salary and benefit policies, and training plans. You could also discuss your overall strategy for human resources, explain the kind of company culture you want to foster, present your philosophy about human resources, or describe how your human resources approach will be different than that of other firms. Skip this section for a very tiny business.

Select and edit the <u>one or more</u> statements that best apply.

☐ **Basic Human Resources Statement**

We recognize that human resources are an extremely important asset. Hence we will screen new applicants very carefully including in-person interviews and reference checks. We will review each employee's performance regularly, and when possible promote from within. Our salaries and benefit packages will be competitive with those offered by other firms in our area.

☐ **Human Resources Strategy Statement**

Our human resources strategy will be (to treat all employees with respect, to create a high performance environment, to

EXPERT ADVICE

Human Resources Plan

In your business plan you typically only detail the individuals and positions that are considered to be key. This section, however, allows you to outline your hiring and human resources plan for all positions—so that you may hire, retain, and motivate the best overall workforce possible. Keep in mind your business strategy as you develop a Human Resources Plan. For example if your strategy emphasizes superior customer service, how will your Human Resources Plan insure that you hire the best customer service people possible? In today's competitive labor market, even a very small business needs to carefully develop a plan for hiring, retaining, and motivating employees at all levels.

OPERATIONSOPERATIONSOPERATIONS

create a positive and productive environment, to be fair and consistent, to empower employees, to involve employees in decision-making as much as possible, to keep our labor costs low). **Important elements of this strategy are** . . . .

. . . .

☐ **Staffing Plan New Business Statement**

New staff will be added as the company achieves predetermined revenue benchmarks. As reflected in the financials, the total number of staff positions will reach . . . . . . by the end of year one, ... by the end of year two, and . . . . . . by the end of year three. Our recruitment strategies for identifying candidates and hiring individuals to fill these positions will be based on a combination of referrals, classified advertising in local newspapers, and . . . . When new hires are accomplished, subsequent orientation and training will be the responsibility of . . . .

[handwritten: ONE AND ONE PART TIME over first blank (#); TWO over third blank (# OF); PRE EXISTING CONTACTS over (OTHER STRATEGIES); THE PRESIDENT over (POSITION TITLE)]

- (#)
- (# OF)
- (# OF)
- (OTHER STRATEGIES)
- (POSITION TITLE)

☐ **Support Staff New Business Statement**

A total of . . . . . support personnel will be hired within the first . . . . . months
(# OF)   (# OF)
to accomplish ongoing operational functions such as . . . . ,
(JOB FUNCTION)
. . . . , and . . . . Specific
(JOB FUNCTION)   (JOB FUNCTION)
positions to be filled in this initial period are:

_____ _____-time $_____ per hour

_____ _____-time $_____ per hour

_____ _____-time $_____ per hour

OPERATIONSOPERATIONSOPERATIONS

☐ Hiring Strategy Statement

We will strive to hire people who (are flexible and creative, have a solid work ethic, are willing to work hard, work well with others, have excellent references, have a record of high performance, a good ability to get along with others, an ability to work with a diverse group of people, work well in a team environment). **We will recruit employees by** (newspaper help-wanted advertising, advertising on the internet, searching resume databases, using employment agencies, offering referral bonuses to current employees). **For most positions we will** (do initial screening by telephone, conduct in-person interviews, have candidates fill out an application form, get references from previous employers or schools, do extensive background checks).

☐ Salaries and Benefits Statement

In setting salaries we will (examine each situation individually, follow a company-wide job grading system, be consistent for comparable positions throughout the organization, match industry standards, aim to set salaries ..... % above the average in our area, above the average in our industry). **Our benefits policies will include** (profit-sharing, bonuses, cash rewards, stock options, paid holidays, paid vacations, personal time, medical insurance, an HMO plan, dental insurance, eye glasses insurance, life insurance, short-term disability insurance, long-term disability insurance, educational assistance).

OPERATIONSOPERATIONSOPERATIONS

☐ **Salary and Benefits Higher than Market Statement**

The company's salary structure will be slightly higher than market rates, and an extremely competitive benefit package will be offered not only to help the recruitment effort, but to increase the chance of retaining employees and maintaining an experienced staff. Benefits offered will include .... weeks of paid vacation, a
(# OF)
comprehensive health (and dental) plan, ..., and
(BENEFIT)
....
(BENEFIT)

☐ **Outside Contractors, Freelancers Statement**

To obtain specialized expertise the company (will, has) engaged the services of outside contractors and freelancers. Here are people that have been lined up to date:

....
(FUNCTION)   (PERSON)

....
(FUNCTION)   (PERSON)

....
(FUNCTION)   (PERSON)

☐ **Recruitment: New Business Statement**

Several approaches will be utilized in parallel in order to recruit the new staff members who will be needed as the company grows, including classified newspaper advertising, a paid incentive referral program for current employees, and
.... Candidates will undergo a thorough
(RECRUITMENT STRATEGY)
interview process with at least .... current employees on separate occasions.
(# OF)

OPERATIONSOPERATIONSOPERATIONS

Wherever possible, competency tests will be administered as a part of the selection process.

☐ **Staff Development: New Business Statement**

In addition to the key personnel, other necessary functions will be accomplished through a combination of new hires (full- and part-time) and independent contractors. In specific, the following new employees are anticipated:

. . . .
(# POSITIONS)   (POSITION TITLE)   (EXPECTED TIME TO HIRE)

. . . .

. . . .

. . . .

The following functions will be handled through contractors:

. . . .
(# POSITIONS)   (FUNCTION)   (EXPECTED TIME TO HIRE)

. . . .

. . . .

. . . .

☐ **Training Statement**

Building a sense of teamwork among all personnel is an essential component for the success of the business. By allocating significant time and resources to staff training, we expect to increase every employee's ability to create positive change in the workplace and to help everyone feel that he or she is an important, con-

OPERATIONSOPERATIONSOPERATIONS

tributing part of the organization. Responsibility for training will come under Human Resources, but key managers from every department will take part in developing or reviewing training materials or in actually delivering training sessions as appropriate. Also included in the budget projections are funds for bringing in outside consultants for staff training purposes as needed.

☐ Improve Employee Capabilities Statement

We believe that our employees are truly one of our most important assets. We intend to further invest in their capabilities and job satisfaction by offering the following programs (full or partial tuition reimbursement, out of house seminars, in house seminars, an informal series of seminars by experts on our staff, reimbursement for professionally related books, an in-house book library, an audio cassette library, a video library, a multimedia training center). Employee capabilities we are particularly interested in improving are . . . .

. . . .

☐ Performance Reviews Statement

All employees will have an annual performance review conducted by the manager to whom they directly report. All managers will complete a standard form and meet with each staff member individually to discuss it. This form will contain specific feedback on job performance, and will also make summary recommendations as to areas for improvement and (salary increases/bonuses).

OPERATIONSOPERATIONSOPERATIONS

☐ **To Increase Morale Statement**

To increase company morale we plan on taking a number of steps. We will (rotate people among jobs, give more emphasis to promotion from within, hold regular company parties, have regular company luncheons, start an employee reward program, be more responsive to employee's concerns, give out gifts adorned with the company logo, redecorate employee work areas, give all-employee briefings on the progress of the company, make an effort to publicly praise notable accomplishments by employees at all levels, increase the interaction between different departments, celebrate company milestones).

☐ **Improve a Particular Function Statement**

We will improve the quality of our . . . . We will (FUNCTION OR DEPARTMENT) hire a new, experienced person to revamp this department. We will set new standards of expectations for this area. We will carefully review the performance of each person in the department. And we will carefully monitor the department as a whole.

☐ **Lower Employee Turnover Statement**

We will decrease employee turnover to less than . . . . . % per year, by (increasing (%) the frequency of employee reviews, revamping our benefits program, by making our wages more competitive, starting an employee bonus program, hiring a human resources manager, holding exit interviews to identify and reduce the reasons that employees are leaving).

OPERATIONSOPERATIONSOPERATIONS

Product/Service Delivery

There are many different ways in which you can approach the discussion of product or service delivery. One approach is to emphasize the steps that you will take to insure that your product or service delivery supports either your business strategy or your product or service positioning strategy. Another approach is to simply summarize how you plan on producing products or delivering services. Still another approach may be to discuss standards you will use.

Select and edit the <u>one or more</u> statements that best apply.

☐ **Basic Product/Service Delivery Statement**

We intend that our . . . . delivery will support our
(PRODUCT OR SERVICE)

positioning plan for our . . . . which is to
(PRODUCT OR SERVICE)

. . . . . (IDENTIFY POSITIONING STRATEGY AS DESCRIBED IN EARLIER PARTS OF THIS BUSINESS PLAN) . . . . . . To meet

this objective we will . . . .

. . . .

☐ **Description of Product Development Approach Statement**

Before giving the go ahead on a new product we will (get customer feedback, do market surveys, do a feasibility study, do a focus group, research comparative offerings). The decision to proceed will be largely based on the following factors . . .

. . . .

The actual (design, engineering, development) of the product will be done by . . .

. . . .

OPERATIONSOPERATIONSOPERATIONS

The following manufacture will be done (by a contract manufacturer, at our facility at, by arrangement with, at . . . .

. . . .

company).

☐ **Description of Service Standards Approach Statement**

These are some of the standards we will use to help insure that we provide high quality service:

1. We will answer our phones within 3 rings.
2. We will provide a free, written estimate within 72 hours.
3. We will begin work within 7 days of receiving a signed agreement.
4. We will not interrupt work for any reason until we finish a job.
5. We will use the highest quality materials available.
6. We will leave the work area clean and neat at the end of each day.
7. We will follow-up after every job to be sure the customer is satisfied.
8. We will guarantee satisfaction for all of our work.

EXPERT ADVICE

Product/Service Delivery

This section focuses on the nitty-gritty of how you are going to fulfill your product/service strategy. It's one thing to say your products or services will be great in one way or another—it's quite another to make it happen. There are many different things that you could discuss in this section. For a new business however, I would suggest that you focus on how your product/service delivery will be different from your competitors. And for an existing business, I would suggest that you focus on possible changes to your product/service delivery.

OPERATIONSOPERATIONSOPERATIONS

☐ **Controlling Costs Statement**

We will control costs by (keeping our labor costs low, getting competitive bids on major purchases, arranging for a long-term delivery contract, using just-in-time inventory methods, watching overhead costs closely, checking variances with budget each month, offering employee's awards for cost-saving ideas, instituting a gain-sharing program, benchmarking all costs with industry standards).

☐ **Quality Control Statement**

We will insure that our quality is high by (having a specific quality control program, having specific standards that must be adhered to, doing spot checks, selecting high quality vendors, double-checking crucial steps, having a rigorous hiring process, appointing a quality control manager, having . . . .

. . . .

personally inspect each job, communicating to all employees that quality is our first priority, benchmark our offerings with those of competitors, conducting customer surveys, making follow-up calls after each assignment).

☐ **State of the Art Focused Statement**

Supporting our strategic goal of being on the cutting edge in new product development is a multifaceted process. To keep our employees up to speed with the latest developments we will (attend seminars, attend trade conferences, meet regularly with outside experts, maintain close relations with universities, subscribe to the appropriate journals, have outside experts give in-house presentations, hire expert consultants, obtain research information from other firms, pursue a joint development project with . . . .

. . . . ,

enter licensing agreements).

☐ Delivering Quality, Personalized Service Statement

In order to deliver high quality, personalized service we will (carefully select all employees, put each employee through a careful training process, make sure each employee understands our way of delivering quality service to each customer, have immediate backup support available for more difficult service issues, give employees enough latitude so that they can respond immediately to almost all customer requests, base employee compensation largely upon customer satisfaction).

☐ Using Computers to Cut Inventory Needs Statement

We will use our computer and software systems to closely monitor inventory requirements. This will allow us to effectively operate with much lower levels of inventory that has been the case in the past—without increasing the risk of stock outs.

☐ Selecting Suppliers Not Just on Price Statement

In the past we have largely selected suppliers on the basis of price. This has produced several problems which we would like to avoid in the future. So now we are using additional criteria for choosing suppliers and assigning outside work. For work involving a cost greater than $ . . . . . , we are adding the following criteria for
(\$)

OPERATIONSOPERATIONSOPERATIONS

the selection of suppliers . . . .

. . . .

For suppliers under a cost of $ . . . . . the additional criteria will be limited to . . . .

(\$)

. . . .

☐ **Relationships with Suppliers Statement**

We believe that maintaining excellent relationships with our suppliers is an impor-

tant part of successfully delivering our . . CEILING SYSTEMS . . . . We pay

(PRODUCTS OR SERVICES)

our suppliers within terms; we treat their sales people and customer service people

with respect; we maintain a relationship with key executives at our core suppliers;

and we let our suppliers know that we appreciate their work. Because of these steps,

our suppliers are willing to really go to bat for us when we need their extra help.

This is particularly important when (specifications must be changed at the last

minutes, we have a rush job, when schedules must be re-arranged, when we want

to meet the needs of a particularly demanding customer, etc.).

☐ WE WILL CONTROL COSTS BY GETTING COMPETITIVE
BIDS ON MAJOR COMPONENTS, USING JUST-IN-TIME
INVENTORY METHODS AND CHECKING VARIANCES WITH
BUDGET EACH MONTH.

OPERATIONSOPERATIONSOPERATIONS

Customer Service/Support

Customer service is an increasingly important aspect of running a successful business. Some organizations make it a centerpiece of their marketing campaigns. Will you handle all aspects of customer service in-house, or will you outsource some of it, to a fulfillment service, for example? If you intend to pay significant attention to customer service, describe how you will do it. Will it be a part of on-going training programs? Will you devise special employee incentives? Will you make an effort to solicit feedback from the customers, and if so, how?

Select and edit <u>one or more</u> statements that best apply.

☐ **Basic Customer/Service Support Statement**

Customer service/support will be handled by . . . .

. . . .

During our normal business hours calls will be handled by the

. . . . (POSITION) . During nonbusiness hours

calls will be taken by . . . .

. . . .

Since customer service/support is an integral part of our business, we will strive to keep our customers satisfied at all times. We will give particular effort to *RETURNING CALLS THAT*

DAY, AS SOON AS WE GOT THE VOICE MESSAGE. WE WILL ALSO TRY NOT TO SAY "NO" TO OUR CUSTOMERS SPECIAL REQUESTS. WE WILL TURN QUOTES AROUND IN 72 HOURS, APPROVAL DRAWINGS IN TWO WEEKS, AND SHIP PRODUCT IN FIVE WEEKS.

EXPERT ADVICE

Customer Service/Support

As the world becomes more and more competitive, customer service and support is becoming an increasingly important grounds for competition. In fact, many firms view customer service/support as an opportunity to market additional products and services to customers. Hence it is important that no matter how small your business that you have a specific, coherent plan for service/support.

OPERATIONSOPERATIONSOPERATIONS

☐ **Improve Customer Service Statement**

We seek to improve our customer service by taking the following steps: (decrease waiting time at our peak service periods, adding some support capability to our World Wide Web site, offering support by e-mail, offering support by fax, offering a fax-back program, expanding our phone capacity, installing a voice mail system, increasing our hours, outsourcing our service, monitoring occasional service calls, seeking customer input, installing toll free customer service lines).

☐ **Customer Service Plan: New Business Statement**

We intend to prioritize customer service and make it a key component of our marketing programs. We believe that providing our customers with what they want, when and how they want it, is the key to repeat business and to word-of-mouth advertising. Not only will we train our employees to deliver excellent service, we will give them the flexibility to respond creatively to client requests. In addition, we will continually monitor our clients' level of satisfaction with our service through surveys and other convenient feedback opportunities.

☐ **Fulfillment: Existing Business Statement**

The new internal information systems to be deployed will have an extremely positive impact on the order fulfillment process. In the past, too much time was wasted in an inefficient order communication process. Now, we expect to reduce order processing time by .... , which will result in faster shipping and higher levels of customer satisfaction.
(AMOUNT OF TIME)

OPERATIONSOPERATIONSOPERATIONS

☐ **Customer Service: Existing Business Statement**

We have discovered that our customer service standards have not kept pace with the levels of service now offered by some of our competitors. Therefore we have designed an extensive employee training program, involving everyone from
.... to ...., with the
(POSITION TITLE)   (POSITION TITLE)
goal of ....
(MEASURABLE GOAL)

☐ **Customer Service: New Business Statement**

An important part of our operating plan is to make contact with customers after the sale/services are rendered. We believe that new sources of revenue can be developed through additional post-sale services, and that our client base can be more effectively retained through this approach.

☐ **Customer Service: Shipping Statement**

Our relatively high cost of shipping has put us at a competitive disadvantage. The current cost of shipping for an average order is $ ......, which we feel can be
($)
reduced by ..... %. We intend to achieve this cost reduction by putting our over-
(%)
all shipping requirements out to bid.

☐ **Using the World Wide Web Statement**

We plan on using the World Wide Web for a significant portion of our service/support effort. On the web we can offer support 24 hours a day, 365 days a year. And on the Web, customers don't have to wait for the next available service representative. Once the service area of our Web site is up, the cost to maintain it will be

OPERATIONSOPERATIONSOPERATIONS

minimal. On our Web site we plan on offering (a choice of text options explaining basic service issues, lists of other resources for help, lists of frequently asked questions and answers, a extensive searchable database of service/support information, the ability to e-mail for help with highly specific questions, current postings of newly discovered service issues).

☐ **Order Turnaround Statement**

We shall turn around all orders in a maximum of . . . .

by . . . .

. . . .

In order to accomplish this we will need to . . . .

. . . .

☐ **Decrease Service Call Time Statement**

We will decrease the time spent of the average service call by about . . . .

. . . .

We will accomplish this by . . . .

. . . .

☐ **Response to Service Calls Statement**

We shall generally respond to service calls within . . . .

. . . .

Even during busier periods we intend to respond no later than . . . .

. . . .

OPERATIONSOPERATIONSOPERATIONS

Emergency or high priority calls we intend to respond to within . . . .

. . . .

☐ **Decrease Waiting Time Statement**

We intend to decrease our average waiting time for (incoming calls, service calls, support calls, our customers). We hope to decrease our response time from typically . . . .

to . . . . by . . . .
                                                           (DATE)

OPERATIONSOPERATIONSOPERATIONS

Facilities

Your location and the facility itself may be an important aspect of your company's business. Describe the advantages and disadvantages of the location. What kind of a facility is it? Will clients be coming there? What kind of equipment will be there, and how will it be furnished? Be sure that you take future growth into account. For how long will this facility be adequate?

Select and edit the <u>one or more</u> statements that best apply.

☐ **Basic Facilities Statement: Existing Business Statement**

The company currently (owns/leases) .... square feet of space located at
        (# OF)
.... This space is used as the primary production facility as
(ADDRESS/CITY, STATE)
well as the main office and administrative headquarters. The total number of full-
or part-time employees working in this facility is ...... , for a square footage per
        (#)
person of .... This facility will continue to meet all of our needs during the
    (#)
remaining period of the current lease, which ends in .... There is an option
        (DATE)
to renew at the end of this period, which we expect to do. If more space is needed
then, additional space is expected to be available nearby at approximately the same
price per square foot.

☐ **Basic Facilities Statement: New Business**

As a service business, the location of our facility and the professional image it presents are essential parts of our marketing strategy. Since our target market is

OPERATIONSOPERATIONSOPERATIONS

. . . . , we feel that our company needs to be locat-
(TARGET MARKET)

ed near other businesses that serve a similar demographic profile,
preferably with parking and public transportation facilities nearby. Rental fees in the range of . . . . . to . . . . . is another impor-
                                    ($)   ($)
tant factor. In the city of . . . . , satisfying
                              (LOCATION)
these criteria means one of the following areas or neighborhoods:

. . . . , ... , or
(NEIGHBORHOOD)   (NEIGHBORHOOD)

. . . .
(NEIGHBORHOOD)

☐ **Home Office Statement**

This business will be operated out of a home office, primarily in
order to reduce expenditures. ~~The space to be utilized for this~~

[handwritten note:] THE OFFICE IS PERFECTLY ADEQUATE SINCE ALL OPERATIONS ARE "BEHIND THE SCENE". CUSTOMERS ARE CONTACTED BY PHONE OR FAX AND THERE IS NO NEED FOR THEM TO PERSONALLY VISIT THE OFFICE. ALL PRODUCTION OPERATIONS WILL BE OUTSOURCED TO LOCAL FABRICATORS, ~~AND~~ SUPPLIERS AND PAINTERS. SINCE MATERIALS WILL BE PURCHASED ON A JUST-IN-TIME FASHION, NO INVENTORY SPACE WILL BE REQUIRED.

☐

(ADDRESS, CITY/TOWN)

EXPERT ADVICE

Facilities

The relative importance of your facilities and the key factors in your facilities will vary dramatically from one business to the next. For a retailer, a highly visible, high-traffic location will probably be essential. For a wholesale operation, which typically has a small profit margin but large space requirements, a low price per square foot may be the ... : Identify the key fac- ... business and stick to ... execute your business ... ber, very few busi- ... re A quality offices— ... gle business requires ... ve.

OPERATIONSOPERATIONSOPERATIONS

our parameters for all of the criteria. With the presence of . . . .
(OTHER RETAILER)
and . . . . in the immediate vicinity, the traffic level is
(OTHER RETAILER)
already high, over . . . . . . cars per day, but not higher than the existing roadways
(# OF)
can handle smoothly. The location is very accessible, and there is ample parking
available. According to the most recent U.S. Census data, the median household
income for the relevant Standard Metropolitan Statistical Area (SMSA) is also very
attractive over $ . . . . . per year. The rent, $ . . . . . per square foot, is at the high end
(\$)   (\$)
of our acceptable range, but still falls within our target parameters.

☐ **Equipment Statement**

A limited amount of specialized equipment is utilized at the facility to (to test,
manufacture, design, package, etc.). including . . . . ,
(EQUIPMENT #1)
. . . . , and . . . . Approximately . . . . . .
(EQUIPMENT #2)   (EQUIPMENT #3)   (# OF)
square feet is required for this operation. In addition to this production equipment, there are over . . . . . . computers in use for applications ranging from
(# OF)
order entry and inventory control to word processing and graphics. Office equipment present at the facility includes . . . . . . copy machines, ... scanners,
(# OF)   (# OF)
and . . . . . . printers.
(# OF)

☐ **Furnishings and Fixtures Statement**

We will be renting an unfurnished facility, and will need to acquire furniture
which will create a professional look and a contemporary feel, since clients will be
coming to the office on a regular basis. In order to reduce initial expenditures, we

OPERATIONSOPERATIONSOPERATIONS

plan to lease these furnishings, which will include desks, chairs, lighting, cabinets, framed works of modern art, potted plants, and a sofa and easy chairs for the waiting area.

☐ Relocation Statement

Our market research shows that the current location of our facility, ..., is one of the primary factors holding back our revenue
(ADDRESS, CITY OR TOWN)
growth. The basic problem with the location is ....
(CURRENT PROBLEM)
After considering several options to address this problem, we have decided to relocate to a new facility at .... This new space offers
(ADDRESS, CITY OR TOWN)
a number of significant advantages over our current location, including

....
(ADVANTAGES)

☐ Expansion Statement

The company's current facility is not large enough to accommodate the new size and scope of the business. We are utilizing ...... square feet at the present time,
(# OF)
and plan to move to a new facility offering at least ...... square feet, which
(# OF)
meets current and anticipated needs for the foreseeable future.

☐ Increase Capacity of Facilities Statement

We will increase the capacity of our (plant, warehouse, office, etc.). We will accomplish this by (using a more efficient floor plan, by using shared offices, by building an addition, by leasing additional space, by moving to a new location).

OPERATIONSOPERATIONSOPERATIONS

☐ **Increase Utilization of Facilities Statement**

We will improve the utilization of our (plant, warehouse, offices, facility, building). We will re-organize the layout to be more efficient, and to be a more effective place to work. We will do this by . . . .

☐ **New Facilities: Existing Business Statement**

Continued growth of our business demands that we increase the number of locations. Our current facilities are located in . . . . Based on
(LOCATION)
research into our current customer base and other parts of the greater metropolitan area with a similar demographic profile, we are planning to open satellite offices in . . . . in . . . . and . . . . in
(AREA)   (MONTH, YEAR)   (AREA)
. . . .
(MONTH, YEAR)

☐ **Facility Improvements Statement**

We plan on making improvements to our current facility in order to (improve our capacity, to accommodate more employees, to make for a more efficient work flow, to make for a more attractive work environment, to make the work environment more consistent with our business image). **These are the specific steps we plan on taking** . . . .

OPERATIONSOPERATIONSOPERATIONS

☐ **Create a More Professional Work Environment Statement**

We will create a more professional work environment. To do this we will (improve the landscaping, clean up the grounds, get new company signs, improve the entrance way, get a new receptionist work station, get new furniture, repaint the walls, buy new or used office cubicles, carpet the floors, encourage everyone to clean up their work area, set up a conference room).

☐ **Upgrade Equipment Statement**

We intend to upgrade the following office equipment: (personal computers, servers, computer printers, phone system, voice mail, copiers, fax machines, postage meters, shipping equipment).

☐ **Automate Functions Statement**

We will automate the following function(s) . . . .

. . . .

We will achieve this by . . . .

. . . .

☐ **Enhance Web Site Statement**

We will expand the capability of our Web site to include (customer support, job postings, product information, complete product catalog, news releases, internal news letters, etc.).

OPERATIONSOPERATIONSOPERATIONS

☐ **Paperless Office Statement**

We will move to a virtually paperless office by .... To do this we will
(ENTER DATE)
need the following additional equipment . . . .

. . . .

CHAPTER 15

Preparing the Financials

PREPARING THE FINANCIALS

Getting started with financial forecasting

Preparing financial forecasts may at first seem like an overwhelming task. However if you are extremely careful and meticulous, and follow the step-by-step guidance in this book very carefully, you can create complete financial forecasts even if you have no previous financial experience.

Some aspects of financial forecasting are relatively easy—such as creating the profit and loss forecast. In fact for a very simple business (such as an unincorporated, part-time business that does not sell on credit, has no inventory, will not need to borrow money and does not plan on significantly expanding) you may only need to create a profit and loss statement to run your business.

But for most businesses you will need to forecast future balance sheets and cash flows. Creating these forecasts is, frankly, not an easy task, especially if you sell on credit or have inventory and do not have a lot of financial experience. But you can do it you follow the advice in this book carefully, and allow yourself an adequate amount of time to perform and carefully double-check the more difficult calculations. I believe that I have explained how to create financials at least as carefully and simply as any other resource on this topic.

If you are in a rush to complete your financials or you don't want to bother to learn how to do all the calculations, you can always order our interactive software that automatically calculates profit and loss projections, cash flow projections, balance sheet projections and key ratio's (Adams Streetwise Business Plan Software—see the ad in the back of this book). But of course if you use software to create your financials you won't learn as much in the process (it would kind of be like cheating in school).

> You can prepare your own financials even if you do not have financial experience.

PREPARING THE FINANCIALS

What financials do you need to create?

If you're planning a really simple business—I suggest you only create profit and loss projections—and save yourself all of the trouble of creating the more difficult cash flow and balance sheet projections.

However, there are very few businesses that are simple enough to only do profit and loss forecasting. In fact I feel that only a part-time home-based business that is unincorporated, does not sell on credit, has no inventory, will not need to borrow money and does not plan on significantly expanding, should only create profit and loss projections.

If your business does not meet the above criteria it is very important that you carefully project cash flow and future balance sheets otherwise your business could get into deep financial trouble and you may not find out soon enough to save it.

So virtually all businesses should create the following forecasts (also called pro-forma's):

- Profit and Loss
- Cash Flow
- Balance Sheets

For most situations I would suggest that you project all of the above pro-forma's (profit and loss, cash flow and balance sheets) on a monthly basis for the next 12 months and on an annual basis for the following two years. By only doing monthly calculations for the next 12 months you can save yourself a lot of calculations and still satisfy the requirements of just about any lender or investor. For a very small business, such as under $500,000 in annual sales I might only project 12 months in the

> All but the small businesses need to create projected cash flows and balance sheets, in addition to profit and loss statements.

PREPARING THE FINANCIALS

future and not beyond. For a business larger than $10 million you may want to project further into the future.

You will also need to create a page listing called "Assumptions and Comments" which details the key assumptions or other comments that relate to your financials. You will need to provide a Starting Balance Sheet showing the current financial status of the company. And if you have an existing business you will need to provide lenders or investors with any previous (or historical) financial statements.

Finally you can complete your financial statements with a summary of "Key Ratio's" which are ratio's based on the financials that gauge the financial health of the company.

Adapting these financials to your own purposes

The financials in this book are designed for a small business with all of the financial issues that a small business may be likely to face. However, some parts of the financials may not be relevant for your business. If a particular item is not relevant for your business you can just leave the item blank or delete the row. For example if your business is a service business and does not have inventory—then just ignore any reference to inventory.

Using Computer Spreadsheets

If you choose to assemble your own financial projection spreadsheets you may find it highly worthwhile to construct them very carefully upfront and make them interact as much as possible with each other, because this will save you time when you make revisions. And my experience is that you will end up making more revisions than think you will when you get started! One of the advantages of using The Adams Streetwise Small Business Software is that you can make a change on one financial and it

> Including key ratios makes your plan look more complete.

PREPARING THE FINANCIALS

automatically makes all of the relevant changes on the other financial projections. Financial spreadsheets created in our software can also be exported to both Excel and Lotus.

Follow this sequence in Creating your Financials:

1. Assumptions and Comments Worksheet
2. Starting Balance Sheet
3. Profit and Loss Forecast
4. Cash Flow Forecast
5. Balance Sheet Forecast
6. Key Ratio's

It is important to follow the above sequence in working on your financial statements. This is the sequence I will be following in this book—and I have found this sequence to be highly effective in teaching people how to assemble financial statements.

Remember however that if you later make a change to your Assumptions and Comments worksheet it will affect results for all relevant numbers in the other financial statements. For example if you reduce your payroll tax rate, you will reduce your expenses on your Profit and Loss projection, reduce your use of funds on your Cash Flow Projection, increase the equity on your Balance Sheet Projection and change your Key Ratio's. So be sure that you are satisfied with your input on each worksheet before proceeding to the next one. And if you go back and make a change on any worksheet make sure that you make appropriate changes on all other worksheets that may be effected.

Follow this sequence in preparing your financials.

PREPARING THE FINANCIALS

Assumptions and Comments

The financials should support the text of your business plan, help you to run your business better, and help you to get financing, if needed.

The trap many people fall into in creating financials, however, is to get hopelessly buried in small details such as creating long lists of office supplies or getting frustrated trying to figure out the latest rules on depreciating assets. Instead, I suggest you make your best quick estimate on less important smaller numbers and give more thought to the numbers that really matter. Of course if you want to, you can always go back later and do a more careful estimate on any particular entry.

Examples of some of the numbers that really matter (and that potential financiers are likely to ask you about) are your sales projection, the average number of days on which you expect to get paid, your profit margins, and when and how you are going to repay any debt.

Expert Advice on Assumptions and Comments

In starting a new business, you can't expect to be 100 percent comfortable with your answers to the assumptions. That is one reason that they are called assumptions and not "certainties" and why you clearly identify your major assumptions for all readers to see. But as you go through the assumptions, keep in mind which assumptions may turn out to be way off and significantly impact your financials. For example, let's say you estimate freight at 1 percent of sales and it actually comes in at 1.5 percent—50 percent over projection. Unless you have a very thin profit margin, this will not dramatically change your financials. On the other hand, if your cost of goods sold is projected to be 20 percent, but actually comes in at 30 percent— then your financials will clearly be dramatically impacted.

> Focus more carefully on the numbers that really matter.

PREPARING THE FINANCIALS

Credit Assumptions

If you are selling on credit, the most important assumption will probably be the number of days you anticipate to get paid in. Potential financiers, especially bankers, are likely to ask you about this assumption. People starting a new business tend to consistently underestimate how long it will take to get paid (and how much effort it will take to get paid). Let's say that your stated terms are "net 30." Chances are that many, if not most, customers will pay you after 30 days. So you need to be sure that you have a good plan for getting paid—and that you are using a realistic estimate for the number of days you anticipate to get paid in.

Payables Assumptions

On the other hand, if you are a new business, you may find it very difficult to get credit at all for your purchases—and if you can you may be held to very strict credit terms.

A Challenging Financial Hurdle

The difficulty of timely payment collection from customers, combined with the difficulty of getting credit from suppliers, can create a challenging financial hurdle for a new business.

Comments

Besides the basic assumptions here, I would recommend that except for a multimillion dollar financing proposal you keep your additional comments to an absolute minimum. Potential financiers know that you have to make a huge number of assumptions in planning a new or growing business—they want to know about only your most critical assumptions. They are looking to finance your business, not to run it.

A new business can not assume that all suppliers will grant credit.

Name of Plan: . . . .

Starting Month: $ . . . .

Starting Year: $ . . . .

Years Covered by Plan: $ . . . .

Commissions: . . . . %

Freight Costs: . . . . %

Payroll Tax Rate: $ . . . .

Income Tax Rate: $ . . . .

Days Inventory: $ . . . .

Cost of Sales: . . . . %

Credit Sales: . . . . %

Days Credit: $ . . . .

Cost of Sales A/P: . . . . %

Cost of Sales Days A/P: $ . . . .

General A/P: . . . . %

Days General A/P: $ . . . .

S-T Interest Rate: . . . . %

L-T Interest Rate: . . . . %

Comments . . . .

. . . .

. . . .

. . . .

. . . .

. . . .

. . . .

. . . .

PREPARING THE FINANCIALS

Filling in the Assumptions

Name of Plan

What is the Name of the plan to be used in page headers on financial reports?

If this is the final copy of your plan for presentation you may want to enter the name of your business on it or you may choose to leave it blank. If you are still working on your rough drafts of your financials this line allows you to clearly label each draft, i.e. draft1, draft2, etc.

Starting Month

What is the Starting Month of the plan?

Enter the starting month of the plan. This, in most instances, should reflect the beginning of your fiscal year.

Starting Year

What is the Starting Year of the plan? (e.g. 1999)

Enter the starting year of the plan.

Years Covered by Plan

What is the Number of Years to be covered by plan?

You can choose to run your plan for 1, 2, 3, 4 or 5 years. Most people create business plans for either one, two or three years. In this fast changing world projections more than 12 months in the future have increasingly little accuracy. The business plan financials are broken out by month for the first year, total for the first year, and then by totals for subsequent years.

ASSUMPTIONS AND COMMENTS

Name of Plan: _____
Starting Month: _____
Starting Year: _____
Years Covered by Plan: _____

Commissions:	0.0%
Freight Costs:	0.0%
Payroll Tax Rate:	0
Income Tax Rate:	0
Days Inventory:	0
Cost of Sales:	0.0%
Credit Sales:	0.0%
Days Credit:	0
Cost of Sales A/P:	0.0%
Cost of Sales Days A/P:	0
General A/P:	0.0%
Days General A/P:	0
S-T Interest Rate:	0.0%
L-T Interest Rate:	0.0%

Comments _____
_____
_____
_____

PREPARING THE FINANCIALS

ASSUMPTIONS AND COMMENTS

Name of Plan: _____
Starting Month: _____
Starting Year: _____
Years Covered by Plan: _____

Commissions: **0.0%**
Freight Costs: **0.0%**
Payroll Tax Rate: **0**

Income Tax Rate: 0
Days Inventory: 0
Cost of Sales: 0.0%
Credit Sales: 0.0%
Days Credit: 0
Cost of Sales A/P: 0.0%
Cost of Sales Days A/P: 0
General A/P: 0.0%
Days General A/P: 0
S-T Interest Rate: 0.0%
L-T Interest Rate: 0.0%

Comments _____
_____
_____
_____

Commissions
What percentage of sales will sales Commissions be?

If your business pays sales commissions enter the average amount here. If you do not pay commissions, enter 0. If your business uses dedicated sales staff or pays out finders fees, what percentage does it represent? If you're not sure divide the total commission paid by your sales for the past year.

Freight Costs
What percentage of sales will Freight costs run?

If your business pays freight or delivery costs enter the average amount here, as a percentage of sales. If you do not have freight costs, enter 0. If you figure freight costs into your cost of goods sold it will be accounted for in inventory value—do not enter it here.

Payroll Tax Rate
What percentage of gross payroll will the Employer's Share of Payroll Taxes plus the cost of employee benefits run?

Here you should estimate all of the employer's share of payroll taxes that you will pay plus any fringe benefits such as health care costs, life insurance, etc. Payroll taxes vary with a lot of different factors such as your firm's unemployment rating, the level of pay of each employee and so many other factors that trying to get an exact estimate can be a tedious chore. So you may want to take a rough estimate of the employer's share of payroll taxes,

PREPARING THE FINANCIALS

say 13%, and add on an additional percentage for fringe benefits.

Income Tax Rate

What percentage of net income do you estimate all Income Taxes (city, state, federal) will run?

A quick way to roughly estimate your tax rate is to take your estimated federal and state tax rate (and local if applicable) and add them together. (i.e. 30% estimated federal tax rate plus 10% estimated state tax rate adds up to a 40% total tax rate.) Note, if you want to be more precise you could take into consideration that currently in the United States the state income tax is deductible from the federal income tax.

Days Inventory

How many Days of Inventory (in other words how many days of sales it would take to exhaust the inventory if it were not replenished) you will stock?

If you believe your amount of inventory on hand will vary between 30 and 60 days inventory on hand, we suggest you follow one of two alternatives. Our first recommendation would be to simply use the average amount of 45 for your Days of Inventory. In your assumptions accompanying your business plan you can state your inventory assumption. Or you could create three scenarios, varying the Days of Inventory from 30 to 45 to 60.

Having inventory will significantly complicate your business planning process. So for example if you are running a house painting service and you buy paint more or

---

ASSUMPTIONS AND COMMENTS

Name of Plan:	_____
Starting Month:	_____
Starting Year:	_____
Years Covered by Plan:	_____
Commissions:	0.0%
Freight Costs:	0.0%
Payroll Tax Rate:	0
Income Tax Rate:	**0**
Days Inventory:	**0**
Cost of Sales:	0.0%
Credit Sales:	0.0%
Days Credit:	0
Cost of Sales A/P:	0.0%
Cost of Sales Days A/P:	0
General A/P:	0.0%
Days General A/P:	0
S-T Interest Rate:	0.0%
L-T Interest Rate:	0.0%

Comments _____
_____
_____
_____

PREPARING THE FINANCIALS

ASSUMPTIONS AND COMMENTS

Name of Plan:	_____
Starting Month:	_____
Starting Year:	_____
Years Covered by Plan:	_____
Commissions:	0.0%
Freight Costs:	0.0%
Payroll Tax Rate:	0
Income Tax Rate:	0
Days Inventory:	0
Cost of Sales:	**0.0%**
Credit Sales:	0.0%
Days Credit:	0
Cost of Sales A/P:	0.0%
Cost of Sales Days A/P:	0
General A/P:	0.0%
Days General A/P:	0
S-T Interest Rate:	0.0%
L-T Interest Rate:	0.0%

Comments _____

_____

_____

_____

less for each job but do not stockpile large quantities of paint, I would recommend that you do not consider the paint to be inventory—but instead an expense item. In other words, as soon as you buy the paint I would consider it expensed and I would not consider it to be inventory on hand. (On your tax returns however you technically should include unused paint as an asset.)

Cost of Sales

What percentage of sales will cost of sales (inventory) be?

Cost of sales are your direct costs of the materials or services that you have sold. For a manufacturing business you would include the costs of the product you are making. You will want to include all expenses that are related such as salaries of manufacturing personnel, raw materials, etc. For a retailer or wholesaler cost of sales is the cost you incurred for products that you have sold, not the cost of products still remaining in inventory.

For a service business, cost of sales is your direct expenses of providing your service, which would typically consist largely of labor costs—that is, the labor costs of the people who are directly providing the service, not the support staff. For a restaurant, cost of sales is the cost of the food and beverages that you purchase.

Cost of Sales does not include costs that are not directly incorporated in a finished product or service. For example, marketing costs such as advertising, literature, and sales commissions are not considered costs of sales.

PREPARING THE FINANCIALS

General and administrative expenses, building rent, utilities, and insurance are also not costs of sales.

For costs that you include under costs of sales be sure not to include them in any other categories such as payroll.

Credit Sales %

Enter % of your sales that will be made on credit. Enter 0 if you will not make sales on credit.

Most non-retail businesses will be at or near 100% credit for this question. Retail businesses may be near 100% cash.

Days Credit

How many days will credit customers take on average to pay you. Enter 0 if you will not make sales on credit.

Enter the average number of days that credit customers will pay you. Don't include in the average the fact that cash customers will pay you instantly, because your cash sales payments will be calculated separately.

If you believe your average amount of days it takes credit customers to pay will vary, such as between 30 and 60 days, we suggest you follow one of two alternatives. Our first recommendation would be to simply use the average amount of 45 for your days credit assumption. Or you could create three scenarios, varying the days of credit assumption from 30 to 45 to 60.

ASSUMPTIONS AND COMMENTS

Name of Plan:	_____
Starting Month:	_____
Starting Year:	_____
Years Covered by Plan:	_____
Commissions:	0.0%
Freight Costs:	0.0%
Payroll Tax Rate:	0
Income Tax Rate:	0
Days Inventory:	0
Cost of Sales:	0.0%
Credit Sales:	**0.0%**
Days Credit:	**0**
Cost of Sales A/P:	0.0%
Cost of Sales Days A/P:	0
General A/P:	0.0%
Days General A/P:	0
S-T Interest Rate:	0.0%
L-T Interest Rate:	0.0%

Comments _____
_____
_____
_____

PREPARING THE FINANCIALS

Cost of Sales A/P %

What percentage of Cost of Sales expenses will be paid for on credit.

For example, if you buy 25% of your inventory or other cost of sales expenses on credit then enter "25".

For this answer focus only on credit for Cost of Sales expenses, not marketing or general administrative expenses.

Days Cost of Sales A/P

How many days will you take to pay for Cost of Sales expenses?

Enter the average number of days that you will pay for inventory or other Cost of Sales expenses that you buy on credit. Don't include in the average any items that you pay for in cash because cash purchases will be calculated separately.

If you believe the average amount of days it takes you to pay for inventory or Cost of Sales expenses varies, such as from 30 to 60 days, we suggest one of the two alternatives. Our first recommendation would be to simply use the average amount of 45 for your days. In your assumptions accompanying your business plan you can state this assumption. Or you could create three scenarios, varying the days you take to pay for direct cost items from 30 to 45 to 60.

General A/P %

What percentage of non-cost of sales (or non-inventory) items or services will be bought on credit?

PREPARING THE FINANCIALS

For example if you buy 75% of non-payroll-related and non-cost of sales items on credit enter "75."

This item includes most non-inventory and non-cost of sales expenses. It includes most marketing and general and administrative costs, but it does not include payroll costs and non-operating costs and depreciation and income taxes.

Days General A/P

How many days will you take to pay for non-cost of sales items or services that you will buy on credit?

Enter the average number of days that you will take to pay for non-cost of sales items or services that you buy on credit. Don't include in the average any items that you pay for in cash because cash purchases will be calculated separately.

S-T Interest Rate

What do you estimate your annual interest rate will be for short-term debt?

Make your best estimate of what your bank or other lender will charge you for short-term loans. If you have no idea, look in today's paper to find the current prime rate and add 2.00 percentage points to it. Bankers and equity lenders are very current with interest rates so if you must estimate, estimate slightly conservatively.

L-T Interest Rate

What do you estimate your annual interest rate will be for long-term debt?

ASSUMPTIONS AND COMMENTS

Name of Plan:	_____
Starting Month:	_____
Starting Year:	_____
Years Covered by Plan:	_____
Commissions:	0.0%
Freight Costs:	0.0%
Payroll Tax Rate:	0
Income Tax Rate:	0
Days Inventory:	0
Cost of Sales:	0.0%
Credit Sales:	0.0%
Days Credit:	0
Cost of Sales A/P:	0.0%
Cost of Sales Days A/P:	0
General A/P:	0.0%
Days General A/P:	**0**
S-T Interest Rate:	**0.0%**
L-T Interest Rate:	**0.0%**

Comments _____

_____

_____

_____

PREPARING THE FINANCIALS

ASSUMPTIONS AND COMMENTS

Name of Plan:	_____
Starting Month:	_____
Starting Year:	_____
Years Covered by Plan:	_____
Commissions:	0.0%
Freight Costs:	0.0%
Payroll Tax Rate:	0
Income Tax Rate:	0
Days Inventory:	0
Cost of Sales:	0.0%
Credit Sales:	0.0%
Days Credit:	0
Cost of Sales A/P:	0.0%
Cost of Sales Days A/P:	0
General A/P:	0.0%
Days General A/P:	0
S-T Interest Rate:	0.0%
L-T Interest Rate:	0.0%

Comments _____

_____

_____

_____

Make your best estimate of what your bank or other lender will charge you for long-term loans. If you have no idea look in today's paper to find the current prime rate and add 3.00 percentage points to it. Bankers and equity lenders are very current with interest rates so if you must estimate, estimate slightly conservatively.

Comments

Comments are an important part of any business plan. Especially if you are seeking equity investment money, we suggest that you consult with a qualified business attorney for specific advice on comments that should accompany financials (and your business plan as a whole) in your particular situation. In any event, comments are important to identify any major assumptions not previously covered. Typical comments may include the following:

- All businesses have risks and hence there is no guarantee or assurance that the projections in these financials will be achieved.
- Sales projections are based upon the assumption of a . . . % market share
- Sales projections assume that the product will be completed by . . .
- Cost projections assume a . . .% inflation rate
- Depreciation costs assume a weighted average depreciation schedule of . . . years
- These projections assume that we will obtain $ . . . in financing by . . . .

PREPARING THE FINANCIALS

Starting Balance Sheet

What Have You Committed to the Business?

Both bankers and equity investors want to see how much money you and your partners have personally put into the business. They don't want to be investing or financing a business if the principals are not personally heavily invested in it. So specifically they will look to see how much equity is in the business.

What Are the Assets?

Beyond what you have committed to the business, investors and particularly bankers want to see what assets the business has. The more solid assets the business has, the better protection for their investment. Bankers particularly like fixed assets that they can seize in an absolute worst case scenario. They like to see cash, inventory, and accounts receivable as well, but they give secondary importance to these assets because they find that when a business starts to run into problems these "softer" assets tend to get expended as the business struggles to survive.

> Bankers particularly like to see fixed assets.

How Good Are the Accounts Receivable?

Bankers, especially, are likely to ask you how solid are your accounts receivable. They might ask for an aging, showing how much money is at 0–30 days, 30–60 days, 60–90 days, and over 90 days.

Are You Current on Your Payables?

Bankers will sometimes ask if you are current on your payables. Like many business people you may be paying beyond

PREPARING THE FINANCIALS

the stated terms, but still within a range that the vendor considers to be good enough to continue to extend you credit. So I would answer the banker that "we are paying vendors within terms that they consider acceptable." If you are way behind on payments to major vendors you should try to bring them into a range that the vendor considers acceptable before seeking financing.

Get a Credit Report

Also you should get a credit report on your business (and also on yourself personally) from a major credit reporting agency such as Dun & Bradstreet. Potential lenders often check these reports before lending. Clear up any disputes or problems on your credit reports before you apply for financing.

Be sure that your total assets equal your total liabilities plus equity

Basically the total liabilities and equity shows who has legal claim to the assets of the business. Hence the total liabilities and equity must always equal the total assets. And this is why a balance sheet is called a balance sheet.

Remember that a balance sheet is a snap shot of your business at one moment in time. This starting balance sheet should reflect your business at the date of the start of the business plan. Often the starting date on the business plan will be a future date. Hence the starting balance sheet will actually be a projection of what the starting balance sheet of the business will be on that future date.

> Getting a credit report can avoid embarrassing situations.

PREPARING THE FINANCIALS

Balance Sheet does not affect Profit and Loss Projection

The Starting Balance Sheet will not impact your profit and loss projection, but it will certainly impact your balance sheet projections and will generally impact your cash flow projections. So if you only want to prepare a profit and loss projection for your business, but no balance sheets or cash flows, then you could skip the starting balance sheet.

Starting Balance Sheet

Assets	Balance
Current Assets	
Cash	$ . . . .
Accounts Receivable	$ . . . .
Inventory	$ . . . .
Other Current Assets	$ . . . .
Total Current Assets	$ . . . .
Long Term Assets	
Depreciable Assets	$ . . . .
Accumulated Depreciation	$ . . . .
Net Depreciable Assets	$ . . . .
Non-Depreciable Assets	$ . . . .
Total Long-Term Assets	$ . . . .
Total Assets	$ . . . .

Liabilities & Equity

	Balance
Current Liabilities	
Cost of Sales A/P	$ . . . .
Non-Cost of Sales A/P	$ . . . .
Short-Term Debt	$ . . . .
Income Taxes Due	$ . . . .
Total Current Liabilities	$ . . . .
Long-Term Debt	$ . . . .
Equity	
Stock & Paid-in Capital	$ . . . .
Retained Earnings	$ . . . .
Total Equity	$ . . . .
Total Liabilities & Equity	$ . . . .

PREPARING THE FINANCIALS

Filling in the Starting Balance Sheet

Assets

Assets are anything that the business currently owns.

Current Assets

Current assets are assets that will be turned into cash within one year or may be converted to cash very quickly. Fixed assets such as equipment, buildings, machinery, etc. are not considered to be current assets even if you are planning to sell them in the near future.

Cash

Cash are your most liquid assets including checking accounts, money market funds, saving accounts.

Accounts Receivable

Accounts receivable is money owed your business by customers as the result of regular business transactions.

Inventory

Inventory includes finished goods, work in process, and raw material. If you entered 0 for cost of sales 0 must be your entry here, or if you entered 0 for days of inventory on hand enter 0 here.

STARTING BALANCE SHEET	
Assets	**Balance**
Current Assets	
Cash	**0**
Accounts Receivable	**0**
Inventory	**0**
Other Current Assets	0
Total Current Assets	0
Long Term Assets	
Depreciable Assets	0
Accumulated Depreciation	0
Net Depreciable Assets	0
Non-Depreciable Assets	0
Total Long-Term Assets	0
Total Assets	0
Liabilities & Equity	
Current Liabilities	
Cost of Sales A/P	0
Non-Cost of Sales A/P	0
Short-Term Debt	0
Income Taxes Due	0
Total Current Liabilities	0
Long-Term Debt	0
Equity	
Stock & Paid-in Capital	0
Retained Earnings	0
Total Equity	0
Total Liabilities & Equity	0

PREPARING THE FINANCIALS

STARTING BALANCE SHEET

Assets	Balance
Current Assets	
Cash	0
Accounts Receivable	0
Inventory	0
Other Current Assets	**0**
Total Current Assets	**0**
Long Term Assets	
Depreciable Assets	**0**
Accumulated Depreciation	**0**
Net Depreciable Assets	0
Non-Depreciable Assets	0
Total Long-Term Assets	0
Total Assets	0
	========
Liabilities & Equity	
Current Liabilities	
Cost of Sales A/P	0
Non-Cost of Sales A/P	0
Short-Term Debt	0
Income Taxes Due	0
Total Current Liabilities	0
Long-Term Debt	0
Equity	
Stock & Paid-in Capital	0
Retained Earnings	0
Total Equity	0
Total Liabilities & Equity	0
	========

Other Current Assets

Other current assets are all other current assets of the business. Examples to be included in this line include pre-paid rent, pre-paid taxes and pre-paid utilities.

Total Current Assets

Total current assets is calculated here by adding up cash, accounts receivable, inventory and other current assets.

Long-Term Assets

Long term assets are assets that are not easily turned into cash, that typically have useful lives greater than one year. Examples are such items as equipment, buildings, land, motor vehicles, etc.

Depreciable Assets

Depreciable assets are assets that depreciate over time such as equipment, motor vehicles, leasehold improvements and buildings. For this entry you should include your purchase price of the items, not their current market or book value.

Accumulated Depreciation

This entry includes all of the depreciation accumulated to date on all of your depreciable assets. As depreciable assets get older they loose value. For example a five-year-old truck has less value than a brand new truck.

Depreciation is an accounting figure that records the deterioration in value of equipment, motor vehicles,

PREPARING THE FINANCIALS

and buildings. Each of these items is assumed to lose a certain percentage of its value each year. Different accounting principles and tax laws apply to different categories of goods. For example you may be able to depreciate a car or truck over 3 years, a computer over 5 years, office furniture over 10 years, leasehold improvements over the life of the lease, buildings over 40 years.

So assuming that you are using simple straight-line depreciation, the matching monthly depreciation figures may be car or trucks: 1/36 of purchase price per month. For computers: 1/60 of purchase price per month; office furniture: 1/120 per month; buildings: 1/480 of purchase price per month.

Do not enter a negative number for accumulated depreciation as the spreadsheet is already formulated to subtract this item and a negative entry would result in the addition, not the subtraction of depreciation. Nor should you enter a percentage, this will result in erroneous data.

Net Depreciable Assets

Net depreciable assets is calculated by subtracting accumulated depreciation from depreciable assets.

Non-Depreciable Assets

Non-depreciable assets are long-term assets that do not depreciate such as land.

STARTING BALANCE SHEET	
Assets	Balance
Current Assets	
Cash	0
Accounts Receivable	0
Inventory	0
Other Current Assets	0
Total Current Assets	0
Long Term Assets	
Depreciable Assets	0
Accumulated Depreciation	0
Net Depreciable Assets	**0**
Non-Depreciable Assets	**0**
Total Long-Term Assets	0
Total Assets	0
Liabilities & Equity	
Current Liabilities	
Cost of Sales A/P	0
Non-Cost of Sales A/P	0
Short-Term Debt	0
Income Taxes Due	0
Total Current Liabilities	0
Long-Term Debt	0
Equity	
Stock & Paid-in Capital	0
Retained Earnings	0
Total Equity	0
Total Liabilities & Equity	0

PREPARING THE FINANCIALS

STARTING BALANCE SHEET

Assets	Balance
Current Assets	
Cash	0
Accounts Receivable	0
Inventory	0
Other Current Assets	0
Total Current Assets	0
Long Term Assets	
Depreciable Assets	0
Accumulated Depreciation	0
Net Depreciable Assets	0
Non-Depreciable Assets	0
Total Long-Term Assets	**0**
Total Assets	**0**
Liabilities & Equity	
Current Liabilities	
Cost of Sales A/P	**0**
Non-Cost of Sales A/P	**0**
Short-Term Debt	**0**
Income Taxes Due	**0**
Total Current Liabilities	0
Long-Term Debt	0
Equity	
Stock & Paid-in Capital	0
Retained Earnings	0
Total Equity	0
Total Liabilities & Equity	0

Total Long-Term Assets
Total long-term assets is calculated by adding up net depreciable assets and non-depreciable assets.

Total Assets
Total assets is calculated by adding up total current assets and total long-term assets

Current liabilities
Current liabilities are liabilities that will be paid within one year.

Cost of Sales Payable
These are amounts that the business owes vendors for purchases of inventory or cost of sales items.

Non-Cost of Sales Payable
These are amounts that the business owes vendors for purchases of non-inventory/non-cost of sales items.

Short-Term Debt
This is borrowed funds or notes that the business owes that are due within one year.

Income Taxes Due
This is all income taxes that the business owes. Sales taxes and any other taxes should be included elsewhere such as under non-cost of sales payables.

PREPARING THE FINANCIALS

Total Current Liabilities

This is the total of costs of sales payable, non-cost of sales payable, short-term debt, and income taxes due.

Long-Term Debt

This is borrowed funds or notes that the business owes that is due in more than one year.

Equity

Equity is the owner's or stockholder's net worth in the business.

Stock and Paid-in Capital

For a corporation or partnership this is the total amount of money that has been invested in the business, including the money to start your business plus any additional capital infusions you have made, not including reinvestment of retained earnings.

For a sole proprietorship both the stock and paid-in capital entry and the retained earnings entry are better thought of as one entry: Net Worth. So to do financials for a sole proprietorship we would recommend setting stock and paid-in capital to zero and consider the retained earnings entry to reflect Net Worth.

Retained Earnings

Retained earnings are net income after tax that has not been distributed to the owner(s) of the business and instead has been kept in the business.

STARTING BALANCE SHEET

Assets	Balance
Current Assets	
Cash	0
Accounts Receivable	0
Inventory	0
Other Current Assets	0
Total Current Assets	0
Long Term Assets	
Depreciable Assets	0
Accumulated Depreciation	0
Net Depreciable Assets	0
Non-Depreciable Assets	0
Total Long-Term Assets	0
Total Assets	0
	========
Liabilities & Equity	
Current Liabilities	
Cost of Sales A/P	0
Non-Cost of Sales A/P	0
Short-Term Debt	0
Income Taxes Due	0
Total Current Liabilities	**0**
Long-Term Debt	**0**
Equity	
Stock & Paid-in Capital	**0**
Retained Earnings	**0**
Total Equity	0
Total Liabilities & Equity	0
	========

PREPARING THE FINANCIALS

STARTING BALANCE SHEET

Assets	Balance
Current Assets	
Cash	0
Accounts Receivable	0
Inventory	0
Other Current Assets	0
Total Current Assets	0
Long Term Assets	
Depreciable Assets	0
Accumulated Depreciation	0
Net Depreciable Assets	0
Non-Depreciable Assets	0
Total Long-Term Assets	0
Total Assets	0
	========
Liabilities & Equity	
Current Liabilities	
Cost of Sales A/P	0
Non-Cost of Sales A/P	0
Short-Term Debt	0
Income Taxes Due	0
Total Current Liabilities	0
Long-Term Debt	0
Equity	
Stock & Paid-in Capital	0
Retained Earnings	0
Total Equity	**0**
Total Liabilities & Equity	**0**
	========

If you are not sure of what the retained earnings of your business is (or what your personal net worth is) you can calculate it by adding up all of your assets and subtracting all of your liabilities. This will give you your net worth or total equity. To determine retained earnings you would then subtract stock and paid-in capital from total equity.

Total Equity

Total equity is the sum of stock and paid-in capital and retained earnings.

Total Liabilities and Equity

Total liabilities and equity is the sum of total liabilities plus total equity. This amount must equal total assets.

If these are not equal, carefully double check each entry for assets and liabilities. Then adjust the retained earnings entry so that total liabilities shows a total equal to total assets.

Do not proceed to the next part of the plan until the Starting Balance sheet "balances."

PREPARING THE FINANCIALS

Profit and Loss Projection

Justifying Sales Forecasts

Both lenders and investors will want to know how you came up with your sales forecast. For an existing business, for example, your sales numbers may reflect your current growth rate or perhaps an accelerated growth rate due to new factors such as the launch of a new product or an enhanced marketing effort. For a new business, sales projections need to be based on some currently existing factor outside the business—such as the estimated size of the potential market, or the sales of similar businesses, or the anticipated sales to specific customers.

Multiple Sales Forecasts

Because it is very difficult, but also very critical, to project sales many people will create multiple sets of financials using different sales forecasts. For example, if you choose to create three sets of financials you may choose to call them the "Weak, Likely, and Strong" scenarios.

However, having created literally hundreds of business financials over the years, I would suggest you focus on creating one set of financials very carefully, rather than creating several different sets—unless you are creating a plan to obtain huge amounts (such as millions of dollars) of financing.

I feel that you are better off with one set of financials for which you have carefully estimated the major assumptions.

> I generally prefer to create one carefully estimated scenario.

Watching Profit Margins

In creating profit and loss projections, I would give careful consideration to profit margins. A large profit margin can make up for a lot of mistakes in running a business. If your projected

PREPARING THE FINANCIALS

Does your financial plan match the text part of your plan?

profit margin is 2 percent, small cost overruns can kill you. But if your projected profit margin is 20 percent, small cost overruns will hardly be noticed. If your profit margin ends up being smaller than projected (or non-existent) in your first run through your financials don't be surprised—this is often the case. Go take a hard look at your expenses and cut back on those that aren't really essential for driving your business ahead.

Does Your Forecast Reflect Your Strategy?

All too often the text part of the business plan is not reflected in the financials and hence never becomes reality. For example, if you say you are going to have a top quality product, but don't allocate adequate funding, then you probably aren't going to achieve your goal. Or if you say you are going to have a first class marketing effort but don't allocate adequate funding, then you are probably not going to achieve this goal either.

At the same time, you need to be careful not to fall into the trap of trying to do a world class effort on all aspects of your business—or you'll run out of money in a hurry. This is where aggressively following strategy becomes crucial. You need to use the strategy that you choose for your business to help decide not just what you will spend a lot of money on—but just as importantly—what areas you will not spend a lot of money on. For example, if your strategy is based on a top quality product, you may want to be careful not to overspend in non-product categories such as marketing and general and administrative expenses.

PREPARING THE FINANCIALS

Bad Debt

If you are selling on credit, you are almost certainly going to have some bad debt. You can handle bad debt by entering in your sales forecast the net sales you expect to eventually get paid for. For example, if you expect to sell $150 worth of goods in January but have a bad debt rate of 2 percent, then your net sales will be $147—the amount you should enter in your January sales forecast.

Profit and Loss Projection

See pages 436-437 for a complete 5-year Profit and Loss Projection form.

Date: . . . .

Sales $ . . . .

Costs

    Cost Of Sales $ . . . .

    Gross Profit $ . . . .

    Gross Profit Margin . . . . %

    Marketing & Sales

        Commissions $ . . . .

        Literature & Mailings $ . . . .

        Advertising & Publicity $ . . . .

        Other Marketing $ . . . .

        Total Marketing & Sales $ . . . .

    General & Administrative

        Payroll $ . . . .

        Payroll Taxes, Benefits $ . . . .

        Facilities & Equip Rent $ . . . .

        Maintenance & Repairs $ . . . .

        Utilities, Phone, Postage $ . . . .

        Insurance $ . . . .

        Supplies $ . . . .

        Freight $ . . . .

        Auto Travel & Entertain. $ . . . .

        Legal & Accounting $ . . . .

        Other Outside Services $ . . . .

        Misc. Taxes, Fees $ . . . .

        Depreciation $ . . . .

        Other G&A Expenses $ . . . .

        Total General & Admin. $ . . . .

Total Operating Costs $ . . . .

        $ . . . .

Operating Profit $ . . . .

Operating Profit Margin . . . . %

Non-Operating Costs

    Interest $ . . . .

Profit Before Income Taxes $ . . . .

Pre-Tax Profit Margin . . . . %

Income Taxes $ . . . .

Net Profit $ . . . .

Net Profit Margin . . . . %

PREPARING THE FINANCIALS

Filling in the Profit and Loss Projection

Sales

Sales should be entered in dollars (or whatever currency you are using), not in units. Sales should be net sales—in other words net sales after adjustments, any discounts, return, etc.

Cost of Sales

Cost of sales is determined by multiplying the Cost of Sales % from the Assumptions Worksheet by Sales. Just leave the entry blank if you do not have any cost of sales.

Cost of sales are your direct costs of the materials or services that you have sold. For a manufacturing business you would include the costs of the product you are making. You will want to include all expenses that are related such as salaries of manufacturing personnel, raw materials, etc. For a retailer or wholesaler, cost of sales is the cost you have incurred for products that you have actually sold—not the cost of products still in inventory.

For a service business, cost of sales is your direct expenses of providing your service, which would typically consist largely of labor costs—that is, the labor costs of the people who are directly providing the service, not the support staff. For a restaurant, cost of sales is the cost of the food and beverages that you purchase.

Gross Profit

Gross profit is calculated by subtracting cost of sales from sales.

PROFIT AND LOSS PROJECTION	
	Jan-99
Sales	**0**
Costs	
Cost Of Sales	**0**
Gross Profit	**0**
Gross Profit Margin	0.0%
Marketing & Sales	
Commissions	0
Literature & Mailings	0
Advertising & Publicity	0
Other Marketing	0
Total Marketing & Sales	0
General & Administrative	
Payroll	0
Payroll Taxes, Benefits	0
Facilities & Equip Rent	0
Maintenance & Repairs	0
Utilities, Phone, Postage	0
Insurance	0
Supplies	0
Freight	0
Auto Travel & Entertain.	0
Legal & Accounting	0
Other Outside Services	0
Misc. Taxes, Fees	0
Depreciation	0
Other G&A Expenses	0
Total General & Admin.	0
Total Operating Costs	0
	0
Operating Profit	0
Operating Profit Margin	0.0%
Non-Operating Costs	
Interest	0
Profit Before Income Taxes	0
Pre-Tax Profit Margin	0.0%
Income Taxes	0
Net Profit	0
Net Profit Margin	0.0%

PREPARING THE FINANCIALS

PROFIT AND LOSS PROJECTION	
	Jan-99
Sales	0
Costs	
Cost Of Sales	0
Gross Profit	0
Gross Profit Margin	**0.0%**
Marketing & Sales	
Commissions	**0**
Literature & Mailings	**0**
Advertising & Publicity	**0**
Other Marketing	**0**
Total Marketing & Sales	**0**
General & Administrative	
Payroll	0
Payroll Taxes, Benefits	0
Facilities & Equip Rent	0
Maintenance & Repairs	0
Utilities, Phone, Postage	0
Insurance	0
Supplies	0
Freight	0
Auto Travel & Entertain.	0
Legal & Accounting	0
Other Outside Services	0
Misc. Taxes, Fees	0
Depreciation	0
Other G&A Expenses	0
Total General & Admin.	0
Total Operating Costs	0
	0
Operating Profit	0
Operating Profit Margin	0.0%
Non-Operating Costs	
Interest	0
Profit Before Income Taxes	0
Pre-Tax Profit Margin	0.0%
Income Taxes	0
Net Profit	0
Net Profit Margin	0.0%

Gross Profit Margin

Gross profit divided by sales. This ratio indicates the core profitability of the business versus sales before subtracting any of the marketing, sales, general and administrative costs of running the business. Like other profit margin ratios, average and recommended gross profit margins will vary widely from one type of business to the next.

Marketing and Sales
Commissions

Commissions are determined by multiplying the commissions % from the Assumptions Worksheet by Sales. If you don't have any commissions then just leave the entry blank.

Literature and Mailings

Include any coupons, brochures, direct mail pieces, catalogs, and other promotional material.

Advertising & Publicity

Include all advertising and publicity expenses, except those listed under other categories such as commissions or literature and mailings.

Other Marketing

All other marketing expenditures not covered in the above categories.

Total Marketing & Sales

Add up all the marketing and sales costs.

PREPARING THE FINANCIALS

General and Administrative (G&A)
Payroll

Gross payroll expenses. Note: if you have already counted some portion of payroll in cost of sales, do not double count it by including it here.

Payroll Taxes, Benefits

Determined by multiplying the Payroll Tax Rate assumption from the Assumptions worksheet by the Payroll.

Facilities & Equipment/Rent

Includes rental and lease payments for facilities and equipment. This figure will usually remain the same throughout the year, unless you need to rent additional equipment, such as for a peak business period.

Maintenance & Repairs

Includes all maintenance and repair work and service contracts.

Utilities, Phone, Postage

Includes all utilities, phone, postage, courier expenses, Internet access, etc.

Insurance

Include all insurance, except any insurance previously included under Payroll Taxes & Benefits.

PROFIT AND LOSS PROJECTION

	Jan-99
Sales	0
Costs	
Cost Of Sales	0
Gross Profit	0
Gross Profit Margin	0.0%
Marketing & Sales	
Commissions	0
Literature & Mailings	0
Advertising & Publicity	0
Other Marketing	0
Total Marketing & Sales	0
General & Administrative	
Payroll	**0**
Payroll Taxes, Benefits	**0**
Facilities & Equip Rent	**0**
Maintenance & Repairs	**0**
Utilities, Phone, Postage	**0**
Insurance	**0**
Supplies	0
Freight	0
Auto Travel & Entertain.	0
Legal & Accounting	0
Other Outside Services	0
Misc. Taxes, Fees	0
Depreciation	0
Other G&A Expenses	0
Total General & Admin.	0
Total Operating Costs	0
	0
Operating Profit	0
Operating Profit Margin	0.0%
Non-Operating Costs	
Interest	0
Profit Before Income Taxes	0
Pre-Tax Profit Margin	0.0%
Income Taxes	0
Net Profit	0
Net Profit Margin	0.0%

PREPARING THE FINANCIALS

PROFIT AND LOSS PROJECTION	
	Jan-99
Sales	0
Costs	
Cost Of Sales	0
Gross Profit	0
Gross Profit Margin	0.0%
Marketing & Sales	
Commissions	0
Literature & Mailings	0
Advertising & Publicity	0
Other Marketing	0
Total Marketing & Sales	0
General & Administrative	
Payroll	0
Payroll Taxes, Benefits	0
Facilities & Equip Rent	0
Maintenance & Repairs	0
Utilities, Phone, Postage	0
Insurance	0
Supplies	**0**
Freight	**0**
Auto Travel & Entertain.	**0**
Legal & Accounting	**0**
Other Outside Services	**0**
Misc. Taxes, Fees	**0**
Depreciation	0
Other G&A Expenses	0
Total General & Admin.	0
Total Operating Costs	0
	0
Operating Profit	0
Operating Profit Margin	0.0%
Non-Operating Costs	
Interest	0
Profit Before Income Taxes	0
Pre-Tax Profit Margin	0.0%
Income Taxes	0
Net Profit	0
Net Profit Margin	0.0%

Supplies

All the various supplies used in operating the business, except for items that directly become part of finished products or services (which would be included under cost of sales). Typical examples are office supplies, cleaning supplies, shipping materials, etc.

Freight

Determined by multiplying the Freight Cost % from the Assumptions worksheet by Sales.

Leave blank if you don't have any freight or delivery costs.

Auto, Travel & Entertainment

This category should include basically any local transportation of employees including auto mileage reimbursement, meals, overnight travel and entertainment expenses.

Legal & Accounting

Includes the fees you pay to external legal and accounting firms. In-house legal or accounting staff should be included in Payroll.

Other Outside Services

Includes cleaning services, landscaping, and all other outside services. You could also include temporary help firms and consultants in this category.

Misc. Taxes and Fees

All taxes and fees except income taxes. Examples include permits, licenses, real estate taxes, inventory taxes, etc.

PREPARING THE FINANCIALS

Depreciation

Monthly portion of depreciation on capital equipment, motor vehicles, buildings and leasehold improvements. Most often this will remain constant over the course of the year.

Depreciation is an accounting figure that records the deterioration in value of equipment, motor vehicles and buildings. Each of these items is assumed to loose a certain percentage of its value each year. Different accounting principles and tax laws apply to different categories of goods. For example you may be able to depreciate a car or truck over 3 years, a computer over 5 years, office furniture over 10 years, leasehold improvements over the life of the lease, buildings over 40 years.

So assuming that you are using simple straight-line depreciation, the matching monthly depreciation figures may be car or trucks: 1/36 of purchase price per month. For computers: 1/60 of purchase price per month. Office furniture: 1/120 per month. Buildings: 1/480 of purchase price per month.

Check with your accountant or the IRS or the tax agency in your country to get the most appropriate depreciation figures for your situation.

Other G&A Expenses

Includes all other operating costs except sales and marketing and cost of sales expenses. You should include a small amount for unforeseeable expenses or cost over-runs.

PROFIT AND LOSS PROJECTION

	Jan-99
Sales	0
Costs	
Cost Of Sales	0
Gross Profit	0
Gross Profit Margin	0.0%
Marketing & Sales	
Commissions	0
Literature & Mailings	0
Advertising & Publicity	0
Other Marketing	0
Total Marketing & Sales	0
General & Administrative	
Payroll	0
Payroll Taxes, Benefits	0
Facilities & Equip Rent	0
Maintenance & Repairs	0
Utilities, Phone, Postage	0
Insurance	0
Supplies	0
Freight	0
Auto Travel & Entertain.	0
Legal & Accounting	0
Other Outside Services	0
Misc. Taxes, Fees	0
Depreciation	**0**
Other G&A Expenses	**0**
Total General & Admin.	0
Total Operating Costs	0
	0
Operating Profit	0
Operating Profit Margin	0.0%
Non-Operating Costs	
Interest	0
Profit Before Income Taxes	0
Pre-Tax Profit Margin	0.0%
Income Taxes	0
Net Profit	0
Net Profit Margin	0.0%

PREPARING THE FINANCIALS

PROFIT AND LOSS PROJECTION	
	Jan-99
Sales	0
Costs	
Cost Of Sales	0
Gross Profit	0
Gross Profit Margin	0.0%
Marketing & Sales	
Commissions	0
Literature & Mailings	0
Advertising & Publicity	0
Other Marketing	0
Total Marketing & Sales	0
General & Administrative	
Payroll	0
Payroll Taxes, Benefits	0
Facilities & Equip Rent	0
Maintenance & Repairs	0
Utilities, Phone, Postage	0
Insurance	0
Supplies	0
Freight	0
Auto Travel & Entertain.	0
Legal & Accounting	0
Other Outside Services	0
Misc. Taxes, Fees	0
Depreciation	0
Other G&A Expenses	0
Total General & Admin.	**0**
Total Operating Costs	**0**
	0
Operating Profit	**0**
Operating Profit Margin	**0.0%**
Non-Operating Costs	
Interest	**0**
Profit Before Income Taxes	0
Pre-Tax Profit Margin	0.0%
Income Taxes	0
Net Profit	0
Net Profit Margin	0.0%

Total G&A
Add up all of the General and Administrative Expenses.

Total Operating Costs
Add up the totals of General and Administrative Costs, Marketing and Sales Costs and Cost of Sales.

Operating Profit
Subtract the Total Operating Costs from Sales.

Operating Profit Margin
Operating profit divided by sales. This ratio indicates the profitability of operating the business versus sales before such costs as interest and taxes.

Non-Operating Costs
Costs that are not directly involved in the operation of the business such as interest expense.

Interest
Multiply your Short-Term Interest Rate and your Long-Term Interest Rate by your Short-Term and Long-Term Debt on your Balance Sheet at the beginning of this month. Then add the total interest for short-term and long-term debt together. You will not be able to finalize this entry until you have finalized the debt amounts on your Balance Sheet. However, I recommend that you carefully take your best guess now at your interest costs and then correct the amount later.

PREPARING THE FINANCIALS

Profit Before Income Taxes
Operating profit less non-operating costs.

Pre-Tax Profit Margin
Profit before income taxes divided by sales. This ratio indicates the profitability of the business versus sales after deducting all costs of operating the business except income taxes.

Income Taxes
Multiply your Income Tax Rate from the Assumptions worksheet by the Profit Before Income Taxes. The result will be negative if your Profit Before Income Taxes is negative—but enter the negative amount anyway. Negative income tax liability from one month will be offset by positive income tax liability in another. Also, a business entity may either be able to get a partial income tax refund if it shows a loss for the year or a tax loss carryforward. Ask your accountant for advice on your specific situation.

Net Profit
Subtract Income Taxes from Profit Before Income Taxes.

Net Profit Margin
Net Profit divided by sales. This ratio indicates the overall profitability of the business versus sales.

PROFIT AND LOSS PROJECTION

	Jan-99
Sales	0
Costs	
Cost Of Sales	0
Gross Profit	0
Gross Profit Margin	0.0%
Marketing & Sales	
Commissions	0
Literature & Mailings	0
Advertising & Publicity	0
Other Marketing	0
Total Marketing & Sales	0
General & Administrative	
Payroll	0
Payroll Taxes, Benefits	0
Facilities & Equip Rent	0
Maintenance & Repairs	0
Utilities, Phone, Postage	0
Insurance	0
Supplies	0
Freight	0
Auto Travel & Entertain.	0
Legal & Accounting	0
Other Outside Services	0
Misc. Taxes, Fees	0
Depreciation	0
Other G&A Expenses	0
Total General & Admin.	0
Total Operating Costs	0
	0
Operating Profit	0
Operating Profit Margin	0.0%
Non-Operating Costs	
Interest	0
Profit Before Income Taxes	**0**
Pre-Tax Profit Margin	**0.0%**
Income Taxes	**0**
Net Profit	**0**
Net Profit Margin	**0.0%**

PREPARING THE FINANCIALS

Cash Flow Projection

It's Crucial if You Sell on Credit

Especially if you sell on credit, the cash flow forecast is a crucial financial forecast instrument. In fact, I refer to my cash flow projection much more often during the course of the year in running the business than the profit and loss projection. The cash flow projection for a business is more likely to swing rapidly and should be updated at least every month for a business selling on credit. If you haven't done cash flow projections before it may seem like a tough task at first—but if you examine just one month on the cash flow, item by item, very carefully, you will go a long way to understanding how cash flow is done.

Especially Important for Growing Businesses

Projecting cash flow is especially important for growing businesses. Growing businesses burn cash. And fast growing businesses burn cash quickly. It is quite possible for a profitable business to be driven into bankruptcy because it ran out of cash to pay its bills. This usually happens when a business must either stock up on inventory, or make and pay for other expenses, before it is able to collect money from customers. This is why in running a small business you must try to hold onto your cash by speeding payments from your customers and extending payables as long as possible to your vendors. It is also why you need to stay on top of your cash flow projections.

Assumptions Versus Reality

Especially in starting a new business you will be surprised how much effort it will take to get credit customers to pay you on a timely basis. Just sending invoices is not going to get all cus-

> Cash flow may swing rapidly.

PREPARING THE FINANCIALS

tomers to pay you. You need to be ready to send overdue letters and make collection calls and be ready to put customers on hold. And you need to be careful about granting credit to begin with. Potential lenders and financiers are very aware of this. So you may want to say a few words to them about how you are going to be sure that you get paid from customers on a timely basis.

Great Deals Burn Cash

In starting or running a business, you need to be careful in taking advantage of "great deals" or "volume savings or discounts" that will eat up your cash. Often I have gotten into cash flow binds because I did not manage my cash carefully enough and allowed expenses to mount or inventory to build more than I had previously planned.

A cash trap to avoid.

Cash Flow Projection

See pages 438-439 for a complete 5-year Cash Flow Projection form.

Date:

Starting Cash $ . . . .

Sources

    Cash Sales $ . . . .

    Credit Sales $ . . . .

    Short-Term Loan Proceeds $ . . . .

    Long-Term Loan Proceeds $ . . . .

    Equity Capital Proceeds $ . . . .

    Total Sources $ . . . .

Uses

    Cost of Sales / Inventory $ . . . .

    Payroll & Related $ . . . .

    Non-Payroll Expenses $ . . . .

    Interest $ . . . .

    Purchase Depreciable Assets $ . . . .

    Purchase Non-Dep. Assets $ . . . .

    Dividends, Owner Pay-Outs $ . . . .

    Short-Term Debt Payments $ . . . .

    Long-Term Debt Payments $ . . . .

    Total Uses Before Taxes $ . . . .

    Income Taxes $ . . . .

    Total Uses After Taxes $ . . . .

Net Change In Cash $ . . . .

Ending Cash Position $ . . . .

PREPARING THE FINANCIALS

Filling in the Cash Flow Projection

Starting Cash

For the first month your Starting Cash entry will be the same as your cash position on your Starting Balance Sheet. For all other months your Starting Cash entry will be the same as your Ending Cash Position from the previous month. So you will have to fill out all items in the one month of your cash flow before you can enter your Starting Cash in the next month.

Sources

These items show the sources that your business will receive cash from.

Cash Sales

Multiply your percentage of sales in cash by your total sales. To get your percentage of cash sales subtract the Credit Sales % (on the Assumptions worksheet) from 100, then multiply the result by Sales from the Profit and Loss Projection.

Credit Sales

Here is the first relatively complex item to calculate. Read the instructions carefully. Consider trying a very, very simple example to make sure you understand it thoroughly. And then make your calculation carefully. And then review your work again.

Start by locating the Days Credit Assumption on the Assumptions worksheet. This will show the number of

CASH FLOW PROJECTION	
	Jan-99
Starting Cash	**0**
Sources	
Cash Sales	**0**
Credit Sales	**0**
Short-Term Loan Proceeds	0
Long-Term Loan Proceeds	0
Equity Capital Proceeds	0
Total Sources	0
Uses	
Cost of Sales / Inventory	0
Payroll & Related	0
Non-Payroll Expenses	0
Interest	0
Purchase Depreciable Assets	0
Purchase Non-Dep. Assets	0
Dividends, Owner Pay-Outs	0
Short-Term Debt Payments	0
Long-Term Debt Payments	0
Total Uses Before Taxes	0
Income Taxes	0
Total Uses After Taxes	0
Net Change In Cash	0
Ending Cash Position	0

PREPARING THE FINANCIALS

CASH FLOW PROJECTION

	Jan-99
Starting Cash	0
Sources	
Cash Sales	0
Credit Sales	0
Short-Term Loan Proceeds	**0**
Long-Term Loan Proceeds	0
Equity Capital Proceeds	0
Total Sources	0
Uses	
Cost of Sales / Inventory	0
Payroll & Related	0
Non-Payroll Expenses	0
Interest	0
Purchase Depreciable Assets	0
Purchase Non-Dep. Assets	0
Dividends, Owner Pay-Outs	0
Short-Term Debt Payments	0
Long-Term Debt Payments	0
Total Uses Before Taxes	0
Income Taxes	0
Total Uses After Taxes	0
Net Change In Cash	0
Ending Cash Position	0

days on average that it takes you to collect cash on credit sales. For example if the Days Credit Assumption is 30 and the current month is January, then during the month of January you should collect 100% of the sales made on credit during the month of December. So you would multiply the sales in December by the Credit Sales % from the Assumptions Worksheet. This would give you the entry you need for cash received in January from previous credit sales.

If your Days Credit Assumption was 60, then you would multiply the sales from November by the Credit Sales % to get your answer.

It's a little more complicated if your Days Credit Assumption does not break on an even month. (For financial purposes it's standard to assume that all months have 30 days and years have 360 days—these calculations are complex enough as it is!). For example let's say that your Days Credit Assumption was 45. Then you would expect during January to collect revenue from the first 15 days of sales during December and the last 15 days of sales during November. So you would multiply 50% (15 days/30 days) of the sales from December and add it to the result of multiplying 50% of the sales from November. Then you would multiply this result by the Credit Sales % to get your answer.

Short-Term Loan Proceeds

Enter proceeds from any short-term loans in this row. You should enter enough proceeds from short-term loans so that the cash flow at the end of the month and

PREPARING THE FINANCIALS

each year reflects a positive balance. Generally you should enter items in this row only after you have completed any other entries to be made on this page. This will make it easier to determine the appropriate level of short-term borrowing that you may need.

Once you have entered short-term loan proceeds you should adjust your Interest Cost on the Profit and Loss Forecast, then if you already calculated the Interest item on the Cash Flow you should re-adjust that entry as well. It is likely that you will have to increase your Short Term Loan Proceeds further to cover your increased interest costs.

Also don't forget to enter repayments of short-term debt in the Uses section. If you are unable to payback short-term debt quickly, then you need to consider other financing options such as long-term debt or additional equity investments.

If any loan proceeds that you receive have been discounted for prepaid interest, add the interest to the net proceeds to obtain the full or gross amount of the loan, and enter that amount here.

Long-Term Loan Proceeds

Enter proceeds from any long-term loans in this row. As with short-term loan proceeds, you can increase long-term loan proceeds to help finance your business. However, short-term swings in financing needs (such as swings within any 12 month period) should be covered by short-term debt.

CASH FLOW PROJECTION

	Jan-99
Starting Cash	0
Sources	
Cash Sales	0
Credit Sales	0
Short-Term Loan Proceeds	0
Long-Term Loan Proceeds	**0**
Equity Capital Proceeds	0
Total Sources	0
Uses	
Cost of Sales / Inventory	0
Payroll & Related	0
Non-Payroll Expenses	0
Interest	0
Purchase Depreciable Assets	0
Purchase Non-Dep. Assets	0
Dividends, Owner Pay-Outs	0
Short-Term Debt Payments	0
Long-Term Debt Payments	0
Total Uses Before Taxes	0
Income Taxes	0
Total Uses After Taxes	0
Net Change In Cash	0
Ending Cash Position	0

PREPARING THE FINANCIALS

CASH FLOW PROJECTION

	Jan-99
Starting Cash	0
Sources	
Cash Sales	0
Credit Sales	0
Short-Term Loan Proceeds	0
Long-Term Loan Proceeds	0
Equity Capital Proceeds	**0**
Total Sources	**0**
Uses	
Cost of Sales / Inventory	**0**
Payroll & Related	0
Non-Payroll Expenses	0
Interest	0
Purchase Depreciable Assets	0
Purchase Non-Dep. Assets	0
Dividends, Owner Pay-Outs	0
Short-Term Debt Payments	0
Long-Term Debt Payments	0
Total Uses Before Taxes	0
Income Taxes	0
Total Uses After Taxes	0
Net Change In Cash	0
Ending Cash Position	0

Equity Capital Proceeds

Enter proceeds from any new equity infusions in this row, such as if a new or current investor contributes an additional amount of money to the business.

Total Sources

Add up all of your sources of cash.

Uses

These items show all of the ways that the business will use cash.

Cost of Sales/Inventory

Calculating cost of sales is somewhat similar to calculating cash from credit sales—but a little bit more complicated.

Start by locating the Cost of Sales Days Accounts Payable (A/P) Assumption on the Assumptions worksheet. This will show the number of days on average that you take to pay for Cost of Sales Items . (Cost of Sales items are your direct costs of the materials or services that you sell. For service businesses Cost of Sales typically consists of labor costs, for a manufacturer it is the direct costs of the goods sold, for a retailer or wholesaler it is inventory.)

For example if the Cost of Sales Days Accounts Payable Assumption is 30 and the current month is January, then during the month of January you will pay for 100% of the Cost of Sales items that you purchased on credit during the month of December.

PREPARING THE FINANCIALS

Notice that I said *purchased* during the month of December— not *sold* during the month of December. The value of Cost of Sales Items that you sold during December directly impacts your Profit and Loss Statement. But it is the value of Cost of Sales Items that you purchased on credit during December that directly impacts your cash uses for Cost of Sales on credit during January.

Next you need to determine the Cost Of Sales Items purchased during December. To determine this value you would subtract Cost of Sales Items on hand at the beginning of December from the Cost of Sales Items on hand at the end of December and then add to this total all of the Cost of Sales Items sold during December.

The inventory on hand at the end of any month should be the Cost of Sales from the Profit and Loss Projection multiplied by the Days Inventory on Hand from the Assumptions Worksheet divided by 30. The inventory on hand at the beginning of any month should be the Cost of Sales *from the previous month* multiplied by the Days Inventory divided by 30.

Next you would multiply the Cost of Sales Items purchased during December by the Cost of Sales Accounts Payable % from the Assumptions Worksheet. This would give you the entry you need for uses of cash for Cost of Sales in January.

If your Cost of Sales Days Accounts Payable Assumption was 60, then you would multiply the Cost of Sales Items purchased during November by the Cost of Sales Accounts Payable % to get your answer.

It's a little more complicated if your Cost of Sales Days Accounts Payable Assumption does not break on an even month. For example let's say that your Cost of Sales Days Accounts Payable Assumption was 45. Then you would expect during

PREPARING THE FINANCIALS

CASH FLOW PROJECTION

	Jan-99
Starting Cash	0
Sources	
Cash Sales	0
Credit Sales	0
Short-Term Loan Proceeds	0
Long-Term Loan Proceeds	0
Equity Capital Proceeds	0
Total Sources	0
Uses	
Cost of Sales / Inventory	0
Payroll & Related	**0**
Non-Payroll Expenses	**0**
Interest	0
Purchase Depreciable Assets	0
Purchase Non-Dep. Assets	0
Dividends, Owner Pay-Outs	0
Short-Term Debt Payments	0
Long-Term Debt Payments	0
Total Uses Before Taxes	0
Income Taxes	0
Total Uses After Taxes	0
Net Change In Cash	0
Ending Cash Position	0

January to pay for Cost of Sales items purchased during the first 15 days of December and the last 15 days of November. So you would multiply 50% (15 days/30 days) of the purchases from December and add it to the result of multiplying 50% of the purchases from November. Then you would multiply this result by the Cost of Sales Accounts Payable % to get your answer.

(Note: If you do not stock Cost of Sales Items (i.e. if you keep no inventory on hand) then your Cost of Sales during any month will be exactly the same as your Cost of Sales purchases during that month (although you may pay for them in a later month if you buy on credit.))

Payroll & Related

Add together Payroll and Payroll Taxes/Benefits from the Profit and Loss Projection from the same month and enter here. In reality your business like most firms probably pays payroll taxes a few days after the payroll period ends and payroll taxes even later than that. However, it is a close enough estimate to assume for forecasting purposes that payroll is on a cash basis.

Non-Payroll Expenses

Start by locating the Days General Accounts Payable on the Assumptions worksheet. This will show the number of days on average that you take to pay for Non-Payroll Expenses (also called General Accounts Payable here). For example if the Days General Accounts Payable Assumption is 30 and the current month is January, then during the month of January you should pay for 100% of

PREPARING THE FINANCIALS

the Non-Payroll Expenses incurred on credit during the month of December. So you would multiply the Non-Payroll Expenses in December by the General Accounts Payable % from the Assumptions Worksheet. This would give you the entry you need for cash used in January to pay for previous Non-Payroll Expense purchases.

To get Non-Payroll Expenses in December you would subtract Payroll, Payroll Taxes/Benefits and Depreciation from the Total General and Administrative on the Profit and Loss Projection. Then you would also add Total Marketing and Sales Costs to this number.

If your Days General Accounts Payable Assumption was 60, then you would multiply the Non-Payroll Expenses from November by the General Accounts Payable % to get your answer.

It's a little more complicated if your Days General Accounts Payable Assumption does not break on an even month. For example let's say that your Days General Accounts Payable Assumption was 45. Then you would expect during January to pay for Non-Payroll Expenses incurred during the first 15 days of December and the last 15 days of November. So you would multiply 50% (15 days/30 days) of the expenses from December and add it to the result of multiplying 50% of the expenses from November. Then you would multiply this result by the General Accounts Payable % to get your answer.

Interest
Simply use the entry for interest for the same month from the Profit and Loss forecast. Interest is

CASH FLOW PROJECTION	
	Jan-99
Starting Cash	0
Sources	
Cash Sales	0
Credit Sales	0
Short-Term Loan Proceeds	0
Long-Term Loan Proceeds	0
Equity Capital Proceeds	0
Total Sources	0
Uses	
Cost of Sales / Inventory	0
Payroll & Related	0
Non-Payroll Expenses	0
Interest	**0**
Purchase Depreciable Assets	0
Purchase Non-Dep. Assets	0
Dividends, Owner Pay-Outs	0
Short-Term Debt Payments	0
Long-Term Debt Payments	0
Total Uses Before Taxes	0
Income Taxes	0
Total Uses After Taxes	0
Net Change In Cash	0
Ending Cash Position	0

PREPARING THE FINANCIALS

CASH FLOW PROJECTION

	Jan-99
Starting Cash	0
Sources	
Cash Sales	0
Credit Sales	0
Short-Term Loan Proceeds	0
Long-Term Loan Proceeds	0
Equity Capital Proceeds	0
Total Sources	0
Uses	
Cost of Sales / Inventory	0
Payroll & Related	0
Non-Payroll Expenses	0
Interest	0
Purchase Depreciable Assets	**0**
Purchase Non-Dep. Assets	**0**
Dividends, Owner Pay-Outs	**0**
Short-Term Debt Payments	**0**
Long-Term Debt Payments	**0**
Total Uses Before Taxes	0
Income Taxes	0
Total Uses After Taxes	0
Net Change In Cash	0
Ending Cash Position	0

assumed to be paid for on a cash basis. Remember interest will change when you change your level of short-term or long-term debt, as well as your short-term or long-term interest rate assumption.

Purchase Depreciable Assets

Enter the full purchase cost of depreciable assets purchased during each period in this row. Examples include equipment, motor vehicles, leasehold improvements and buildings.

Purchase Non-Depreciable Assets

Enter the full purchase cost of any non-depreciable assets purchased during each period in this row. Land is an example of a non-depreciable asset.

Dividends, Owner Pay-Outs

Enter any dividends or pay-outs to owners in this row.

Short-Term Debt Payments

Enter any payments of principal of short-term debt in this row. Interest payments should not be included here.

Long-Term Debt Payments

Enter any payments of principal of long-term debt in this row. Interest payments should not be included here.

PREPARING THE FINANCIALS

Total Uses Before Taxes
Total all of your uses of cash, except income taxes.

Income Taxes
Take your income tax liability estimates from your profit and loss statement and enter them into the appropriate month you will be required to pay income tax estimates or settlements. Contact the IRS or your accountant for information on when tax payments will be due for your situation.

Total Uses After Taxes
Add income taxes to total uses before taxes.

Net Change in Cash
This row reflects the change in your cash position during the month. It is determined by subtracting all cash uses during the period from all cash sources.

Ending Cash Position
This row reflects the amount of cash that you will have on hand at the end of the period. It is determined by adding the Starting cash to the Net change in cash. The ending cash position for one period is the same as the starting cash for the following period.

CASH FLOW PROJECTION

	Jan-99
Starting Cash	0
Sources	
Cash Sales	0
Credit Sales	0
Short-Term Loan Proceeds	0
Long-Term Loan Proceeds	0
Equity Capital Proceeds	0
Total Sources	0
Uses	
Cost of Sales / Inventory	0
Payroll & Related	0
Non-Payroll Expenses	0
Interest	0
Purchase Depreciable Assets	0
Purchase Non-Dep. Assets	0
Dividends, Owner Pay-Outs	0
Short-Term Debt Payments	0
Long-Term Debt Payments	0
Total Uses Before Taxes	**0**
Income Taxes	**0**
Total Uses After Taxes	**0**
Net Change In Cash	**0**
Ending Cash Position	**0**

PREPARING THE FINANCIALS

Balance Sheet Projection

Less Important than Cash Flow

In running your business on a day-to-day basis, the balance sheet is much less important than the cash flow forecast and the profit and loss forecast. If you've got adequate cash to pay your bills and are making a profit—then you're probably going to avoid financial problems. In fact, I spend almost no time looking at the balance sheets for my business. However, bankers will give them some attention, especially if the business looks like it is headed toward trouble. Sometimes bank lending will be dependent upon achieving certain balance sheet conditions, such as maintaining a minimum net worth. Generally, however, cash flow projections are becoming increasingly important for businesses and balance sheets increasingly less important.

Spend Less Time on the Balance Sheet

I would suggest that you spend relatively little time trying to work on your balance sheet as opposed to your cash flow and your income statement.

Monthly Balance Sheets Versus Annual Balance Sheets

Unless the bank is overly concerned about them, I would pay scant attention to the monthly balance sheets. Banks and investors tend to pay a lot more attention to your ending balance sheet for the year—especially if it is prepared by an outside accounting firm.

> Bankers look at balance sheets, both historical and projected.

PREPARING THE FINANCIALS

Using the Balance Sheet to Find Cash

One way to use the balance sheet is to help find more cash. Can underutilized fixed assets be sold for cash? Can needed fixed assets be sold and perhaps leased back. Is there a lot of money tied up in receivables that payment can be accelerated on? Is the inventory excessive?

Balance Sheet Projection

See pages 440-441 for a complete 5-year Balance Sheet Projection form.

Period Ending: . . . .

Assets

Current assets

Cash	$ . . . .
Accounts Receivable	$ . . . .
Inventory	$ . . . .
Other Current Assets	$ . . . .
Total Current Assets	$ . . . .

Long-Term Assets

Depreciable Assets	$ . . . .
Accumulated Depreciation	$ . . . .
Net Depreciable Assets	$ . . . .
Non-Depreciable Assets	$ . . . .
Total Long-Term Assets	$ . . . .

Total Assets $ . . . .

Liabilities & Equity

Current Liabilities

Short-Term Debt	$ . . . .
Cost of Sales A/P	$ . . . .
Non-Cost of Sales A/P	$ . . . .
Income Taxes Due	$ . . . .
Total Current Liabilities	$ . . . .

Long-Term Debt $ . . . .

Equity

Stock & Paid-in Capital	$ . . . .
Retained Earnings	$ . . . .
Total Equity	$ . . . .

Total Liabilities & Equity $ . . . .

PREPARING THE FINANCIALS

Filling in the Balance Sheet Projection

Assets

Assets are anything that the business currently owns.

Current Assets

Current assets are assets that will be turned into cash within one year or may be converted to cash very quickly. Fixed assets such as equipment, buildings, machinery, etc. are not considered to be current assets even if you are planning to sell them in the near future.

Cash

Cash are your most liquid assets including checking accounts, money market funds, savings accounts. Fill in this entry with the final number in the Ending Cash Position from the Cash Flow Projection. Remember all Balance Sheet entries reflect the financial status of the company at the *end* of the period, not the beginning. So for example the January column, represents the last the of January.

Accounts Receivable

Accounts receivable is money owed your business by customers as the result of regular business transactions bought on credit.

To determine the Accounts Receivable balance you must total all of the sales on credit that have been made and not yet paid for.

First turn to the Assumptions worksheet and note the entry for Days Credit. Let's assume that the current

BALANCE SHEET PROJECTION	
Period Ending:	Jan-99
Assets	
Current assets	
Cash	**0**
Accounts Receivable	**0**
Inventory	0
Other Current Assets	0
Total Current Assets	0
Long-Term Assets	
Depreciable Assets	0
Accumulated Depreciation	0
Net Depreciable Assets	0
Non-Depreciable Assets	0
Total Long-Term Assets	0
Total Assets	0
Liabilities & Equity	
Current Liabilities	
Short-Term Debt	0
Cost of Sales A/P	0
Non-Cost of Sales A/P	0
Income Taxes Due	0
Total Current Liabilities	0
Long-Term Debt	0
Equity	
Stock & Paid-in Capital	0
Retained Earnings	0
Total Equity	0
Total Liabilities & Equity	0

PREPARING THE FINANCIALS

BALANCE SHEET PROJECTION

Period Ending:	Jan-99
Assets	
Current assets	
Cash	0
Accounts Receivable	0
Inventory	**0**
Other Current Assets	0
Total Current Assets	0
Long-Term Assets	
Depreciable Assets	0
Accumulated Depreciation	0
Net Depreciable Assets	0
Non-Depreciable Assets	0
Total Long-Term Assets	0
Total Assets	0
Liabilities & Equity	
Current Liabilities	
Short-Term Debt	0
Cost of Sales A/P	0
Non-Cost of Sales A/P	0
Income Taxes Due	0
Total Current Liabilities	0
Long-Term Debt	0
Equity	
Stock & Paid-in Capital	0
Retained Earnings	0
Total Equity	0
Total Liabilities & Equity	0

month is January. If Days Credit is 30 or less, then divide the number of days by 30 and multiply the result by Credit Sales % from the Assumptions Worksheet and by January Sales from the Profit and Loss Projection.

If Days Credit is greater than 30 but not greater than 60, you multiply the Credit Sales % by 100% of January Sales: this gives you January credit sales outstanding. Then you take Days Credit and subtract 30, and then divide the result by 30. The resulting number you multiply by December Sales and by Credit Sales %, this gives you December credit sales outstanding. Then you add together January and December credit sales outstanding.

If Days Credit is greater than 60 but not greater than 90, you multiply the Credit Sales % by the sum of 100% of January Sales and 100% of December Sales: this gives you January and December credit sales outstanding. Then you take Days Credit and subtract 60, and then divide the result by 30. The resulting number you multiply by November Sales and by Credit Sales %, this gives you November credit sales outstanding. Then you add together January and December and November credit sales outstanding.

The process work similar for Days Credit outstanding, greater than 90.

Inventory

Inventory includes finished goods, work in process and raw material. Inventory is also another name for Cost of Sales Items that are kept in supply.

PREPARING THE FINANCIALS

Locate the Days Inventory on the Assumptions worksheet, divide by 30, and then multiply by the current month's Sales from the Profit and Loss Projection and then multiply by the Cost of Sales % from the Assumptions Worksheet. This will give you the inventory on hand at the end of the month, with one exception.

The exception is that if your sales suddenly fall significantly you may end up with more inventory on hand than you need at the end of a month, even if you don't buy any new inventory during the month. In this extreme case your inventory on hand would be your inventory on hand at the of the previous month less any inventory used during the current month. This exception will only occur if your sales are highly erratic.

Other Current Assets

Other current assets are all other current assets of the business. Examples to be included in this line include pre-paid rent, pre-paid taxes and pre-paid utilities.

Total Current Assets

Total current assets is calculated here by adding up cash, accounts receivable, inventory and other current assets.

Long-Term Assets

Long term assets are assets that are not easily turned into cash and typically include such items as equipment, buildings, land, motor vehicles, etc.

BALANCE SHEET PROJECTION

Period Ending:	Jan-99
Assets	
Current assets	
Cash	0
Accounts Receivable	0
Inventory	0
Other Current Assets	**0**
Total Current Assets	**0**
Long-Term Assets	
Depreciable Assets	0
Accumulated Depreciation	0
Net Depreciable Assets	0
Non-Depreciable Assets	0
Total Long-Term Assets	0
Total Assets	0
Liabilities & Equity	
Current Liabilities	
Short-Term Debt	0
Cost of Sales A/P	0
Non-Cost of Sales A/P	0
Income Taxes Due	0
Total Current Liabilities	0
Long-Term Debt	0
Equity	
Stock & Paid-in Capital	0
Retained Earnings	0
Total Equity	0
Total Liabilities & Equity	0

PREPARING THE FINANCIALS

BALANCE SHEET PROJECTION

Period Ending:	Jan-99
Assets	
Current assets	
Cash	0
Accounts Receivable	0
Inventory	0
Other Current Assets	0
Total Current Assets	0
Long-Term Assets	
Depreciable Assets	**0**
Accumulated Depreciation	**0**
Net Depreciable Assets	**0**
Non-Depreciable Assets	**0**
Total Long-Term Assets	**0**
Total Assets	0
Liabilities & Equity	
Current Liabilities	
Short-Term Debt	0
Cost of Sales A/P	0
Non-Cost of Sales A/P	0
Income Taxes Due	0
Total Current Liabilities	0
Long-Term Debt	0
Equity	
Stock & Paid-in Capital	0
Retained Earnings	0
Total Equity	0
Total Liabilities & Equity	0

Depreciable Assets

Depreciable assets are assets that depreciate over time such as equipment, motor vehicles, leasehold improvements and buildings. For this entry you should include your purchase price of the items, not their current market or book value.

Accumulated Depreciation

This entry includes all of the depreciation accumulated to date on all of your depreciable assets. It is calculated by adding depreciation from the Profit and Loss Projection to the Starting Accumulated Depreciation on the Starting Balance Sheet. For more information refer to the discussion of Depreciation under the Profit and Loss Projection section.

Net Depreciable Assets

Net depreciable assets is calculated by subtracting accumulated depreciation from depreciable assets.

Non-Depreciable Assets

Non depreciable assets are long-term assets that do not depreciate such as land.

Total Long-Term Assets

Total long-term assets is calculated by adding up net depreciable assets and non-depreciable assets.

PREPARING THE FINANCIALS

Total Assets

Total assets is calculated by adding up total current assets and total long-term assets

Liabilities and Equity

Liabilities and equity shows who has claims to the business assets.

Current Liabilities

Current liabilities are liabilities that will be paid within one year.

Short-Term Debt

This is borrowed funds or notes that the business owes that is due within one year. This is calculated by taking the starting short-term debt from the starting balance sheet, adding in short-term loan proceeds, and subtracting short-term debt payments from the cash flow.

Cost of Sales Payable

These are amounts that the business owes vendors for purchases of inventory or other cost of sales items.

Start by locating the Cost of Sales Days Accounts Payable (A/P) Assumption on the Assumptions worksheet. This will show the number of days on average that you take to pay for Cost of Sales Items . (Cost of Sales items are your direct costs of the materials or services that you sell. For service businesses Cost of Sales typically consists of labor costs, for a manufacturer it is the

BALANCE SHEET PROJECTION

Period Ending:	Jan-99
Assets	
Current assets	
Cash	0
Accounts Receivable	0
Inventory	0
Other Current Assets	0
Total Current Assets	0
Long-Term Assets	
Depreciable Assets	0
Accumulated Depreciation	0
Net Depreciable Assets	0
Non-Depreciable Assets	0
Total Long-Term Assets	0
Total Assets	**0**
	========
Liabilities & Equity	
Current Liabilities	
Short-Term Debt	**0**
Cost of Sales A/P	**0**
Non-Cost of Sales A/P	0
Income Taxes Due	0
Total Current Liabilities	0
Long-Term Debt	0
Equity	
Stock & Paid-in Capital	0
Retained Earnings	0
Total Equity	0
Total Liabilities & Equity	0
	========

PREPARING THE FINANCIALS

direct costs of the goods sold, for a retailer or wholesaler it is inventory.)

For example if the Cost of Sales Days Accounts Payable Assumption is 30 and the current month is January, then at the end of the month of January you will have outstanding 100% of the Cost of Sales items that you purchased on credit during the month.

Notice that I said *purchased* during the month of January—not *sold* during the month of January. The value of Cost of Sales Items that you *sold* during January directly impacts your Profit and Loss Statement. But it is the value of Cost of Sales Items that you *purchased* on credit during January directly impacts ending balance for Cost of Sales Payable.

Next you need to determine the Cost Of Sales Items purchased during January. To determine this value you would subtract Cost of Sales Items on hand at the beginning of January from the Cost of Sales Items on hand at the end of January and then add to this total all of the Cost of Sales Items sold during January.

The inventory on hand at the end of any month should be the Cost of Sales from the Profit and Loss Projection multiplied by the Days Inventory on Hand from the Assumptions Worksheet divided by 30. The inventory on hand at the beginning of any month should be the Cost of Sales multiplied by the Days Inventory divided by 30. (See the note under Inventory for the extreme exception to this rule).

Next you would multiply the Cost of Sales Items purchased during January by the Cost of Sales Accounts Payable % from the Assumptions Worksheet. This would give you the entry you need for Cost of Sales Payable for January.

PREPARING THE FINANCIALS

If your Cost of Sales Days Accounts Payable Assumption was 60, then you would add up the Cost of Sales Items purchased during January and December and multiply by the Cost of Sales Accounts Payable % to get your answer.

It's a little more complicated if your Cost of Sales Days Accounts Payable Assumption does not break on an even month. For example let's say that your Cost of Sales Days Accounts Payable Assumption was 45. Then at the end of January you would add up 100% (30 days/30 days) of your January Costs of Sales purchases plus 50% (15 days/30 days) of your December Cost of Sales purchases. Then you would multiply this result by the Cost of Sales Accounts Payable % to get your answer.

Non-Cost of Sales Payable

These are the amounts that the business owes vendors for purchases of current items other than inventory or cost of sales items.

Start by locating the Days General A/P Assumption on the Assumptions worksheet. This will show the number of days on average that you take to pay for Non Cost of Sales Payables.

For example if the Days General A/P is 30 and the current month is January, then at the end of the month of January you will have outstanding 100% of the Non Cost of Sales purchases that you made on credit during the month. To get this entry you would multiply January non-payroll expenses (Take Total Operating Costs from the Profit and Loss Projection and subtract Cost of Sales,

BALANCE SHEET PROJECTION	
Period Ending:	Jan-99
Assets	
Current assets	
Cash	0
Accounts Receivable	0
Inventory	0
Other Current Assets	0
Total Current Assets	0
Long-Term Assets	
Depreciable Assets	0
Accumulated Depreciation	0
Net Depreciable Assets	0
Non-Depreciable Assets	0
Total Long-Term Assets	0
Total Assets	0
Liabilities & Equity	
Current Liabilities	
Short-Term Debt	0
Cost of Sales A/P	0
Non-Cost of Sales A/P	**0**
Income Taxes Due	0
Total Current Liabilities	0
Long-Term Debt	0
Equity	
Stock & Paid-in Capital	0
Retained Earnings	0
Total Equity	0
Total Liabilities & Equity	0

PREPARING THE FINANCIALS

BALANCE SHEET PROJECTION

Period Ending:	Jan-99
Assets	
Current assets	
Cash	0
Accounts Receivable	0
Inventory	0
Other Current Assets	0
Total Current Assets	0
Long-Term Assets	
Depreciable Assets	0
Accumulated Depreciation	0
Net Depreciable Assets	0
Non-Depreciable Assets	0
Total Long-Term Assets	0
Total Assets	0
Liabilities & Equity	
Current Liabilities	
Short-Term Debt	0
Cost of Sales A/P	0
Non-Cost of Sales A/P	0
Income Taxes Due	**0**
Total Current Liabilities	**0**
Long-Term Debt	0
Equity	
Stock & Paid-in Capital	0
Retained Earnings	0
Total Equity	0
Total Liabilities & Equity	0

Payroll, Payroll Taxes/Benefits, and Depreciation) by the General A/P % from the Assumptions Worksheet.

If your Days General A/P was 60, then you would add up the non-payroll expenses purchased during January and December and multiply by the General A/P % to get your answer.

It's a little more complicated if your Days General A/P Assumption does not break on an even month. For example let's say that your Days General A/P Assumption was 45. Then at the end of January you would add up 100% (30 days/30 days) of your January non-payroll expenses plus 50% (15 days/30 days) of your December non-payroll expenses. Then you would multiply this result by the General A/P % to get your answer.

Income Taxes Due

Add up all income taxes incurred and subtract all income taxes paid.

Start with Income Taxes Due from the Starting Balance Sheet and add this to the Income Tax entries from the Profit and Loss Projection for all previous months (since the Starting Balance Sheet was dated) and the current month. Then subtract the sum of all the Income Tax entries in the Cash Flow from all previous months and the current month.

Total Current Liabilities

This is the total of costs of sales payable, non cost of sales payable, short-term debt, and income taxes due.

PREPARING THE FINANCIALS

Long-Term Debt

This is borrowed funds or notes that the business owes that are due in more than one year.

Equity

Equity is the owner's net worth in the business.

Stock and Paid-in Capital

For a corporation or partnership this is the total amount of money that has been invested in the business, including the money to start your business plus any additional capital infusions you have made, not including investment of retained earnings.

Start with Stock and Paid-In Capital from the Starting Balance Sheet and then add in all Equity Capital infusions from prior months and the current month from the Cash Flow Projection and then subtract all Dividends/Owner Pay-Outs from prior months and the current month (also from the Cash Flow Projection).

Retained Earnings

Retained earnings are the net income after tax that has not been distributed to the owner(s) of the business.

This should actually be the last number that you fill in on the financial statements (except for the Key Ratio's).

You first should "back into" the Retained Earnings number by first jumping ahead to the last row: Total Liabilities and Equity. Since the Balance Sheet must "balance" Total Liabilities and Equity must equal Total

BALANCE SHEET PROJECTION

Period Ending:	Jan-99
Assets	
Current assets	
Cash	0
Accounts Receivable	0
Inventory	0
Other Current Assets	0
Total Current Assets	0
Long-Term Assets	
Depreciable Assets	0
Accumulated Depreciation	0
Net Depreciable Assets	0
Non-Depreciable Assets	0
Total Long-Term Assets	0
Total Assets	0
Liabilities & Equity	
Current Liabilities	
Short-Term Debt	0
Cost of Sales A/P	0
Non-Cost of Sales A/P	0
Income Taxes Due	0
Total Current Liabilities	0
Long-Term Debt	**0**
Equity	
Stock & Paid-in Capital	**0**
Retained Earnings	**0**
Total Equity	0
Total Liabilities & Equity	0

PREPARING THE FINANCIALS

BALANCE SHEET PROJECTION

Period Ending:	Jan-99
Assets	
Current assets	
Cash	0
Accounts Receivable	0
Inventory	0
Other Current Assets	0
Total Current Assets	0
Long-Term Assets	
Depreciable Assets	0
Accumulated Depreciation	0
Net Depreciable Assets	0
Non-Depreciable Assets	0
Total Long-Term Assets	0
Total Assets	0
Liabilities & Equity	
Current Liabilities	
Short-Term Debt	0
Cost of Sales A/P	0
Non-Cost of Sales A/P	0
Income Taxes Due	0
Total Current Liabilities	0
Long-Term Debt	0
Equity	
Stock & Paid-in Capital	0
Retained Earnings	0
Total Equity	**0**
Total Liabilities & Equity	**0**

Assets—so you can just insert the Total Assets number in the Total Liabilities and Equity entry. Next you can determine Total Equity by subtracting the Long Term debt and Current Liabilities from the entry for Total Liabilities and Equity. Then you can subtract Stock and Paid-in Capital from Total Equity and this will leave you with Retained Earnings.

Then you can double-check your financial statements by using another method to determine Retained Earnings. (See double-checking Your Financials a few paragraphs further along in the text.)

Total Equity

Total Equity is the sum of stock and paid-in capital and retained earnings.

Since the total of liabilities and equity must equal the total of assets, you can calculate Total Equity by subtracting Long-Term Debt and Current Liabilities from Total Assets.

Total Liabilities and Equity

Total liabilities and equity is the sum of total liabilities plus total equity. This amount must equal total assets.

So for this entry you can just go ahead and use the total assets number. Then you can double check your work as explained under the Retained Earnings text.

PREPARING THE FINANCIALS

A Quick Method for Double-Checking Your Financials

It is essential to double-check your financial projections, because it is very easy to have one or more errors which can through your results way off. If bankers or investors pick up on a major error they will be leery of providing you with financing. Even if you aren't seeking financing, a major error in your financials could prove a disaster for your business, for example if they falsely give you confidence to spend more money than you can afford to spend.

Double check your financials by using the following method to double check your Retained Earnings figure. Start with the Retained Earnings entry from the Starting Balance Sheet and add to it all Net Profit (after tax) from the date of the Starting Balance Sheet up through the current period. Then from the Cash Flow Projection add all Equity Capital Proceeds and subtract all Dividends/Owner PayOuts. The resulting number must equal the Retained Earnings number that you derived using the "Backing In" method explained under the Retained Earnings text.

Don't be frustrated if your numbers don't at first match up. If you don't regularly assemble financial statements it will probably take you a while to get your financials right. Very carefully go back and review each step of your work.

If you just can't seem to get your financials to balance yourself you may want to hire an accountant to help you or you may want to consider getting our interactive software that automatically does virtually all of the calculations (see ad at the rear of book).

Don't get frustrated if your financials don't double-check on the first pass.

PREPARING THE FINANCIALS

Revising Your Financials

Chances are that even if your financials double-check correctly you won't be satisfied with your first pass through your work. I often find for example that my profit margin is too low and that I want to go in and reduce costs.

Be careful that when you go back and make even small revisions that you make the changes on all the related financials. For example if you change your Short-Term Interest Rate on the Assumptions worksheet you would have to make changes on the Profit and Loss Projection, the Cash Flow Projection, the Balance Sheet Projection and also on your Key Ratio's. One of the great advantages of using our interactive software is that you can change one assumption in one place and the software automatically recalculates all of the financial statement projections.

Revising financials is an important means of managing a business.

PREPARING THE FINANCIALS

KEY RATIOS AND ANALYSIS

Less Important than Cash Flow

If your cash flow looks solid and your business is profitable, I generally wouldn't be too concerned with ratios. Yes, some banks and some bankers may be very rigid in insisting that your business currently meet, or projects to meet, their ratio requirements. And some bankers will be much more concerned with some ratios than others—which will differ from one banker to the next. But it is a competitive world. If your business otherwise has a solid plan for repaying it's financing, you will usually be able to find someone to finance you even if your ratios are less than desirable.

Makes the Plan Look More Polished

Including ratios in your business plan makes it look more polished for potential lenders and investors. It makes you appear more astute. And it makes less work for them.

When Not to Include Ratios

Ratios are an extra plus for a business plan. Your plan will not be incomplete if you do not include them. I have never given a bank a business plan including ratios. For example, if you don't understand the ratios or if any of the ratios look weak—you would probably be better off not including them in your plan.

> It's a nice touch to include ratios—but it's only crucial for larger ventures.

Ratios and Analysis

Date ....

Quick Ratio ....

Current Ratio ....

Debt to Equity Ratio ....

Debt to Assets Ratio ....

Return on Equity Ratio ....

Return on Assets Ratio ....

Sales Break Even $ ....

Working Capital $ ....

PREPARING THE FINANCIALS

Filling in the Key Ratios and Analysis

Here are the key ratios and financial analysis and the formulas that are used to derive them:

Quick Ratio

$$\frac{\text{Current Assets — Inventory}}{\text{Current Liabilities}}$$

Also called the Acid Test, this ratio should usually be greater than one. The ratio tests the very short-term liquidity versus current obligations of the business. Inventory is not included because it is assumed that inventory can not be as quickly turned into cash as other current assets such as bank accounts and accounts receivable.

Current Ratio

$$\frac{\text{Current Assets}}{\text{Current Liabilities}}$$

This ratio should usually be greater than two. This ratio tests the short-term liquidity of the business.

Debt to Equity Ratio

$$\frac{\text{Total Liabilities}}{\text{Total Equity}}$$

This ratio should usually be one or less, but benchmarks for this ratio vary considerably among different

RATIOS AND ANALYSIS	
	Jan-99
Quick Ratio	————
Current Ratio	————
Debt to Equity Ratio	————
Debt to Assets Ratio	———
Return on Equity Ratio	———
Return on Assets Ratio	———
Sales Break Even	0
Working Capital	0
	========

PREPARING THE FINANCIALS

RATIOS AND ANALYSIS

	Jan-99
Quick Ratio	_____
Current Ratio	_____
Debt to Equity Ratio	_____
Debt to Assets Ratio	_____
Return on Equity Ratio	_____
Return on Assets Ratio	_____
Sales Break Even	0
Working Capital	0
	========

industries. This ratio indicates how heavy the debt load of the business is versus the equity. A high debt to equity ratio may indicate the business may be considered by potential lenders to be at its debt capacity and too risky a candidate for additional debt financing.

Debt to Assets Ratio

$$\frac{\text{Total Liabilities}}{\text{Total Assets}}$$

This ratio should be .5 or less, but benchmarks for this ratio vary considerably among different industries. This ratio is almost identical to the debt to equity ratio, except that the debt load is compared to assets plus equity, instead of just equity.

Return on Equity Ratio

$$\frac{\text{Net Profit}}{\text{Total Equity}}$$

This ratio should be high enough to make it worthwhile for investors to make equity investments in the business. This ratio should reflect an expected return high enough to offset risks of the investment. Because virtually all new and/or small businesses have a lot of risks, investors expect to earn much higher returns than if they invested in larger, more stable businesses.

PREPARING THE FINANCIALS

Return on Assets Ratio

$$\frac{\text{Net Profit}}{\text{Total Assets}}$$

This ratio shows how effectively the business uses it's total assets in earning net profits. This ratio should at least be significantly higher than the highest interest rate the firm will be paying on its debt financing.

Sales Break Even

$$\frac{\text{Fixed Costs}}{1 - (\text{cost of goods \%} + \text{commission \%} + \text{freight \%})}$$

This value indicates the amount of sales that you need to achieve to reach break-even.

Your break-even level should be significantly lower than your most likely sales projection.

Cost of goods sold, commissions and freight are all costs that vary with sales.

Working Capital

Current Assets — Current Liabilities

Working capital measures the amount of funds that the business has available to pay for the daily operations of the business. This number should be positive and should be large enough to easily cover the expected ebbs and flows of running the business.

RATIOS AND ANALYSIS

	Jan-99
Quick Ratio	_____
Current Ratio	_____
Debt to Equity Ratio	_____
Debt to Assets Ratio	_____
Return on Equity Ratio	_____
Return on Assets Ratio	_____
Sales Break Even	0
Working Capital	0
	=========

PREPARING THE FINANCIALS

Alternative Calculation Method

For several of the above ratios (Debt to Equity Ratio, Debt to Assets Ratio, Return on Equity Ratio, Return on Total Assets Ratio), there is an alternative, slightly more complex, method than we have used for the calculation. For our calculations we have used the equity or assets at the end of the period, as reflected on the balance sheet. Instead, you could determine these ratios using the average equity or assets employed during the period. To determine the average equity or assets employed you take the starting amount and the ending amount and divide by 2. However, it is very unlikely that any potential banker or investor will ask you refine these ratios.

Annualizing Returns

For use of capital ratios (Return on Equity Ratio, Return on Total Assets Ratio) we have used the return for each period shown. In other words the return in each monthly column is on a monthly basis, whereas the return for each year is on an annual basis. As an alternative you could annualize the monthly return ratios by multiplying them by 12. So a return that may currently show 1% per month, would instead show 12% per year.

> The alternative calculation method is more precise, but also more work.

CHAPTER 16

Sample Plans

RAINBOW KITES, INC.

BUSINESS PLAN: RAINBOW KITES, INC.

Note: This business plan (for a fictitious business) was created by editing and adapting the pre-written text provided earlier in this book. It took me only four hours to produce this entire plan using our companion software to automate both the writing of the text and the creation of the financials.

Summary

Business Concept

The kite industry has expanded rapidly in the past several years and growth is expected to continue at a strong pace for the foreseeable future. This offers excellent opportunities for new companies to enter this market. We intend to address the needs of customers in this market who seek higher quality, higher priced kites. We will address this need by importing, selling and distributing higher end kites in the United States and Canada. Distinguishing characteristics of our business will be top quality products, special emphasis on higher end independent retailers, and a high level of service.

Current Situation

We are a start-up, incorporated in 1998 in the State of California. The principal owner is Tom Anderson whose title is President and who has many years of experience in the toy industry. Other key personnel include Nancy Anderson, his spouse who has experience in customer service, bookkeeping, and office work. At this time we are seeking additional equity capital to compliment our own equity investment and seeking to arrange a bank line for inventory and receivables financing. We have firm commitments to distribute several highly sought after overseas kite manufacturers and have verbal commitments from independent retailers primarily along the West Coast to stock our products. We hope to ship our first products within six months of finalizing financing arrangements.

Key Success Factors

The success of our business will be largely a result of superior products, superior service, extra attention to detail throughout our operation, personnel, and our high level of experience in the industry. In particular, what really sets us apart from the competition is that we are ONLY going to sell high end kites and we are ONLY going to sell to higher end outlets. This will allow us to give absolutely top service and product selection for these accounts without getting distracted from the very different product and service demands of the more mass market outlets.

Financial Situations/Needs

In order to effectively launch the business, we project a total need for $300,000 in equity financing. Principal uses of the funds will be to finance operations until cash flow becomes positive and to create a stronger balance sheet in order to help secure additional bank lending to finance against inventory and receivables. To date we have raised $132,000 from founders, Tom and Nancy Anderson, and their relatives. We project that the company will be profitable within two years. We project that within three years of reaching breakeven that this new investment could be cashed out by either the founding partners purchasing this investment stake or by replacing the investment stake with additional bank financing.

Vision

Vision Statement

Our vision of what our company will become in the future is to have developed relationships with key retailers so strong that they will view us more as indispensable partners than just another supplier. We will work closely with each retailer we serve to recommend product assortment unique for their customer base, appropriate stocking levels, pricing and display assortments. We will constantly seek out and work with the manufacturers we represent to deliver the most innovative and exciting products possible to the retailers we serve.

Milestones

1. Overseas manufacturers agreements in place . . . done.
2. Verbal commitments from many West Coast retailers . . . done.
3. Presentation to potential investors . . . underway now.
4. Presentation to potential banks for inventory and receivable financing . . . underway now.
5. Financing commitments in place . . . 60 days.
6. Product catalog completed . . . 30 days.
7. Additional sales reps being recruited . . . underway now.
8. Sales rep selection finalized . . . 60 days.
9. Warehouse lease signed . . . 90 days.
10. First written orders from retailers . . . 75 days.
11. First orders to manufacturers . . . 110 days.
12. First shipments from our warehouse . . . 160 days.

Market Analysis

The Overall Market

The overall size of the industry is currently $150 million in the United States and Canada. Because the industry includes a very diverse group of product types with significantly different characteristics, it is more meaningful to break out analysis of the industry into roughly two groups. The first group and by far the larger unit volume are lower end kites sold primarily through mass market outlets such as discount department stores. The second group are higher end kites that are sold largely at independent and specialty chain stores. While the unit volume is much less, the dollar volume is approximately the same ($75 million) as that for lower end kites because the average price point is much higher.

Changes in the Market

The most significant development in this marketplace recently has been the shift in toy and kite business away from independent stores to national mass marketers over the past decade. However, recently this trend has slowed as independent toy and novelty retailers have become better at differentiating themselves and their product selections from those offered by national mass marketers.

Market Segments

The market is primarily segmented by distribution channel. The mass market retailers are looking for low-priced products and a high percentage of their products are licensed merchandise, for example based upon kid's cartoon characters. Independent specialty retailers however are trying increasingly to be as different from the mass merchants as possible and are generally selling much higher priced product and seldom want merchandise based upon licensed cartoon characters.

It should be pointed out that there are few stores that sell just kite merchandise—even among independent specialty stores most of the volume in kites is sold at stores that sell a wide assortment of other merchandise such as toys or other novelty items.

Target Market and Customers

Our target market is independent and small chain merchants that are committed to selling higher end kite products.

We particularly want to focus on accounts that just sell higher end kite products and that are committed to stocking a selection of at least a dozen different kite products. These accounts we feel offer the best growth potential and will benefit the most by the help we can bring to them in selecting and displaying our higher end merchandise.

Customer Needs

The basic need of target retail customers is to differentiate their store from mass market stores and give customers a reason for shopping their store and paying significant premiums for their products instead of getting a low-end product at a discount department store.

These stores really appreciate stocking a line that is not sold at mass market accounts. They also appreciate dealing with an importer who is committed to specialty stores exclusively, not mass market accounts.

Customer Buying Decisions

The buying decision is almost always made at an in-person sales presentation. The personal touch appears to be essential for moving buyers to action for this product because at these high end retailers are very demanding about the product quality being stocked in their stores. They insist upon seeing finished products, not just mock-ups or catalog pages. Some purchases are made at trade shows, but only a small percentage.

Competitive Analysis

Industry Overview

Across the United States and Canada there are many firms that distribute kites. The vast majority however distribute only one or two low end kites as a very small part of their overall distribution business.

There are several distribution firms that offer between a dozen and as many as one hundred kite products. These firms represent many different products and the sale of kites represents a very small fraction of their business. These firms also to a wide variety of outlets including mass merchant accounts.

Changes in the Industry

The big change in the kite industry over the last few years has been the concentration of lower end kite sales in mass market accounts, along with a strengthening market for higher end kites in upscale specialty accounts.

Current distributors representing larger kite product lines, while still selling to a wide variety of outlets, have tended to focus most of their efforts on selling lower end products to mass market type accounts—where their revenue is much greater.

Opportunities

While the competition is well established in and gives a lot of focus to current major markets for this product, they are much less aggressively pursuing the higher end kite market. This market offers terrific potential because it has significant growth potential, and the competition is not well entrenched here. Furthermore, this market differs from the other markets in the many important ways. While this market may not be the largest, it appears a very solid opportunity for a newer competitor.

Threats and Risks

Because we are a small firm, we do not anticipate a meaningful or prompt reaction to our market entrance from our larger and more established competitors. We think a strong reaction from existing distribution firms is particularly unlikely because the primary competitors derive only a very small percentage of their business from kite sales, and even that revenue is largely from mass market accounts that we plan on avoiding. However, we have developed contingency plans for certain reactions that competitors may make. If a competitor lowers their prices on the exact same product we are offering we will match their price on that product. But we intend as much as possible to emphasize products that our competitors are not selling to begin with.

Strategy

Key Competitive Capabilities

We are better positioned than our main competitors to take advantage of the increasing demands of upscale independent specialty stores to sharply differentiate their kite selection from those of mass merchants. Because we are going to focus exclusively on importing higher end kites for independent specialty stores we will be much better able to serve their needs than current distributors who handle many items other than kites and also give their primary attention to larger mass merchandise customers.

Tom Anderson's extensive experience in the toy business and his solid knowledge of the kite market in North America, his personal contacts at independent retailers on the West Coast, and his contacts at overseas suppliers give us a strong competitive advantage.

Nancy Anderson's background in running offices and handling customer service issues will give us a strong service advantage.

Key Competitive Weaknesses

Our primary weakness is that we are a new business competing largely against established firms. To significantly build sales, we must not just find new customers—we must take customers away from existing firms. However, by offering a superior selection of kites and focusing exclusively on upscale independent stores we feel will can quickly open accounts at many retailers and build strong relationships. Cofounder Tom Anderson has had many discussion with owners and buyers at retailers that confirm this opinion.

Another disadvantage we have is stronger personal ties with accounts on the West Coast of the United States and Canada than in other parts these countries. We plan on offsetting this weakness by hiring experienced commission reps for other territories. We have already had preliminary discussions with several highly successful reps and these reps have shown interest in continuing discussions with us.

Financially, we do need additional funding. But after the targeted funding is in place we will have ample financing for the foreseeable future.

Strategy

Our strategy is to focus 100% of our efforts on the market for upscale kites. By focusing all of our effort and energy on this particular niche, we expect to quickly develop and maintain a leadership position. While other firms try to be all things to all people, we believe that our singular focus will give us significant advantages. Most of the firms serving this niche now also serve much larger markets and give only secondary attention to the upscale. On the other hand, our firm will give our total focus to this niche; our key people will stay in personal touch with customers in this niche; and we will be able to respond to changes in this market much faster than our competitors.

We will offer the best, most highly personalized service in the marketplace we serve. Especially being a very small, owner-operated company, we intend to use this to our advantage to be absolutely certain that every one of our customers receives excellent service. We will go out of our way to make sure that our customers know that they truly matter to us. For example we will carefully recommend seasonal inventory plans for each store that reflects the customer traffic that the store receives. We will also make display suggestions and create a number of displays that can be adopted to the needs of particular stores. Sales reps and inhouse employees who deal with customers will be carefully trained and will be given wide latitude for insuring that customers are always satisfied.

Products/Services

Product/Service Description

Our underlying philosophy in selecting products has been to choose lines that will bring excitement, surprise and satisfaction to demanding higher end customers. We personally test each individual product. Special attention is giving to ease of assembly, durability, and general overall attraction.

We prefer to choose lines that we can represent exclusively, but because our first priority is on representing top-of-the-line merchandise, we have agreed to take on two leading lines on a non-exclusive basis.

A complete draft copy of our first catalog detailing our initial product lines and products is available upon request.

An important component of our business is not just our products but our service. These are some of the important service elements we offer:

- Stocking of all products offered in our West Coast warehouse, avoiding long waits to fill orders from overseas
- Detailed advice on inventory planning and sales forecasting for individual stores
- Display fixtures custom built to suit the needs of our customers
- Full returnability for any product defects
- Coordination of co-operative advertising programs with manufacturers

Positioning of Products/Services

We intend to position our business not just as a distributor of products, but a partner bringing a high level of service to the stores that we enter into business with.

We will work with stores through merchandise selection and display options to significantly increase the sales and profitability of their kite business. By doing this we expect to develop a strong loyalty among our customers.

Sales and Marketing

Marketing Strategy

Our basic marketing strategy is to work with our retailers on a one-to-one basis to develop unique marketing programs for them. Especially because we want to develop close working relationships with our customers, we want to establish accounts in as personable a way as possible too. Hence we will overwhelmingly emphasis in-person sales calls to build accounts.

We will closely integrate all of our marketing and sales efforts to project a consistent image of our company and a consistent positioning of our products or services. We will build this image around our name, "Rainbow Kites, Inc.", and will emphasize to retailers what the wonderful color and excitement of a well-done display of top quality kites can add to their store.

While we will attend some trade shows and produce a color catalog, these marketing initiatives are seen as supporting, not competing, with our independent sales representatives.

Sales Tactics

Our primary sales method is face-to-face selling by independent reps A particularly important aspect of our sales process is that we will fly all of our independent reps to our West Coast office to extensively train them in our product line, in building displays, and in building a bigger kite business for our customers.

We will insist that our independent reps represent only noncompeting, non-kite lines. We will stay in close phone contact with our reps in addition to having sales meetings with them at least four times per year, usually at major trade shows.

We will pay our reps on a "ledger" basis, giving them commission on all sales in their exclusive territories even if the account phoned the order in directly to our main office.

Advertising

We will have a small advertising budget, devoted exclusively to trade publications designed to reach buyers and owners of upscale independent stores. The objective of our trade advertising will be limited to reinforcing the image of our company and the excitement of stocking upscale kites. All ads will be four-color and between 1/4 and 1/8 page in size. Each ad will prominently feature our logo and a bright, colorful, changing display of upscale kites.

We will also work with our retailers to obtain co-op advertising funds for their own local advertising. Currently, very little co-op money is being provided by kite manufacturers, but we believe that we can make more funds available, especially if we work with a United States ad agency to develop effective advertising layouts and copy that our retailers could use.

Publicity

Our publicity effort will be three fold. First, we will send news releases to trade magazine to try to get product or company feature coverage in front of the eyes of retailers. Second, we will product a few generic press releases about kites that our retailers can use to try to obtain publicity coverage for their stores in local publications. Third, we shall have a quarterly newsletter for retailers that we are currently serving or hope to be serving. We anticipate sending 1,000 copies of the news release out our first year and gradually increasing to 2,000 copies by our third year. In the newsletter we will highlight not just our products, but also display ideas and success stories of stores who increased their kite sales.

Trade Shows, et. al.

We will have a small booth or table top display at four national conventions each year, including the National Toy Show in February in New York, The Toy and Hobby Show in April in Toronto, The International Gift Show in Las Vegas, and the West Coast Toy and Gift Fair in May. We will emphasize not just our products but the custom-built displays that we are producing for retailers.

We will also provide limited funds for display space for our independent reps at regional trade shows that they attend. Typically we will pay for one table top display.

Operations

Key Personnel

The Company will be managed by the two founding partners, whose individual areas of expertise covers many of the functional aspects of the business. Tom Anderson will serve as the President of the Company, and will be responsible for Product Selection and Sales & Marketing. Nancy Anderson will be the Vice President, in charge of Administration. She will be responsible for customer service, accounting, shipping and the general administration of the business.

Tom Anderson has a long history of experience in the toy business and specifically in kites. For several years he grew the kite business at Ocean Gifts and Toys in Los Angeles into one of the largest and most profitable exciting in the country. Tom has a many industry contacts and an in-depth knowledge of the kite and toy business. See Tom's resume for further details.

Nancy Anderson directed a staff of twelve as the manager of customer service for LA Selections, a major local jobber of novelty goods. She has also held a wide variety of other inside business and operations positions. See Nancy's resume for further details.

Organizational Structure

The organizational structure is very simple. The independent commissioned reps will report to Tom Anderson. Support staff at the office and warehouse will report to Nancy. Because Tom will frequently go on buying trips to the Far East or be on the road selling, Nancy will be able to support any day-to-day needs that the reps may have. However even when Tom is on the road he will be in constant touch by computer or phone.

Product/Service Delivery

In order to deliver high quality, personalized service we will carefully select all employees—especially sales reps and customer service representatives who deal directly with customers. Tom is currently interviewing candidates for sales reps. We will carefully review references not from past employers or manufacturers but from retailers whom these sales reps have served. We will also make sure that each employee understands our way of delivering quality service to each customer. We will have immediate backup support available by phone from our office for more difficult service issues. And we will give employees enough latitude so that they can respond immediately to almost all customer requests or complaints—which in this industry usually means granting prompt credit for damaged merchandise.

Customer Service/Support

We intend to prioritize customer service and make it a key component of our marketing programs. We believe that providing our customers with what they want, when and how they want it, is the key to repeat business and to word-of-mouth advertising. Not only will we train our employees to deliver excellent service, we will give them the flexibility to respond creatively to client requests. In addition, we will continually monitor our clients' level of satisfaction with our service through surveys and other convenient feedback opportunities.

Initially we expect to have few enough accounts so that Nancy and one additional employee can handle all customer service issues. Having just one employee to train should help insure that Nancy can help make the new hire a top performer. As our business grows we intend to hire additional customer service people one at a time and pay a premium over market labor rates to attract and retain quality help.

Shipping problems are a huge issue with the firms that we compete with largely because they insist on using surface shipping methods to keep their costs down to charge low prices to keep their mass merchant accounts happy.

We intend to use air freight to import our kites from the Far East. This will add to our costs slightly. But because all of our products are more expensive it makes more sense for us. It will also allow us to have much thinner inventories in our warehouse without risking stocking out.

Our relatively high cost of shipping has put us at a competitive disadvantage. The current cost of shipping for an average order is $ . . . , which we feel can be reduced by . . . %. We intend to achieve this cost reduction by putting our overall shipping requirements out to bid.

RAINBOW KITES, INC. RAINBOW KITES, INC.

Facilities

We plan to lease approximately 10,000 square feet of space as soon as our financing is finalized. We have a specific property in mind and have a tentative agreement with the landlord's agent. This building located near LAX airport has 8,500 feet of warehouse space and a small 850 square foot office. The lease rate is $6.35 per foot triple net for a 2 year lease with the option for two additional years at an increase of 5.9% per year.

The building is located in a busy industrial neighborhood, but because we do not intend to have customers visit us we have decided we are better off with a lower-rent location than a location that could double as a fancy showroom.

RAINBOW KITES, INC. RAINBOW KITES, INC.

Assumptions and Comments Worksheet

Name of Plan:	Rainbow Kites, Inc.
Starting Month:	Jan-2000
Years:	5
Commissions:	**10.00**
Freight Costs:	**3.00**
Payroll Tax Rate:	**13.00**
Income Tax Rate:	**35.00**
Days Inventory:	**90**
Cost of Sales:	**60.00**
Credit Sales?:	y
Credit Sales %:	**100.00**
Days Credit:	**60**
Cost of Sales A/P?:	y
Cost of Sales A/P %:	**100.00**
Cost of Sales Days A/P:	**30**
General A/P?:	y
General A/P %:	**100.00**
Days General A/P:	**30**
S-T Interest Rate:	**10.00**
L-T Interest Rate:	**11.00**
Expense Headings	

RAINBOW KITES, INC. RAINBOW KITES, INC.

Starting Balance Sheet

Rainbow Kites, Inc.
Starting Balance Sheet

	Balance
Assets	
Current Assets	
Cash	110,100
Accounts Receivable	0
Inventory	0
Other Current Assets	0
Total Current Assets	110,100
Long Term Assets	
Depreciable Assets	10,400
Accumulated Depreciation	800
Net Depreciable Assets	9,600
Non-Depreciable Assets	0
Total Long-Term Assets	9,600
Total assets	119,700
Liabilities & Equity	
Current Liabilities	
Cost of Sales A/P	0
Non-Cost of Sales A/P	0
Short-Term Debt	0
Income Taxes Due	0
Total Current Liabilities	0
Long-Term Debt	0
Equity	
Stock & Paid-in Capital	132,000
Retained Earnings	-12,300
Total Equity	119,700
Total Liabilities & Equity	119,700
Note: Total Assets must equal	
Total Liabilities & Equity	

RAINBOW KITES, INC. RAINBOW KITES, INC.

Profit and Loss Forecast

Rainbow Kites, Inc.
Profit and Loss Projection

	Jan-2000	Feb-2000	Mar-2000	Apr-2000	May-2000	Jun-2000	Jul-2000	Aug-2000	Sep-2000	Oct-2000	Nov-2000	Dec-2000	Total 2000	2001	2002	2003	2004
Sales	0	0	0	0	60,000	80,000	100,000	120,000	140,000	160,000	180,000	200,000	1,040,000	3,000,000	4,000,000	4,500,000	5,000,000
Costs																	
Cost Of Sales	0	0	0	0	36,000	48,000	60,000	72,000	84,000	96,000	108,000	120,000	624,000	1,800,000	2,400,000	2,700,000	3,000,000
Gross Profit	0	0	0	0	24,000	32,000	40,000	48,000	56,000	64,000	72,000	80,000	416,000	1,200,000	1,600,000	1,800,000	2,000,000
Gross Profit Margin	0.0%	0.0%	0.0%	0.0%	40.0%	40.0%	40.0%	40.0%	40.0%	40.0%	40.0%	40.0%	40.0%	40.0%	40.0%	40.0%	40.0%
Marketing & Sales																	
Commissions	0	0	0	0	6,000	8,000	10,000	12,000	14,000	16,000	18,000	20,000	104,000	300,000	400,000	450,000	500,000
Literature & Mailings	0	2,000	2,000	2,000	2,000	2,000	2,000	2,000	2,000	2,000	2,000	2,000	22,000	30,000	30,000	30,000	30,000
Advertising & Publicity	0	5,000	5,000	5,000	5,000	5,000	5,000	5,000	5,000	5,000	5,000	5,000	55,000	80,000	80,000	80,000	80,000
Other Marketing	0	3,000	3,000	3,000	3,000	3,000	3,000	3,000	3,000	3,000	3,000	3,000	33,000	50,000	50,000	50,000	50,000
Total Marketing & Sales	0	10,000	10,000	10,000	16,000	18,000	20,000	22,000	24,000	26,000	28,000	30,000	214,000	460,000	560,000	610,000	660,000
General & Admin.																	
Payroll	6,700	7,700	7,700	8,900	9,600	9,600	9,600	11,200	11,200	11,200	11,200	11,200	115,800	160,000	180,000	200,000	220,000
Payroll Taxes, Benefits	871	1,001	1,001	1,157	1,248	1,248	1,248	1,456	1,456	1,456	1,456	1,456	15,054	20,800	23,400	26,000	28,600
Facilities & Equip Rent	0	0	8,500	8,500	8,500	8,500	8,500	8,500	8,500	8,500	8,500	8,500	85,000	108,000	112,000	117,000	122,000
Maintenance & Repairs	0	0	400	400	400	400	400	400	400	400	400	400	4,000	5,000	5,000	5,000	5,000
Utilities, Phone, Postage	600	600	1,200	1,200	1,200	1,200	1,200	1,200	1,200	1,200	1,200	1,200	13,200	16,000	16,000	16,000	16,000
Insurance	100	100	400	400	400	400	400	400	400	400	400	400	4,200	5,000	5,000	5,000	5,000
Supplies	200	200	200	200	200	200	200	200	200	200	200	200	2,400	2,500	2,500	2,500	2,500
Freight	0	0	0	0	1,800	2,400	3,000	3,600	4,200	4,800	5,400	6,000	31,200	90,000	120,000	135,000	150,000
Auto Travel & Entertain.	300	300	3,500	3,500	3,500	3,500	3,500	3,500	3,500	3,500	3,500	3,500	35,600	5,500	5,500	5,500	5,500
Legal & Accounting	1,000	1,000	1,000	1,000	1,000	1,000	1,000	1,000	1,000	1,000	1,000	1,000	12,000	12,000	12,000	12,000	12,000
Other Outside Services	200	200	600	600	600	600	600	600	600	600	600	600	6,400	8,000	8,000	8,000	8,000
Misc. Taxes, Fees	100	100	100	100	100	100	100	100	100	100	100	100	1,200	1,200	1,200	1,200	1,200
Depreciation	200	200	400	400	400	400	400	400	400	400	400	400	4,400	4,800	4,800	4,800	4,800
Other G&A Expenses	500	500	500	500	500	500	500	500	500	500	500	500	6,000	6,000	6,000	6,000	6,000
Total General & Admin.	10,771	11,901	25,501	26,857	29,448	30,048	30,648	33,056	33,656	34,256	34,856	35,456	336,454	444,800	501,400	544,000	586,600
Total Operating Costs	10,771	21,901	35,501	36,857	45,448	48,048	50,648	55,056	57,656	60,256	62,856	65,456	550,454	904,800	1,061,400	1,154,000	1,246,600
Operating Profit	-10,771	-21,901	-35,501	-36,857	-21,448	-16,048	-10,648	-7,056	-1,656	3,744	9,144	14,544	-134,454	295,200	538,600	646,000	753,400
Operating Profit Margin	0.0%	0.0%	0.0%	0.0%	-35.7%	-20.1%	-10.6%	-5.9%	-1.2%	2.3%	5.1%	7.3%	-12.9%	9.8%	13.5%	14.4%	15.1%
Non-Operating Costs																	
Interest	0	0	0	0	0	0	0	1,250	1,250	2,083	2,083	2,500	9,167	30,000	30,000	5,000	0
Profit Before Income Taxes	-10,771	-21,901	-35,501	-36,857	-21,448	-16,048	-10,648	-8,306	-2,906	1,661	7,061	12,044	-143,621	265,200	508,600	641,000	753,400
Pre-Tax Profit Margin	0.0%	0.0%	0.0%	0.0%	-35.7%	-20.1%	-10.6%	-6.9%	-2.1%	1.0%	3.9%	6.0%	-13.8%	8.8%	12.7%	14.2%	15.1%
Income Taxes	0	0	0	0	0	0	0	0	0	0	0	0	0	92,820	178,010	224,350	263,690
Net Profit	-10,771	-21,901	-35,501	-36,857	-21,448	-16,048	-10,648	-8,306	-2,906	1,661	7,061	12,044	-143,621	172,380	330,590	416,650	489,710
Net Profit Margin	0.0%	0.0%	0.0%	0.0%	-35.7%	-20.1%	-10.6%	-6.9%	-2.1%	1.0%	3.9%	6.0%	-13.8%	5.7%	8.3%	9.3%	9.8%

RAINBOW KITES, INC. RAINBOW KITES, INC.

Cash Flow Forecast

Rainbow Kites, Inc.
Cash Flow Projection

	Jan-2000	Feb-2000	Mar-2000	Apr-2000	May-2000	Jun-2000	Jul-2000	Aug-2000	Sep-2000	Oct-2000	Nov-2000	Dec-2000	2001	2002	2003	2004
Starting Cash	110,100	102,529	90,828	354,127	317,670	280,422	91,374	19,726	100,420	36,514	77,175	23,235	24,279	493	85,383	123,083
Sources																
Cash Sales	0	0	0	0	0	0	0	0	0	0	0	0	0	0	0	0
Credit Sales	0	0	0	0	0	0	60,000	80,000	100,000	120,000	140,000	160,000	2,880,000	3,833,333	4,416,667	4,916,667
Short-Term Loan Proceeds	0	0	0	0	0	0	0	150,000	0	100,000	0	50,000	0	0	0	0
Long-Term Loan Proceeds	0	0	0	0	0	0	0	0	0	0	0	0	0	0	0	0
Equity Capital Proceeds	0	0	300,000	0	0	0	0	0	0	0	0	0	0	0	0	0
Total Sources	0	0	300,000	0	0	0	60,000	230,000	100,000	220,000	140,000	210,000	2,880,000	3,833,333	4,416,667	4,916,667
Uses																
Cost of Sales / Inventory	0	0	0	0	0	144,000	84,000	96,000	108,000	120,000	132,000	144,000	1,888,500	2,495,000	2,756,250	3,050,000
Payroll & Related	7,571	8,701	8,701	10,057	10,848	10,848	10,848	12,656	12,656	12,656	12,656	12,656	180,800	203,400	226,000	248,600
Non-Payroll Expenses	0	3,000	13,000	26,400	26,400	34,200	36,800	39,400	42,000	44,600	47,200	49,800	711,667	842,033	917,367	987,367
Interest	0	0	0	0	0	0	0	1,250	1,250	2,083	2,083	2,500	30,000	30,000	5,000	0
Purchase Depreciable Assets	0	0	15,000	0	0	0	0	0	0	0	0	0	0	0	0	0
Purchase Non-Dep. Assets	0	0	0	0	0	0	0	0	0	0	0	0	0	0	0	0
Dividends, Owner Pay-Outs	0	0	0	0	0	0	0	0	0	0	0	0	0	0	0	0
Short-Term Debt Payments	0	0	0	0	0	0	0	0	0	0	0	0	0	0	250,000	50,000
Long-Term Debt Payments	0	0	0	0	0	0	0	0	0	0	0	0	0	0	0	0
Total Uses Before Taxes	7,571	11,701	36,701	36,457	37,248	189,048	131,648	149,306	163,906	179,339	193,939	208,956	2,810,967	3,570,433	4,154,617	4,335,967
Income Taxes	0	0	0	0	0	0	0	0	0	0	0	0	92,820	178,010	224,350	263,690
Total Uses After Taxes	7,571	11,701	36,701	36,457	37,248	189,048	131,648	149,306	163,906	179,339	193,939	208,956	2,903,787	3,748,443	4,378,967	4,599,657
Net Change In Cash	-7,571	-11,701	263,299	-36,457	-37,248	-189,048	-71,648	80,694	-63,906	40,661	-53,939	1,044	-23,787	84,890	37,700	317,010
Ending Cash Position	102,529	90,828	354,127	317,670	280,422	91,374	19,726	100,420	36,514	77,175	23,235	24,279	493	85,383	123,083	440,093

RAINBOW KITES, INC. RAINBOW KITES, INC.

Balance Sheet Forecast

Rainbow Kites, Inc.
Balance Sheet Projection

Period Ending:	Jan-2000	Feb-2000	Mar-2000	Apr-2000	May-2000	Jun-2000	Jul-2000	Aug-2000	Sep-2000	Oct-2000	Nov-2000	Dec-2000	2001	2002	2003	2004
Assets																
Current assets																
Cash	102,529	90,828	354,127	317,670	280,422	91,374	19,726	100,420	36,514	77,175	23,235	24,279	493	85,383	123,083	440,093
Accounts Receivable	0	0	0	0	60,000	140,000	180,000	220,000	260,000	300,000	340,000	380,000	500,000	666,667	750,000	833,333
Inventory	0	0	0	0	108,000	144,000	180,000	216,000	252,000	288,000	324,000	360,000	450,000	600,000	675,000	750,000
Other Current Assets	0	0	0	0	0	0	0	0	0	0	0	0	0	0	0	0
Total Current Assets	102,529	90,828	354,127	317,670	448,422	375,374	379,726	536,420	548,514	665,175	687,235	764,279	950,493	1,352,049	1,548,083	2,023,426
Long-Term Assets																
Depreciable Assets	10,400	10,400	25,400	25,400	25,400	25,400	25,400	25,400	25,400	25,400	25,400	25,400	25,400	25,400	25,400	25,400
Accumulated Depreciation	1,000	1,200	1,600	2,000	2,400	2,800	3,200	3,600	4,000	4,400	4,800	5,200	10,000	14,800	19,600	24,400
Net Depreciable Assets	9,400	9,200	23,800	23,400	23,000	22,600	22,200	21,800	21,400	21,000	20,600	20,200	15,400	10,600	5,800	1,000
Non-Depreciable Assets	0	0	0	0	0	0	0	0	0	0	0	0	0	0	0	0
Total Long-Term Assets	9,400	9,200	23,800	23,400	23,000	22,600	22,200	21,800	21,400	21,000	20,600	20,200	15,400	10,600	5,800	1,000
Total Assets	111,929	100,028	377,927	341,070	471,422	397,974	401,926	558,220	569,914	686,175	707,835	784,479	965,893	1,362,649	1,553,883	2,024,426
Liabilities & Equity																
Current Liabilities																
Short-Term Debt	0	0	0	0	0	0	0	150,000	150,000	250,000	250,000	300,000	300,000	300,000	50,000	0
Cost of Sales A/P	0	0	0	0	144,000	84,000	96,000	108,000	120,000	132,000	144,000	156,000	157,500	212,500	231,250	256,250
Non-Cost of Sales A/P	3,000	13,000	26,400	26,400	34,200	36,800	39,400	42,000	44,600	47,200	49,800	52,400	59,933	71,100	76,933	82,767
Income Taxes Due	0	0	0	0	0	0	0	0	0	0	0	0	0	0	0	0
Total Current Liabilities	3,000	13,000	26,400	26,400	178,200	120,800	135,400	300,000	314,600	429,200	443,800	508,400	517,433	583,600	358,183	339,017
Long-Term Debt	0	0	0	0	0	0	0	0	0	0	0	0	0	0	0	0
Equity																
Stock & Paid-in Capital	132,000	132,000	432,000	432,000	432,000	432,000	432,000	432,000	432,000	432,000	432,000	432,000	432,000	432,000	432,000	432,000
Retained Earnings	-23,071	-44,972	-80,473	-117,330	-138,778	-154,826	-165,474	-173,780	-176,686	-175,025	-167,965	-155,921	16,459	347,049	763,699	1,253,409
Total Equity	108,929	87,028	351,527	314,670	293,222	277,174	266,526	258,220	255,314	256,975	264,035	276,079	448,459	779,049	1,195,699	1,685,409
Total Liabilities & Equity	111,929	100,028	377,927	341,070	471,422	397,974	401,926	558,220	569,914	686,175	707,835	784,479	965,893	1,362,649	1,553,883	2,024,426

RAINBOW KITES, INC. RAINBOW KITES, INC.

Key Ratios

Rainbow Kites, Inc.
Ratios and Analysis

	Jan-2000	Feb-2000	Mar-2000	Apr-2000	May-2000	Jun-2000	Jul-2000	Aug-2000	Sep-2000	Oct-2000	Nov-2000	Dec-2000	2000	2001	2002	2003	2004
Quick Ratio	34.18	6.99	13.41	12.03	1.91	1.92	1.48	1.07	0.94	0.88	0.82	0.80	0.80	0.97	1.29	2.44	3.76
Current Ratio	34.18	6.99	13.41	12.03	2.52	3.11	2.80	1.79	1.74	1.55	1.55	1.50	1.50	1.84	2.32	4.32	5.97
Debt to Equity Ratio	0.03	0.15	0.08	0.08	0.61	0.44	0.51	1.16	1.23	1.67	1.68	1.84	1.84	1.15	0.75	0.30	0.20
Debt to Assets Ratio	0.03	0.13	0.07	0.08	0.38	0.30	0.34	0.54	0.55	0.63	0.63	0.65	0.65	0.54	0.43	0.23	0.17
Return on Equity Ratio	-0.10	-0.25	-0.10	-0.12	-0.07	-0.06	-0.04	-0.03	-0.01	0.01	0.03	0.04	-0.52	0.38	0.42	0.35	0.29
Return on Assets Ratio	-0.10	-0.22	-0.09	-0.11	-0.05	-0.04	-0.03	-0.01	-0.01	0.00	0.01	0.02	-0.18	0.18	0.24	0.27	0.24
Sales Break Even	39,893	81,115	131,485	136,507	139,437	139,437	139,437	146,133	146,133	146,133	146,133	146,133	1,537,978	1,906,667	2,005,185	2,107,407	2,209,630
Working Capital	99,529	77,828	327,727	291,270	270,222	254,574	244,326	236,420	233,914	235,975	243,435	255,879	255,879	433,059	768,449	1,189,899	1,684,409

CHAPTER 17

Sample Plans

LAWN MASTERS OF NEWTON

LAWN MASTERS OF NEWTON

BUSINESS PLAN: LAWN MASTERS OF NEWTON

Note: This business plan (for a fictitious business) was created by editing and adapting the pre-written text provided earlier in this book.

Summary

Business Concept

Lawn Masters of Newton is part of the lawn maintenance industry. Our target market is homeowners in the Newton, Massachusetts community. Our principal service is lawn care, including seeding, fertilizing, mowing, and shrubbery and tree care. Our service differs from competitors in that we offer a complete set of services offered on an a la carte basis. Our intention is that the company will become the leading provider of lawn maintenance services in Newton.

We have been successful in providing lawn maintenance services, with a special emphasis on one-stop shopping. We have an excellent reputation and are best known for our customer service and flexibility, which differentiates us from our competitors. The company is profitable and has great potential for growth and for becoming a leader in the local market area. To best take advantage of our growth opportunities, the company would like to purchase new maintenance equipment and move to a larger facility. These expenditures will allow us to finance and support our planned growth, without sacrificing the quality of service that we are known for.

Current Situation

The company was founded as a corporation in the Commonwealth of Massachusetts on April 1, 1986. Currently the company is well established in its market, with sales in our past fiscal year reaching $1,350,000. In recent years our sales have been growing steadily. The major challenge the firm is facing at this point is expansion in order to increase market share. It intends to respond to this challenge by purchasing new equipment so that we are able to put more teams in the field, by moving to a larger facility, and by launching several innovative marketing and publicity efforts.

LAWN MASTERS OF NEWTON

In the next few years, it is estimated that lawn maintenance services in Newton, Massachusetts will grow by at least 10–20%. This growth will be driven by the aging of the population base, the increasing value of residential property in Newton, and the robust overall economic situation in New England. We know that we are not the only company to see the business opportunities created by this expected growth, but we do feel that our one-stop, menu-oriented service structure is a unique response to the situation that will help us stand out in what will be a crowded marketplace.

Key Success Factors

The success of our business has been and will continue to be largely a result of our ability to deliver dependable, high quality lawn maintenance services custom tailored to each customer's needs.

More specifically, the key factors that can be identified as being particularly important in our firm's ability to succeed are:

1. A comprehensive set of lawn maintenance services—we can do it all
2. A very flexible, menu-oriented system for choosing services
3. An especially well-trained staff, able to deal professionally with customers
4. A very well-organized set of operating procedures that guarantees our dependability

Another major asset is our highly talented and experienced management team. The three key individuals complement each other well, combining backgrounds in diverse group of important areas. Jack Duffy brings expertise in finance and management, Ed Davis brings expertise in lawn maintenance techniques and operations, and Janice Kendall brings expertise in sales and marketing. Together, these strengths cover all of the major aspects of the business with solid experience and a proven record of success.

We are, above all, very customer-focused, committed to solving all of our related customer's needs and doing everything we possibly can to keep them satisfied. This approach will insure that we retain a highly satisfied clientele and get referrals.

LAWN MASTERS OF NEWTON

Financial Situation/Needs

At this time we are seeking $30,000 in a credit line, and $180,000 in an asset-backed loan. The credit line will be used for moving expenses, improvements to the new facility, and early season advertising expenditures. The loan will be used to purchase equipment (utility truck and associated tools) for the ten new crews which will be needed to service our expanded customer base. We will be able to pay down the loan completely in 18 months, a process we will begin in August, 1998. The credit line will be cleared before the end of 1998.

LAWN MASTERS OF NEWTON

Goals

Vision Statement

Highly personalized service has always been the hallmark of Lawn Masters of Newton. As a very small, owner-operated company, we are able to be very flexible in the way we provide yard maintenance services and do whatever we can to accommodate our customer's needs—from mowing and pruning to fertilizing, mulching and weed control.

Now, we intend to be a stand-out even more as the best managed and most professionally operated firm operating in the City of Newton, Massachusetts. In a field filled with small mom-and-pop operators who run their businesses by the seat of their pants, we intend to distinguish ourselves by planning our services and operations very carefully; having rigorous hiring and training programs; having specific policies and standards for serving customers; and carefully monitoring the quality of our service. We are also going to carefully communicate to our customers the key differences and advantages in doing business with us so our target customers know that choosing us as a supplier is the safe choice for consistent, high quality service. These steps, we believe, will allow Lawn Masters of Newton to double our sales revenue during 1998.

Milestones

Important milestones for our business the upcoming year are:

Move to new facility	1/15/98
Obtaining financing for new equipment	2/01/98
Launching an upgrade of our services, The Total Lawn Maintenance Package	3/01/98
Launching a new advertising campaign	3/01/98
Adding local cable television advertising to our sales effort	3/01/98
Launching a Web site	3/01/98
Achieving sales of $2.2M	9/15/99

LAWN MASTERS OF NEWTON

Market Analysis

The Overall Market

We estimate the total current market for residential yard maintenance services in Newton, Massachusetts at about $12.5 million. We have derived this number by estimating the percentage of Newton homeowners (20%) who contract for these services and multiplying that number of customers (25,000 occupied housing units * 20% = 5,000) times an average annual fee for mowing, pruning and spring and fall clean-up, ($2500).

The current market for this service appears to be growing because several more companies offering these services just opened their doors in the last two years and all of the firms appear to be prospering. Furthermore, as discussed in the customer needs section of this plan, the overall market may be able to grow further if a new business can offer new service dimensions that meet needs not currently being served by existing competitors.

Changes in the Market

As the market for yard maintenance services continues to mature, buyers have become increasingly discerning and increasingly aware of and interested in the key feature/benefit differences from one competitor's offering to the next. As a result many, but not all, buyers are placing much added importance on features and performance and how well the service appears to serve their needs, and are placing less emphasis on price. We believe, for instance, that it will be to our competitive advantage to offer a full range of services—from mowing and pruning to seeding, weeding and insect control—so that customers will not have to contract a variety of different firms to accomplish all of their needs.

Market Segments

The market can be broken into basically three segments: the full-service segment for consumers who are more interested in a comprehensive approach and are less concerned with price; the midrange segment for consumers who want more than a bare bones package; and the economy segment for consumers who are most concerned with price. While some yard maintenance companies are on the borderline between these groupings, this

LAWN MASTERS OF NEWTON

segmentation applies to most service offerings, and most potential consumers are generally likely to only consider options within one segment at any one time.

Target Market and Customers

We intend to direct all of our effort within the City of Newton, Massachusetts. To reach our sales goals, we estimate that we will need to achieve about 20% market share — not enough to provoke an aggressive competitive response.

While we could easily travel to surrounding towns to provide yard maintenance services, we feel that from a marketing standpoint we are much better off focusing on Newton. One advantage is that we will be able to build sales momentum more easily by purchasing larger ads in one local newspaper. We feel that we will also be able to more quickly build a word-of-mouth reputation. The demographics of Newton, of course, are particularly good for our business.

Customer Characteristics

All of our prospective customers share the need for professional yard maintenance services. Most of them have the following characteristics: two-income homeowners; own at least quarter-acre lots with lawns, shrubs and trees; college educated; concerned with the environment and the proper use of pesticides and other chemical treatments. Many, but not all, of our target customers are middle-aged or elderly.

Customer Needs

Even within the market segment that we are targeting, customer needs vary significantly from one buyer to the next. Most companies are currently dealing with this broad range of market demands by specializing in servicing a narrow portion of the market segment; i.e., just offering lawn mowing, or focusing exclusively on reseeding and fertilizing services. We intend to take a "menu" approach, in which customers can pick and choose any level of services they need.

Customer Buying Decisions

The buying decision is almost always made at an in-person sales presentation. The personal touch appears to be essential for moving buyers to action for yard maintenance services because homeowners in Newton feel very protective and proprietary about their property. To support the sales presentation pricing incentives are not very important in closing the sale—but testimonials, especially from nearby neighbors, are.

Buyers in this market tend to put a lot of weight on the company rather than just on the particular merits of the product or service being offered. We intend to make this work to our advantage by carefully developing a very specific and favorable image for ourselves.

When we sell to married couples both the husband and the wife play a role in the decision making. Usually the husband plays the key decision-making role, but the other spouse must at least acquiesce for the purchase decision to move ahead. For this reason, we have found that it is highly desirable to be able to make the sales presentation when both spouses are home.

LAWN MASTERS OF NEWTON

Competitive Analysis

Industry Overview

Competition in the yard maintenance field is highly limited by locality. Customers are reluctant to use service providers based in distant locations and even tend to do business with a service organization that specifically focuses on their city or town. As a result, in our target market of Newton, Massachusetts, there are only eight significant direct competitors. Because these companies are private, exact sales information is not available, but based on their number of employees, we estimate that no one competitor dominates and that the market share for each firm ranges between 10% and 15%.

The actual competition in this industry is rather mild. Customers do not to switch firms very often and do not tend to carefully comparison shop before making buying decisions. Market shares have tended to be relatively stable. Competitors do not make aggressive marketing moves, such as running predatory or comparative advertising campaigns. There is little competition on price, and price incentives or promotions are rare. Relationships are of primary importance. Customers tend not to seriously consider unsolicited overtures from new vendors, and it takes a strong reason for them to specifically request a presentation from a new vendor.

The industry obviously has pronounced seasonal swings. The first quarter tends to account for less than 10% of sales. The second and third quarters represent the vast majority, over 80%, of sales. Some fall clean-up work extends into the fourth quarter, bringing in, like the first quarter, about 10% of the annual revenue. Seasonality in this industry has important implications—because the billings have to take place during the spring and summer months, it is essential to carry out any sales or marketing activities during the late winter so that customers can be signed up and ready by late March or early April.

Ease of entry in this industry can be characterized as moderately difficult. Barriers do not involve capital requirements or staffing issues, but rather the difficulty of developing a customer base from scratch.

Most firms in this industry are sole proprietorships or closely held corporations. These ownership patterns have been relatively steady for years. Debt loads in the industry tend to be relatively marginal, in the range of 20% of total capitalization.

LAWN MASTERS OF NEWTON

Nature of Competition

Competition focuses on the quality of service, particularly on reliability. Price is seldom emphasized and tends not to vary much between most firms. Instead, firms try to emphasize to their customers how their service is better than that of their competitors. For example, they might mention in their advertising or sales pitches the number of years in service in Newton and the guaranteed availability of crews and equipment.

Companies strive not only to build relationships with their current customers, but also to emphasize to new customers how strong and beneficial a long-term relationship with them will be. The emphasis is on selling not a particular product or service, but the whole company. Often extra intangibles, such as direct knowledge of an established customer's specific landscaping situation, are emphasized to show that the value of the whole relationship is greater than the sum of the actual services that are being sold.

Changes in the Industry

The industry is currently experiencing a period of moderate growth caused by the aging of the population base, the increasing value of residential property in Newton, and the robust economy. In the years ahead, this trend is expected to continue. We believe that there will be more and more customers, and that they will be looking for one single source for their yard maintenance needs. This gives a huge advantage to firms that offer an extremely flexible and broad array of services, and a disadvantage to those that don't.

Primary Competitors

Name	Green Lawns, Inc.
Location	123 Washington Street, Newton, MA
Sales	$1.3 million (est.)
Profitability	unknown
Number of employees	50 (peak)
Years in business	30
Strategy	Full service
Competitive strengths	Large client base
	Offer wide range of services

LAWN MASTERS OF NEWTON

Competitive weaknesses	Lack of modern management
Other pertinent info	

Name	Total Lawn
Location	88 Mt. Auburn Street, Watertown, MA
Sales	$2 million (est.)
Profitability	unknown
Number of employees	70 (peak)
Years in business	25
Strategy	Full service
Competitive strengths	Large client base
	Offer wide range of services
Competitive weaknesses	Lack of modern management
	Not focused in Newton
Other pertinent info	

Name	Landscaping Specialists
Location	78 Boylston Street, Newton, MA
Sales	unknown
Profitability	unknown
Number of employees	65 (est.)
Years in business	about 20
Strategy	Commercial and residential
Competitive strengths	Modern equipment
	Offers top quality commercial services
Competitive weaknesses	Perceived to be oriented toward businesses
Other pertinent info	Owned by holding company with several other similar businesses operating in different parts of Greater Boston

LAWN MASTERS OF NEWTON

Competitive Company Matrix

Main competitors	Green Lawns	Total Lawn	Landscaping Specialists
Industry rank	3	2	1
Overall competitiveness	1	2	3
Estimated sales	$1.2M	$2M	$2M+
Sales trend	up	steady	up
Estimated profits	$300K	$400K	$500K+
Financial strength	high	unknown	high
Apparent strategy	Full-service	Full-service	Full-service, Res. And Com.
Seen by customers as	Familiar	Outsiders	Business-oriented
Loyalty of customers	High	Medium	unknown
Quality reputation	Medium	Medium	High
Sales strength	Medium	Medium	High
Advertising strength	Low	Low	High
Use of promotions	Low	Low	Medium
#1 Strength	Service range	Service range	High Quality work
#1 Weakness	Disorganized	Disorganized	Non-residential focus

Our number one competitor is Green Lawns Inc. They compete largely by being a full service provider. Their major competitive strength is their years and years of full-service delivery in Newton. They have succeeded in the market because they have a local focus and they will agree to do just about anything.

Our number two competitor is Total Lawn. They compete largely by being a full service provider. Their major competitive strength is their large client base and the economies of scale that offers them. They have succeeded in the market because they operate in several communities and offer a wide range of services.

Our number three competitor is Landscaping Specialists. They compete largely by emphasizing quality and the most up-to-date equipment. Their major competitive strength is their professionalism They have succeeded in the market because they dominate the profitable commercial services sector.

Competitive Products/Services

Service	Complete lawn maintenance
Competitor	Green Lawns Inc.
Dollar sales	$1.3M
Sales trend	Up
Profitability estimate	$300K
Price	$2495
Target Buyers	Newton homeowners
Primary positioning	Full service
Features/attributes most emphasized in ads/sales pitches or packaging	1. Full service 2. Local experience
Sales methods	Flyers, telephone
Advertising budget	Minimal
Advertising themes	unknown
Promotional/incentive programs	Referral incentive ($100 off)
Competitive strengths	Full service Track record
Competitive weaknesses	Not well-managed
Other pertinent info	Their crews often appear and act unprofessionally

Service	Complete lawn maintenance
Competitor	Total Lawn
Dollar sales	$2M
Sales trend	Steady
Profitability estimate	$400K
Price	$2295
Target Buyers	Homeowners in Metrowest area

LAWN MASTERS OF NEWTON

Primary positioning	Full Service
Features/attributes most emphasized in ads/sales pitches or packaging	1. Full Service 2. Reliable
Sales methods	Telemarketing
Advertising budget	None
Advertising themes	unknown
Promotional/incentive programs	unknown
Competitive strengths	Full service Well-established
Competitive weaknesses	Lack of professionalism Lack of community focus
Service	**Complete lawn maintenance**
Competitor	Landscaping Specialists
Dollar sales	$2M - $3M
Sales trend	Up
Profitability estimate	$500K+
Price	$2750
Target Buyers	Homeowners in greater Boston
Primary positioning	Modern and Professional
Features/attributes most emphasized in ads/sales pitches or packaging	1. Up-to-date eqpt and techniques 2. Broad range of experience
Sales methods	Telemarketing Door-to-door Direct Mail Newspaper
Advertising budget	>$200K
Advertising themes	The best and most up-to-date
Promotional/incentive programs	Referral incentives Start early, save money

LAWN MASTERS OF NEWTON

Competitive strengths	Well-capitalized
	Well-managed
Competitive weaknesses	Not focused on residential services

Opportunities

An examination of the competitive offerings finds several weaknesses. The most important weakness is the fragmentation of services offered. Some firms only mow lawns and prune shrubs. Others only do reseeding and care for new lawns. Still others specialize in weed and pest control. Such fragmentation makes one-stop shopping difficult if not impossible. This weakness is particularly important because it is of major concern to many buyers; they want one company to do exactly what they need, no more, no less. That is the role we intend to play.

In addition, we do not feel that most of our competitors run their businesses as efficiently as possible. We will be the only service organization in Newton, for instance, to schedule crews by computer, to communicate with the field via mobile communications technologies, to have serious staff training programs, and to offer customer feedback and evaluation through our Internet web page.

Threats and Risks

We do not anticipate a meaningful or prompt reaction to our marketing initiatives from our competitors. However, we have developed contingency plans for certain reactions that competitors may make. If competitors lower their price, we will match their move. We plan to watch for other competitive actions, such as special offers or service changes, and we plan to react swiftly to any competitive move. Reacting to competitive moves will in the short run hurt our profit margins, but will in the long run preserve our market share.

LAWN MASTERS OF NEWTON

STRATEGY

Key Competitive Capabilities

We have a strong competitive advantage in our superior ability in overall management. Important differences between our capabilities and those of our main competitors are vastly superior scheduling, staff training, and customer feedback systems. We believe that our highly visible management differences will help make us appear in the consumer's mind to be a more reliable service provider.

Another key competitive advantage lies in the flexibility of our service concept. Potential customers can literally select from a menu of options that covers every aspect of lawn maintenance. There is no dimension of the service we will not provide—none of our competitors can make that claim. Other firms give lip service to the importance of their customers, but leave a lot to be desired in how far they go to serving them. But we will definitely go the extra mile in serving and responding to our customers' needs.

Key Competitive Weaknesses

Being a small, locally owned firm we have several inherent advantages in facing large, national competitors—but there are some disadvantages as well. The larger competitors have economies of scale, large buying power, and a brand name identity. None of them have successfully penetrated our target market community yet, but they could. The professionalism and flexible service package that currently distinguishes us could be matched by a larger, well-funded national company. If a competitor like this does emerge, we will attempt to overcome them by dramatically increasing our local advertising and stressing our local ties, our in-depth knowledge of the Newton community, and all of the good works we participate in as a member of this community.

Main Strategy

Our strategy will be to offer the best, most highly personalized service in the marketplace we serve. Especially being a very small, owner-operated company, we intend to use this to our advantage to be absolutely certain that every one of our customers receives excellent service. We will go out of our way to make sure our customers know that they

LAWN MASTERS OF NEWTON

truly matter to us. We intend to be very flexible in the way we provide service, and to do whatever we can to accommodate our customer's needs. Employees who deal with customers will be carefully trained and will be given wide latitude for insuring that customers are always satisfied.

Implementing this strategy means building a broad line of services to meet a broad range of needs for our customers. The market trend is towards one-stop shopping. Currently, customers are increasingly giving a larger share of their business to vendors who provide multiple services. And vendors who have the broadest product lines have the most advantage in working with customers in the lawn maintenance field. This strategy is also one of the fastest and strongest ways that we can differentiate our company from the competition.

We understand that we will be setting a new standard of customer service. We are going to go well beyond the definitions of old and take customer service to a new level. In addition to just plain treating customers well and being responsive to their needs, we are going to provide additional services to customers. Initially these new services are going to include on-line feedback and scheduling of special services via our Website, and a completely nontoxic, nonchemical option to weed treatment problems.

Positioning of Products/Services

We will position ourselves as providing highly customized solutions to customers with particularly demanding or specific requirements—and in our community, almost every homeowner believes that they have particularly demanding or specific requirements. We will be highly flexible and responsive in adapting our services to the needs of consumers in Newton. The types of buyers who are most likely to benefit from our approach will be single-family homeowners with full acre lots and plenty of trees and shrubs.

Product/Service Description

We provide one comprehensive lawn maintenance service, but we offer many different options, including:

— Spring clean-up

LAWN MASTERS OF NEWTON

— Tree and shrub trimming
— Fertilizing
— Mulching
— Weed control
— Insect control
— Mowing
— Leaf removal
— Winter prep
— Seeding
— Sodding

Our underlying philosophy in developing this spectrum of services has been to present ourselves as the one-stop solution for all lawn maintenance needs. Important objectives are to manage each account carefully to lead to profitability and repeat business. We insure that we achieve these objectives by following up frequently to see that every customer is satisfied, and to give them a feedback/evaluation and special services request vehicle at our Website.

Our revenue break out (FY '97) by service is:

Product/Service:	Unit Sales	Revenue	Percent of Total:
1. Spring clean-up	300	90,000	6.6%
2. Fertilizing & mulching	150	150,000	11.1%
3. Trimming	200	75,000	5.5%
4. Weed control	150	75,000	5.5%
5. Insect control	60	50,000	3.7%
6. Seeding	200	200,000	14.8%
7. Sodding	125	200,000	14.8%
8. Mowing	300	300,000	22.2%
9. Leaf removal	400	120,000	8.8%
10. Winter prep	300	90,000	6.6%
TOTAL		1,350,000	

LAWN MASTERS OF NEWTON

We offer the following services:

Name	Spring clean-up
Brief description	Remove debris, selective seeding, repair damage
Key features	Tree and shrub surgery optional
Sales	$90K
Price	$300

Name	Fertilizing & mulching
Brief description	Prep for partial or complete reseeding
Key features	Non-toxic chemicals used
Sales	$150K
Price	$1000

Name	Trimming
Brief description	Optional add-on to annual service package
Key features	Flat fee for basic level of trees and shrubs
Sales	$75K
Price	$400

Name	Weed control
Brief description	Several applications throughout the year to remove weeds
Key features	Nontoxic chemicals used
Sales	$75K
Price	$500

Name	Insect control
Brief description	Several applications throughout the year to eliminate insects
Key features	Nontoxic chemicals used
Sales	$50K
Price	$800

LAWN MASTERS OF NEWTON

Name	Seeding
Brief description	Complete reseeding
Key features	Guaranteed results
Sales	$200K
Price	$1000

Name	Sodding
Brief description	Complete sodded lawn
Key features	Guaranteed results
Sales	$200K
Price	$1500

Name	Mowing
Brief description	Once/week, 6 months
Key features	On-going customer evaluation
Sales	$300K
Price	$1000

Name	Leaf removal
Brief description	Two visits
Key features	Can contract for this service alone
Sales	$120K
Price	$300

Name	Winter prep
Brief description	Feed lawn, secure trees and shrubs
Key features	Will store lawn furniture and equipment
Sales	$90K
Price	$300

LAWN MASTERS OF NEWTON

Future Products/Services

We are planning a new service, to be launched next year (1999), which can be described as a local supply and support center for homeowners who wish to do some of their own yard work. Specialized tools and equipment will be available for purchase or rental. Top soil, fertilizer, sand, and stones of various sorts will also be available. This support center will complete our goal of offering some product or service for every aspect of lawn maintenance, including the do-it-yourselfers.

Marketing Strategy

Our marketing program will support our overall company strategy by emphasizing the flexibility and comprehensiveness of our service offerings, as well as the efficiency and professionalism with which we work. This will be reflected in all of our marketing, including our sales presentations, our advertising, and our literature.

Our marketing objective is to increase sales to $2.5M by 9/15/98, the end of this season. We want to increase our customer base to approximately 1,000 homeowners, which would bring our market share to about 20%.

Our marketing strategy will be based around an aggressive sales effort. In-person sales presentations, scheduled at the potential customer's home on the weekends or in the evenings, will be the core of our selling effort. Other marketing activities including advertising and publicity will be geared to increasing the receptiveness of potential customers to agreeing to meet with our salespeople.

This strategy will be supported by advertising in the local newspapers, the *Tab*, the *Graphic*, and the *Chronicle*. Our selling effort will consist, in part, of responding to and selling inquiries generated by this advertising.

Our marketing program will have three major components, focused on developing qualified leads for sales presentations and on strengthening our image as the most professional lawn maintenance organization operating in the City of Newton.

Program 1: A Referral Incentive program, in which current customers who refer a potential new account receives a rebate on their annual service bill equal to 10% of the annual service bill of the referred account.

LAWN MASTERS OF NEWTON

Program 2. A Free Service Consultation, which is how the at-home sales presentations will be represented. A well-trained and professionally attired consultant will inspect the potential customer's grounds, give an expert opinion as to any unusual needs, and make an overall recommendation as to an annual service plan.

Program 3. A well-publicized effort to support and work with the Newton Community Gardening organization at Nahanton Park as a gesture of goodwill of contribution to the community.

Sales Tactics

Our sales process begins when the potential customer responds to our advertising by telephoning us for more information. We have found that rather than providing more information over the phone, our best chance of closing the sale is to arrange an appointment to visit the prospect in person. We have found it is fairly easy to persuade potential customers to agree to see a representative of our company in person. The most difficult part of the sales process however is closing the sale. Closing the sale requires not only knowledge of the service but also strong sales skills. We have found that the unique advantages of our service that are important to emphasize in sales calls are our flexibility and professionalism.

An important part of our sales process is uncovering the key concerns and needs of the buyer—which often differ from one customer to the next. Because of this it is important to have bright and engaging sales people who can think on their feet and who are also effective in establishing a rapport with their customers.

Senior people in the company will do most of this sales work. This is an important competitive element because customers prefer to deal with the management and they are able to be sure that the company will do everything possible to land the sale and to keep the customer happy.

We will support our sales effort with the following collateral: brochures, flyers, and testimonial sheets.

LAWN MASTERS OF NEWTON

Advertising

While our service has several strong, unique competitive advantages, we will focus on just one in our advertising in order to more clearly distinguish ourselves from the competition in a meaningful way—rather than confuse consumers with multiple messages. The benefit we will focus on is our flexibility; that is, the customizable nature of our service offerings. We have developed the following unique selling proposition that will an important focus of all our advertising: "Whatever It Takes to Let You Enjoy Your Yard This Summer."

The purpose of our advertising is to support our sales efforts. It will do this by increasing awareness of our company and its services. This in turn will make it easier for salespeople to get appointments with buyers and achieve their sales goals.

We will advertise in the following local newspapers: the *Tab*, the *Graphic* and the *Chronicle*. This will allow us to zero in on the Newton market and help position our firm as being closer to the local community than firms that advertise in more broadly circulated media.

We will also experiment with cable television advertising, featuring short interviews with satisfied customers recorded in their own yards.

Finally, we intend to employ the following low-cost advertising techniques: delivering leaflets door to door, putting flyers on car windshields, leaving flyers at other businesses, and car/truck advertising.

We will run our advertising daily during the early spring (March and April), and start to scale it back gradually throughout the summer. Another daily push will start after Labor Day and run through September, focusing on leaf removal and winter preparation services.

Promotions/Incentives

We will run one major sales promotion as an early sign-up discount during the month of March. Discounts off of standard pricing will typically run about 5% to 10%. We will promote this sales incentive with coupons and flyers, mailings to current customers, and newspaper and radio advertising.

LAWN MASTERS OF NEWTON

We will also use giveaways to attract new customers and to build loyalty with current customers. We will give away items which depend on a good lawn, such as croquet sets and badminton games.

We see our World Wide Web site playing primarily an operations support role—but it will also have some promotional role. On the site we will offer service information, basic information about lawn maintenance, suggestions on how to use our service more effectively, links to related sites, discount coupons that may be printed out, and information on how to reach us. We will promote our Web site on all our literature, by listing our Web address everywhere our street address is listed such as on business cards and on our stationary, and in our advertising.

We will offer free estimates and evaluations without any obligation. We will use this free offer as an opportunity to familiarize the prospect with our business, emphasize our competitive advantages, and try to close the sale.

Publicity

The main purpose of our publicity is to increase the general awareness of our services. Our publicity is also intended to emphasize our commitment to Newton and to inform customers and potential customers of new developments concerning our services.

Our publicity campaign will emphasize our involvement with the Community Gardeners of Newton by sending press releases and video tapes, and arranging media interviews. We will target local newspapers, radio stations, and cable television shows.

We will produce and send a newsletter every month to promote our company and our services. We will send approximately 500 copies to current customers, and another 1,000 or more to prospects. In the newsletter we will highlight items of interest to people who care about lawn maintenance. There will be an editorial column by the President of the Company, a Q&A feature, tips, short anecdotes drawn from actual experiences in Newton, and updates on our involvement with the Newton Community Gardeners.

LAWN MASTERS OF NEWTON

Trade Shows, Business-to-Business Shows, Consumer Shows

The city of Newton sponsors several events that are appropriate for our participation, including a Spring Festival, a July fourth event, and an Octoberfest. All of these events are held on the grounds of the City Hall, and local business are invited to rent booth space and exhibit. Our objective in attending these events is to get names of possible leads, build relationships with current customers, emphasize our unique services, and portray our firm as a major player in the this business in the Newton community.

We will make an effort to gather names of prospects at the show by having a drawing and a guest book. We will follow-up with attendees after the show by phoning to arrange a face-to-face meeting.

LAWN MASTERS OF NEWTON

OPERATIONS

Key Personnel

The company has three employees who can considered to be key. Jack Duffy, President and CEO, is responsible for management, finances, accounting and other administration issues. He has been with Lawn Masters of Newton for over ten years, and previously held the position of Regional Manager for Home Depot in New England. Ed Davis, Vice President, will be responsible for services and overall operations, including training and supervision of all the work crews. He has been with Lawn Masters of Newton for five years and has a degree in environmental studies from the University of Massachusetts. Janice Kendall will be responsible for sales, marketing, and customer relations. She is new to our company and was most recently an Assistant Director for Publicity with the Massachusetts Audubon Society.

The compensation and incentives plan offered to key personnel is designed to give these individuals a significant stake in the company's success as a way of encouraging top performance and of retaining them in their positions. In addition to salaries, compensation for key personnel will include profit sharing (set at 10% of pre-tax earnings) and bonuses based on newly registered accounts.

Board of Directors

Members of the board of directors have been selected for their ability to bring specialized skills and experience to the company. In addition to the three principals involved in daily operations, these directors will include Frank White, whose expertise lies in the area of small business law, Stan Novak, who works extensively with several community organizations in Newton in a fundraising capacity, and Bill Miles, who is the Chairman of the Newton Community Gardeners organization. These non-management directors will not be compensated for their participation.

Organizational Structure

Our organizational structure is very informal, without written descriptions of specific areas of responsibilities. This is primarily because the three key members of the management team work very closely across many aspects of the company's operations. As a

LAWN MASTERS OF NEWTON

matter of practice however, here is who takes the primary role in each of the major functional areas:

Finance: Jack Duffy

Marketing and Sales: Janice Kendall

Operations/Office: Ed Davis

Being a very small company, our selection and use of outside contractors and service providers is an important part of our operation. Here is a breakout of the key outsiders that will be supporting our business:

Accounting: Arnold Financial Services, taxes and strategic planning

Legal: White & Associates, review and prepare legal documents

Graphics & Design: Desktop Graphics Inc., brochures and other collateral

Human Resources Plan

We recognize that human resources are an extremely important asset, especially in a service business in which work is performed on customer's property. Our competitors do not generally recognize this fact, and in general, the personnel standards in the lawn maintenance industry are very low. Often, unskilled, unqualified individuals are hired, paid minimum wage, and worked hard until they leave. Field staff of this sort obviously do not reflect well on the company.

At Lawn Masters of Newton, we have decided that although all of our field staff are seasonal workers, we will nevertheless hire only people who are qualified or who can be trained to do the work as required, and who can interact with customers in a friendly and professional manner. Thus, we screen new applicants very carefully, including in-person interviews and reference checks. We will strive to hire people who have a solid work ethic and work well with others. Working well with others is especially important in our system of three-person work crews, each having a consistent set of scheduled assignments and a crew leader.

We will recruit employees by newspaper help-wanted advertising, and offering referral bonuses to current employees. We will review each employee's performance regularly, and when possible promote from within.

LAWN MASTERS OF NEWTON

The company's salary structure will be higher than market rates, and an extremely competitive benefit package will be offered (most of our competitors offer no benefits at all to seasonal workers) not only to help the recruitment effort, but to increase the chance of retaining employees for the entire lawn maintenance season and hopefully bringing them back next year. Benefits offered will include paid vacation days after the season (accrued at a rate of 1.25 days/month of employment), and a comprehensive health plan (employer pays 50%).

Training

Building a sense of teamwork among all personnel is an essential component for the success of the business. By allocating significant time and resources to staff training, we expect to increase every employee's ability to provide valuable services for our customers, and to feel that he or she is an important, contributing part of the organization. Responsibility for training will come under Operations (Ed Davis), but all three members of the management team have taken part in developing or reviewing training materials or in actually delivering training sessions as appropriate.

Due to the short, seasonal nature of the business, all employees need feedback on their performance with a much greater frequency than the normal annual review process. Lawn Masters of Newton uses a standard form, completed on a weekly basis by the crew leader. This form contains specific feedback on job performance, and also makes summary recommendations as to areas for improvement.

Service Delivery

Here are some of the standards we have adopted to help insure that we provide high quality service:

1. We will answer our phones within 3 rings.
2. We will provide a free, written estimate within 48 hours.
3. We will begin work within 3 days of receiving a signed agreement.
4. We will not interrupt work for any reason until we finish a job.
5. We will use the highest quality equipment and supplies available.

LAWN MASTERS OF NEWTON

6. We will leave the property clean and neat at the end of each day.
7. We will follow-up after every job to be sure the customer is satisfied.
8. We will guarantee satisfaction for all of our work.

Our strategy is built around offering highly personalized service to our customers. Integral to this approach is the careful selection of field staff, in-depth training so that they may respond quickly to customer requests, and in-depth back-up support for more difficult requests.

Quality Control Changes

Overall responsibility for control is handled by Ed Davis. After a major review of our current procedures, which included soliciting input from customers, we have redesigned certain aspects of the process. In particular, we will institute new incentive programs and emphasize training and rewards to help motivate employees to ensure that our high quality standards are being met.

Customer Service/Support

We intend to prioritize customer service and make it a key component of our marketing programs. We believe that providing our customers with what they want in the area of lawn maintenance, when and how they want it is the key to repeat business and to word-of-mouth advertising. Not only will we train our employees to deliver excellent service, we will give them the flexibility to respond creatively to client requests. In addition, we will continually monitor our clients' level of satisfaction with our service through surveys and convenient feedback opportunities.

We plan on using the World Wide Web for a significant portion of our service/support effort. On the Web we can offer support 24 hours a day, 365 days a year. And on the Web, customers don't have to wait for the next available service representative. Once the service area of our Web site is up the cost to maintain it will be minimal. On our Web site we plan on offering a choice of text options explaining basic service issues, lists of frequently asked questions and answers about lawn maintenance, and the ability to e-mail for help with highly specific questions and any requested changes in the scheduled maintenance plan.

LAWN MASTERS OF NEWTON

Facilities

The company's current facility is not large enough to accommodate the new size and scope of the business. We are utilizing approximately 2,000 square feet at the present time, located on Wells Avenue in an industrial section of Newton, for equipment storage and maintenance as well as office space. We plan to move to a new facility, within the same industrial park development, offering at least twice the space (4,000 square feet), which will meet current and anticipated needs for the foreseeable future. The move is scheduled to take place in January, 1998.

LAWN MASTERS OF NEWTON

Assumptions and Comments Worksheet

Name of Plan:	Lawn Masters of Newton
Starting Month:	Jan-1998
Years:	3
Commissions:	**0.00**
Freight Costs:	**0.00**
Payroll Tax Rate:	**13.00**
Income Tax Rate:	**35.00**
Days Inventory:	**0**
Cost of Sales:	**0.00**
Credit Sales?:	N
Credit Sales %:	**100.00**
Days Credit:	**30**
Cost of Sales A/P?:	n
Cost of Sales A/P %:	**0.00**
Cost of Sales Days A/P:	**0**
General A/P?:	y
General A/P %:	**100.00**
Days General A/P:	**30**
S-T Interest Rate:	**10.00**
L-T Interest Rate: Expense Headings	**11.00**

LAWN MASTERS OF NEWTON

Starting Balance Sheet

Lawn Masters of Newton
Starting Balance Sheet

	Balance
Assets	
Current Assets	
Cash	22,330
Accounts Receivable	18,250
Inventory	0
Other Current Assets	1,200
Total Current Assets	41,780
Long Term Assets	
Depreciable Assets	78,400
Accumulated Depreciation	25,300
Net Depreciable Assets	53,100
Non-Depreciable Assets	0
Total Long-Term Assets	53,100
Total assets	94,880
Liabilities & Equity	
Current Liabilities	
Cost of Sales A/P	0
Non-Cost of Sales A/P	3,200
Short-Term Debt	0
Income Taxes Due	0
Total Current Liabilities	3,200
Long-Term Debt	0
Equity	
Stock & Paid-in Capital	10,000
Retained Earnings	81,680
Total Equity	91,680
Total Liabilities & Equity	94,880
Note: Total Assets must equal	
Total Liabilities & Equity	

LAWN MASTERS OF NEWTON

Profit and Loss Forecast

Lawn Masters of Newton
Profit and Loss Projection

	Jan-1998	Feb-1998	Mar-1998	Apr-1998	May-1998	Jun-1998	Jul-1998	Aug-1998	Sep-1998	Oct-1998	Nov-1998	Dec-1998	Total 1998	1999	2000	2001	2002
Sales	36,000	75,000	225,000	305,000	305,000	305,000	300,000	285,000	280,000	215,000	105,000	57,000	2,493,000	2,750,000	3,000,000	3,000,000	3,000,000
Costs																	
Cost Of Sales	0	0	0	0	0	0	0	0	0	0	0	0	0	0	0	0	0
Gross Profit	36,000	75,000	225,000	305,000	305,000	305,000	300,000	285,000	280,000	215,000	105,000	57,000	2,493,000	2,750,000	3,000,000	3,000,000	3,000,000
Gross Profit Margin	100.0%	100.0%	100.0%	100.0%	100.0%	100.0%	100.0%	100.0%	100.0%	100.0%	100.0%	100.0%	100.0%	100.0%	100.0%	100.0%	100.0%
Marketing & Sales																	
Commissions	0	0	0	0	0	0	0	0	0	0	0	0	0	0	0	0	0
Literature & Mailings	0	4,000	20,000	20,000	20,000	5,000	5,000	5,000	5,000	0	0	0	84,000	90,000	90,000	90,000	90,000
Advertising & Publicity	0	3,000	70,000	70,000	70,000	50,000	50,000	50,000	50,000	0	0	0	413,000	425,000	425,000	425,000	425,000
Other Marketing	2,500	2,500	2,500	2,500	2,500	2,500	2,500	2,500	2,500	2,500	2,500	2,500	30,000	35,000	40,000	40,000	40,000
Total Marketing & Sales	2,500	9,500	92,500	92,500	92,500	57,500	57,500	57,500	57,500	2,500	2,500	2,500	527,000	550,000	555,000	555,000	555,000
General & Admin.																	
Payroll	7,000	9,500	64,000	108,000	108,000	108,000	108,000	108,000	103,000	89,000	42,000	15,000	869,500	935,000	1,010,000	1,010,000	1,010,000
Payroll Taxes, Benefits	910	1,235	8,320	14,040	14,040	14,040	14,040	14,040	13,390	11,570	5,460	1,950	113,035	121,550	131,300	131,300	131,300
Facilities & Equip Rent	4,500	12,000	12,000	12,000	12,000	12,000	12,000	12,000	12,000	12,000	12,000	12,000	136,500	152,000	164,000	164,000	164,000
Maintenance & Repairs	2,000	2,000	2,000	2,000	2,000	2,000	2,000	2,000	2,000	2,000	2,000	2,000	24,000	35,000	40,000	40,000	40,000
Utilities, Phone, Postage	3,000	3,000	3,000	3,000	3,000	3,000	3,000	3,000	3,000	3,000	3,000	3,000	36,000	37,000	37,000	37,000	37,000
Insurance	4,500	4,500	4,500	4,500	4,500	4,500	4,500	4,500	4,500	4,500	4,500	4,500	54,000	56,000	56,000	56,000	56,000
Supplies	1,200	1,200	6,500	12,000	12,000	12,000	12,000	12,000	12,000	7,000	2,500	1,800	92,200	102,000	102,000	102,000	102,000
Freight	0	0	0	0	0	0	0	0	0	0	0	0	0	0	0	0	0
Auto Travel & Entertain.	1,000	1,500	4,500	6,500	6,500	6,500	6,500	6,500	6,500	4,000	1,500	1,500	53,000	55,000	55,000	55,000	55,000
Legal & Accounting	1,500	1,500	1,500	1,500	1,500	1,500	1,500	1,500	1,500	1,500	1,500	1,500	18,000	18,000	18,000	18,000	18,000
Other Outside Services	600	600	600	600	600	600	600	600	600	600	600	600	7,200	7,500	7,500	7,500	7,500
Misc. Taxes, Fees	0	6,000	300	200	0	0	0	0	0	0	0	0	6,500	13,000	13,000	13,000	13,000
Depreciation	4,000	6,400	6,400	6,400	6,400	6,400	6,400	6,400	6,400	6,400	6,400	6,400	74,400	76,800	76,800	76,800	76,800
Other G&A Expenses	1,500	1,500	1,500	1,500	1,500	1,500	1,500	1,500	1,500	1,500	1,500	1,500	18,000	20,000	20,000	20,000	20,000
Total General & Admin.	31,710	50,935	115,120	172,240	172,040	172,040	172,040	172,040	166,390	143,070	82,960	51,750	1,502,335	1,628,850	1,730,600	1,730,600	1,730,600
Total Operating Costs	34,210	60,435	207,620	264,740	264,540	229,540	229,540	229,540	223,890	145,570	85,460	54,250	2,029,335	2,178,850	2,285,600	2,285,600	2,285,600
Operating Profit	1,790	14,565	17,380	40,260	40,460	75,460	70,460	55,460	56,110	69,430	19,540	2,750	463,665	571,150	714,400	714,400	714,400
Operating Profit Margin	5.0%	19.4%	7.7%	13.2%	13.3%	24.7%	23.5%	19.5%	20.0%	32.3%	18.6%	4.8%	18.6%	20.8%	23.8%	23.8%	23.8%
Non-Operating Costs																	
Interest	0	1,604	1,577	1,551	1,524	1,497	1,470	1,444	1,417	1,390	1,364	1,337	16,175	12,191	8,340	4,490	640
Profit Before Income Taxes	1,790	12,961	15,803	38,709	38,936	73,963	68,990	54,016	54,693	68,040	18,176	1,413	447,490	558,959	706,060	709,910	713,760
Pre-Tax Profit Margin	5.0%	17.3%	7.0%	12.7%	12.8%	24.3%	23.0%	19.0%	19.5%	31.6%	17.3%	2.5%	17.9%	20.3%	23.5%	23.7%	23.8%
Income Taxes	627	4,536	5,531	13,548	13,628	25,887	24,146	18,906	19,143	23,814	6,362	495	156,623	195,636	247,121	248,469	249,816
Net Profit	1,163	8,425	10,272	25,161	25,308	48,076	44,844	35,110	35,550	44,226	11,814	918	290,867	363,323	458,939	461,441	463,944
Net Profit Margin	3.2%	11.2%	4.6%	8.2%	8.3%	15.8%	14.9%	12.3%	12.7%	20.6%	11.3%	1.6%	11.7%	13.2%	15.3%	15.4%	15.5%

LAWN MASTERS OF NEWTON

Cash Flow Forecast

Lawn Masters of Newton
Cash Flow Projection

	Jan-1998	Feb-1998	Mar-1998	Apr-1998	May-1998	Jun-1998	Jul-1998	Aug-1998	Sep-1998	Oct-1998	Nov-1998	Dec-1998	1999	2000	2001	2002
Starting Cash	22,330	46,593	82,418	181,772	217,817	246,408	262,967	311,293	349,886	388,919	374,128	382,426	386,127	847,471	1,350,039	1,853,276
Sources																
Cash Sales	36,000	75,000	225,000	305,000	305,000	305,000	300,000	285,000	280,000	215,000	105,000	57,000	2,750,000	3,000,000	3,000,000	3,000,000
Credit Sales	0	0	0	0	0	0	0	0	0	0	0	0	0	0	0	0
Short-Term Loan Proceeds	0	0	0	0	0	0	0	0	0	0	0	0	0	0	0	0
Long-Term Loan Proceeds	0	175,000	0	0	0	0	0	0	0	0	0	0	0	0	0	0
Equity Capital Proceeds	0	0	0	0	0	0	0	0	0	0	0	0	0	0	0	0
Total Sources	36,000	250,000	225,000	305,000	305,000	305,000	300,000	285,000	280,000	215,000	105,000	57,000	2,750,000	3,000,000	3,000,000	3,000,000
Uses																
Cost of Sales / Inventory	0	0	0	0	0	0	0	0	0	0	0	0	0	0	0	0
Payroll & Related	7,910	10,735	72,320	122,040	122,040	122,040	122,040	122,040	116,390	100,570	47,460	16,950	1,056,550	1,141,300	1,141,300	1,141,300
Non-Payroll Expenses	3,200	22,300	43,300	128,900	136,300	136,100	101,100	101,100	101,100	101,100	38,600	31,600	989,275	1,065,667	1,067,500	1,067,500
Interest	0	1,604	1,577	1,551	1,524	1,497	1,470	1,444	1,417	1,390	1,364	1,337	12,191	8,340	4,490	640
Purchase Depreciable Assets	0	175,000	0	0	0	0	0	0	0	0	0	0	0	0	0	0
Purchase Non-Dep. Assets	0	0	0	0	0	0	0	0	0	0	0	0	0	0	0	0
Dividends, Owner Pay-Outs	0	0	0	0	0	0	0	0	0	0	0	0	0	0	0	0
Short-Term Debt Payments	0	0	0	0	0	0	0	0	0	0	0	0	0	0	0	0
Long-Term Debt Payments	0	0	2,917	2,917	2,917	2,917	2,917	2,917	2,917	2,917	2,917	2,917	35,004	35,004	35,004	35,004
Total Uses Before Taxes	11,110	209,639	120,114	255,408	262,781	262,554	227,527	227,501	221,824	205,977	90,341	52,804	2,093,020	2,250,311	2,248,294	2,244,444
Income Taxes	627	4,536	5,531	13,548	13,628	25,887	24,146	18,906	19,143	23,814	6,362	495	195,636	247,121	248,469	249,816
Total Uses After Taxes	11,737	214,175	125,645	268,956	276,409	288,441	251,673	246,407	240,967	229,791	96,703	53,299	2,288,656	2,497,432	2,496,763	2,494,260
Net Change In Cash	24,263	35,825	99,355	36,044	28,591	16,559	48,327	38,593	39,033	-14,791	8,297	3,701	461,344	502,568	503,237	505,740
Ending Cash Position	46,593	82,418	181,772	217,817	246,408	262,967	311,293	349,886	388,919	374,128	382,426	386,127	847,471	1,350,039	1,853,276	2,359,016

LAWN MASTERS OF NEWTON

Balance Sheet Forecast

Lawn Masters of Newton
Balance Sheet Projection

Period Ending:	Jan-1998	Feb-1998	Mar-1998	Apr-1998	May-1998	Jun-1998	Jul-1998	Aug-1998	Sep-1998	Oct-1998	Nov-1998	Dec-1998	1999	2000	2001	2002
Assets																
Current assets																
Cash	46,593	82,418	181,772	217,817	246,408	262,967	311,293	349,886	388,919	374,128	382,426	386,127	847,471	1,350,039	1,853,276	2,359,016
Accounts Receivable	0	0	0	0	0	0	0	0	0	0	0	0	0	0	0	0
Inventory	0	0	0	0	0	0	0	0	0	0	0	0	0	0	0	0
Other Current Assets	1,200	1,200	1,200	1,200	1,200	1,200	1,200	1,200	1,200	1,200	1,200	1,200	1,200	1,200	1,200	1,200
Total Current Assets	47,793	83,618	182,972	219,017	247,608	264,167	312,493	351,086	390,119	375,328	383,626	387,327	848,671	1,351,239	1,854,476	2,360,216
Long-Term Assets																
Depreciable Assets	78,400	253,400	253,400	253,400	253,400	253,400	253,400	253,400	253,400	253,400	253,400	253,400	253,400	253,400	253,400	253,400
Accumulated Depreciation	29,300	35,700	42,100	48,500	54,900	61,300	67,700	74,100	80,500	86,900	93,300	99,700	176,500	253,300	330,100	406,900
Net Depreciable Assets	49,100	217,700	211,300	204,900	198,500	192,100	185,700	179,300	172,900	166,500	160,100	153,700	76,900	100	-76,700	-153,500
Non-Depreciable Assets	0	0	0	0	0	0	0	0	0	0	0	0	0	0	0	0
Total Long-Term Assets	49,100	217,700	211,300	204,900	198,500	192,100	185,700	179,300	172,900	166,500	160,100	153,700	76,900	100	-76,700	-153,500
Total Assets	96,893	301,318	394,272	423,917	446,108	456,267	498,193	530,386	563,019	541,828	543,726	541,027	925,571	1,351,339	1,777,776	2,206,716
Liabilities & Equity																
Current Liabilities																
Short-Term Debt	0	0	0	0	0	0	0	0	0	0	0	0	0	0	0	0
Cost of Sales A/P	0	0	0	0	0	0	0	0	0	0	0	0	0	0	0	0
Non-Cost of Sales A/P	22,300	43,300	128,900	136,300	136,100	101,100	101,100	101,100	101,100	38,600	31,600	30,900	87,125	88,958	88,958	88,958
Income Taxes Due	0	0	0	0	0	0	0	0	0	0	0	0	0	0	0	0
Total Current Liabilities	22,300	43,300	128,900	136,300	136,100	101,100	101,100	101,100	101,100	38,600	31,600	30,900	87,125	88,958	88,958	88,958
Long-Term Debt	0	175,000	172,083	169,166	166,249	163,332	160,415	157,498	154,581	151,664	148,747	145,830	110,826	75,822	40,818	5,814
Equity																
Stock & Paid-in Capital	10,000	10,000	10,000	10,000	10,000	10,000	10,000	10,000	10,000	10,000	10,000	10,000	10,000	10,000	10,000	10,000
Retained Earnings	64,593	73,018	83,289	108,451	133,759	181,835	226,678	261,788	297,338	341,564	353,379	354,297	717,620	1,176,559	1,638,000	2,101,944
Total Equity	74,593	83,018	93,289	118,451	143,759	191,835	236,678	271,788	307,338	351,564	363,379	364,297	727,620	1,186,559	1,648,000	2,111,944
Total Liabilities & Equity	96,893	301,318	394,272	423,917	446,108	456,267	498,193	530,386	563,019	541,828	543,726	541,027	925,571	1,351,339	1,777,776	2,206,716

LAWN MASTERS OF NEWTON

Key Ratios

Lawn Masters of Newton
Ratios and Analysis

	Jan-1998	Feb-1998	Mar-1998	Apr-1998	May-1998	Jun-1998	Jul-1998	Aug-1998	Sep-1998	Oct-1998	Nov-1998	Dec-1998	1998	1999	2000	2001	2002
Quick Ratio	2.14	1.93	1.42	1.61	1.82	2.61	3.09	3.47	3.86	9.72	12.14	12.53	12.53	9.74	15.19	20.85	26.53
Current Ratio	2.14	1.93	1.42	1.61	1.82	2.61	3.09	3.47	3.86	9.72	12.14	12.53	12.53	9.74	15.19	20.85	26.53
Debt to Equity Ratio	0.30	2.63	3.23	2.58	2.10	1.38	1.10	0.95	0.83	0.54	0.50	0.49	0.49	0.27	0.14	0.08	0.04
Debt to Assets Ratio	0.23	0.72	0.76	0.72	0.68	0.58	0.52	0.49	0.45	0.35	0.33	0.33	0.33	0.21	0.12	0.07	0.04
Return on Equity Ratio	0.02	0.10	0.11	0.21	0.18	0.25	0.19	0.13	0.12	0.13	0.03	0.00	0.80	0.50	0.39	0.28	0.22
Return on Assets Ratio	0.01	0.03	0.03	0.06	0.06	0.11	0.09	0.07	0.06	0.08	0.02	0.00	0.54	0.39	0.34	0.26	0.21
Sales Break Even	34,210	60,435	207,620	264,740	264,540	229,540	229,540	229,540	223,890	145,570	85,460	54,250	2,029,335	2,178,850	2,285,600	2,285,600	2,285,600
Working Capital	25,493	40,318	54,072	82,717	111,508	163,067	211,393	249,986	289,019	336,728	352,026	356,427	356,427	761,546	1,262,281	1,765,518	2,271,258

CHAPTER 18

Forms

PROFIT AND LOSS PROJECTION

Date	Jan. ___	Feb. ___	Mar. ___	Apr. ___	May ___	June ___	July ___
Sales							
Costs							
Cost Of Sales							
Gross Profit							
Gross Profit Margin							
Marketing & Sales							
Commissions							
Literature & Mailings							
Advertising & Publicity							
Other Marketing							
Total Marketing & Sales							
General & Administrative							
Payroll							
Payroll Taxes, Benefits							
Facilities & Equip Rent							
Maintenance & Repairs							
Utilities, Phone, Postage							
Insurance							
Supplies							
Freight							
Auto Travel & Entertain.							
Legal & Accounting							
Other Outside Services							
Misc. Taxes, Fees							
Depreciation							
Other G&A Expenses							
Total General & Admin.							
Total Operating Costs							
Operating Profit							
Operating Profit Margin							
Non-Operating Costs							
Interest							
Profit Before Income Taxes							
Pre-Tax Profit Margin							
Income Taxes							
Net Profit							
Net Profit Margin							

CASH FLOW PROJECTION

Date	Jan. ___	Feb. ___	Mar. ___	Apr. ___	May ___	June ___	July ___
Starting Cash							
Sources							
Cash Sales							
Credit Sales							
Short-Term Loan Proceeds							
Long-Term Loan Proceeds							
Equity Capital Proceeds							
Total Sources							
Uses							
Cost of Sales / Inventory							
Payroll & Related							
Non-Payroll Expenses							
Interest							
Purchase Depreciable Assets							
Purchase Non-Dep. Assets							
Dividends, Owner Pay-Outs							
Short-Term Debt Payments							
Long-Term Debt Payments							
Total Uses Before Taxes							
Income Taxes							
Total Uses After Taxes							
Net Change In Cash							
Ending Cash Position							

Aug. ___	Sept. ___	Oct. ___	Nov. ___	Dec. ___	Yr. 2	Yr. 3	Yr. 4	Yr. 5

BALANCE SHEET PROJECTION

Period Ending	Jan. ___	Feb. ___	Mar. ___	Apr. ___	May ___	June ___	July ___
Assets							
Current assets							
Cash							
Accounts Receivable							
Inventory							
Other Current Assets							
Total Current Assets							
Long-Term Assets							
Depreciable Assets							
Accumulated Depreciation							
Net Depreciable Assets							
Non-Depreciable Assets							
Total Long-Term Assets							
Total Assets							
Liabilities & Equity							
Current Liabilities							
Short-Term Debt							
Cost of Sales A/P							
Non-Cost of Sales A/P							
Income Taxes Due							
Total Current Liabilities							
Long-Term Debt							
Equity							
Stock & Paid-in Capital							
Retained Earnings							
Total Equity							
Total Liabilities & Equity							

INDEX

INDEX

INDEX

INDEX

INDEX

This stand-alone software package completely automates the process of creating a business plan. It includes all of the text and worksheets in this book, plus additional sample plans and short videos describing how to create business plans.

To write the text portion of the plan you scroll on your computer through the broad range of pre-written text options available for each part of the plan. Just click to select from the available options, then customize by editing them on the computer to fit your situation. Then press print...and your text is done. You'll save lots of typing time and you'll be able to make your first draft in literally minutes.

You'll save even more time by using the software to create your financials. Just enter your basic information (such as assumptions, sales, basic costs) and the software will do the rest of the work. Profit and loss projections, cash flow projections, balance sheet projections and key ratio's will automatically be calculated.

Want to change an assumption (such as a lower interest rate) or see what happens with different sales projections? By just re-entering the number you wish to change, all of the financial spreadsheets will automatically recalculate. Then press print . . . and your financials are done.

Adams Streetwise Small Business Software is completely self-contained, but if you prefer you can export the text to any word processor. The financials can be exported to Excel and Lotus or if you prefer you can even start your work using one of these spreadsheet programs.

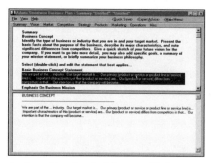

Just scroll and select from multiple pre-written text options. Then make your final edits or add additional copy.

Adams Streetwise
Business Plan Software

To order call 1-800-872-5627
Price: $99.95, plus $4.50 for shipping and handling.

SPECIFICATIONS
Includes both: CD-ROM (Multimedia) Version and 3.5" Disk (Lite) Version

Windows 95 or higher, Windows 3.1, or Windows NT ● 486 PC or higher ● Sound Blaster or compatible audio ● 4 MB RAM (8 recommended) ● 5 MB free hard disk space

Questions about Adams Streetwise Complete Business Plan Software

Question: What is the biggest advantage of using the software, instead of just following the book.

Answer: It's faster. With the software you get integrated financials that are ready to go. You don't have to make sure that you are entering the correct formula into the correct square on the worksheet (or cell on your computer). Instead the work is already done for you. Just enter your data and the software does the calculations.

Question: How easy is it to create different scenario's using the computer, such as scenario's for "weak", "likely" and "strong" sales assumptions.

Answer: You just go to the profit and loss projection and change the sales column. That's all there is to it! All of your variable costs will instantly change. Your profit and loss projections, your cash flow projections, your balance sheet projections and your key ratio's will all be automatically recalculated.

Question: How long does it take to understand the software if I have little experience using computers?

Answer: This software is extremely easy to use. Within a few minutes you should be up and running. The menu's are easy to follow. And should you need it, help is available on-line and in the manual.

Question: How long will it take to create a complete business plan using the software.

Answer: Realistically most users will require approximately one day to create a full plan. However, some highly experienced business people have created complete 10-20 page plans including full financials in as little as four hours.

Question: Can I return the software if it does not meet my expectations?

Answer: Absolutely, we offer a no-questions-asked 30-day money back guarantee.

Change your sales projection—your profit and loss, cash flow, and balance sheet projections will all automatically recalculate.

Your break-even point, your debt ratio, your profit margin, and other key ratios are all automatically calculated.

Also available at software retailers nationwide:

How to order: If you cannot find this software at your favorite retail outlet, you may order it directly from the publisher. Call for price information. BY PHONE: Call 1-800-872-5627 (in Massachusetts 781-767-8100). We accept Visa, Mastercard, and American Express. $5.95 will be added to your total order for shipping and handling. BY MAIL: Write out the full title of the software you'd like to order and send payment, including $5.95 for shipping and handling to: Adams Media Corporation, 260 Center Street, Holbrook, MA 02343. 30-day money-back guarantee.

Bob Adams is one of the foremost authorities on small business. He received an MBA from Harvard Business School and has written numerous business books including the best-selling *Adams Streetwise Small Business Start-Up*. He produced the "Streetwise Business Tips" series for *First Business*, the national television news show produced by the United States Chamber of Commerce, and is often quoted in business publications.